# Garfield BEEFS UP

## BY JIM DAVIS

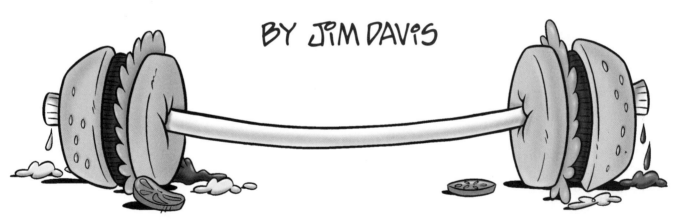

## Ballantine Books • New York

A Ballantine Book
Published by The Ballantine Publishing Group

www.randomhouse.com/BB/

Library of Congress Catalog Card Number: 00-191291

ISBN: 0-345-44109-5

Manufactured in the United States of America

First Edition: October 2000

10 9 8 7 6 5 4 3 2 1

# Garfield's Code of Nevers

**NEVER**
put off until tomorrow what you can eat today

**NEVER**
diet on a day ending in "y"

**NEVER**
swim in the gravy boat

**NEVER**
lick yourself at the dinner table

**NEVER**
floss a pit bull

**NEVER**
buy seafood off a pickup truck with an Iowa license plate

**NEVER**
snore while the boss is talking

**NEVER**
eat the "mystery meat"

**NEVER**
buy used underwear

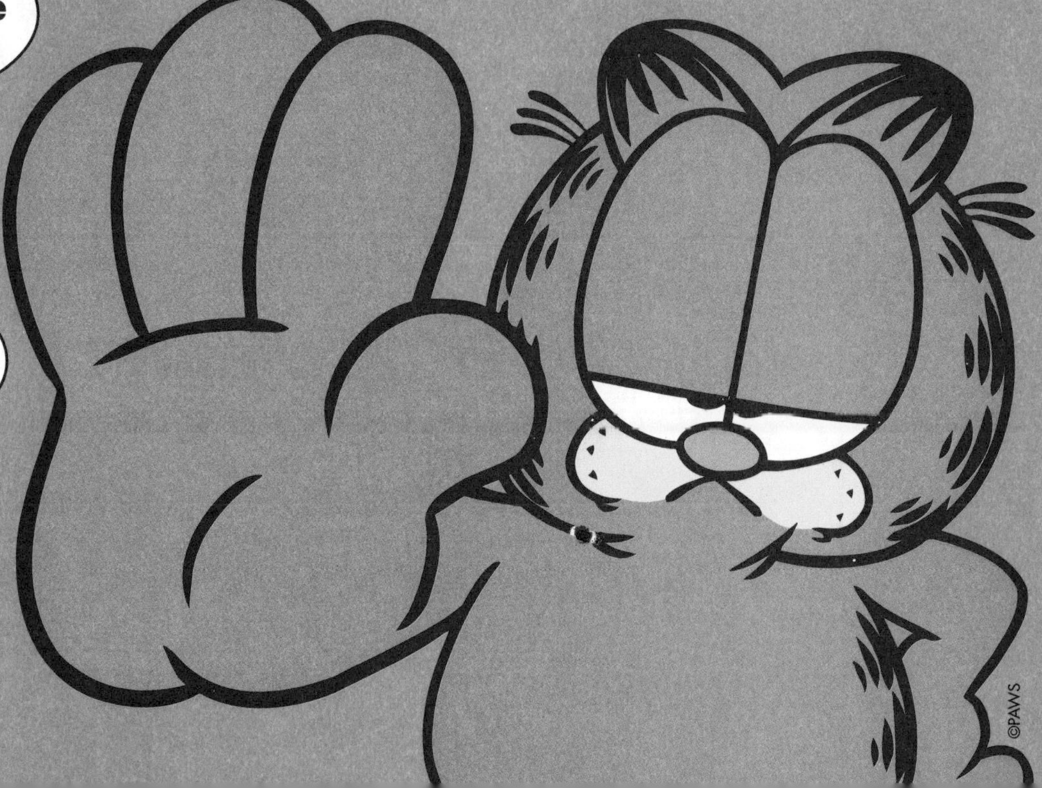

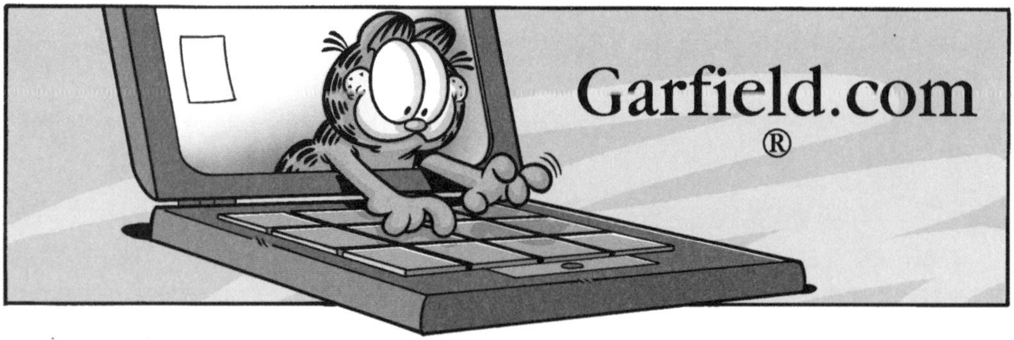
Garfield.com
®

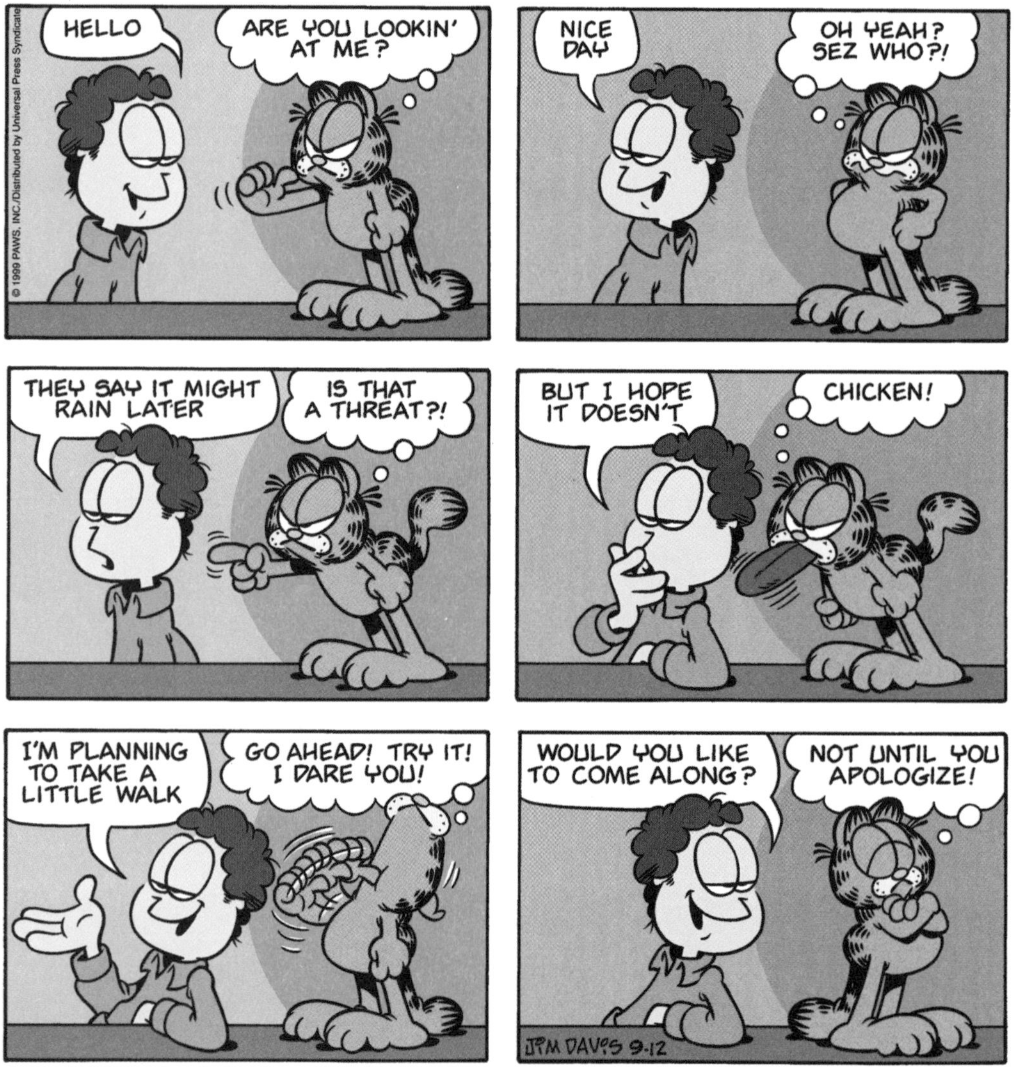
© 1999 PAWS, INC./Distributed by Universal Press Syndicate
HELLO
ARE YOU LOOKIN' AT ME?
NICE DAY
OH YEAH? SEZ WHO?!
THEY SAY IT MIGHT RAIN LATER
IS THAT A THREAT?!
BUT I HOPE IT DOESN'T
CHICKEN!
I'M PLANNING TO TAKE A LITTLE WALK
GO AHEAD! TRY IT! I DARE YOU!
WOULD YOU LIKE TO COME ALONG?
NOT UNTIL YOU APOLOGIZE!
JIM DAVIS 9-12

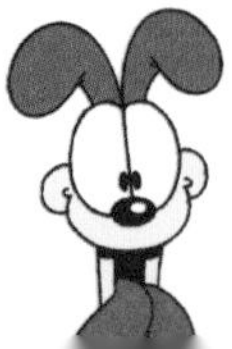

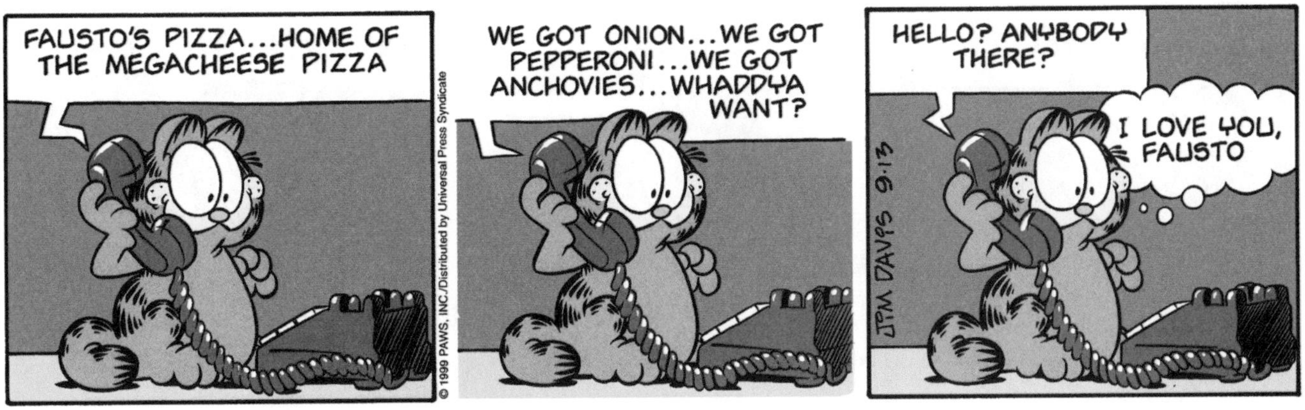
FAUSTO'S PIZZA...HOME OF THE MEGACHEESE PIZZA
WE GOT ONION...WE GOT PEPPERONI...WE GOT ANCHOVIES...WHADDYA WANT?
HELLO? ANYBODY THERE?
I LOVE YOU, FAUSTO
JIM DAVIS 9-13



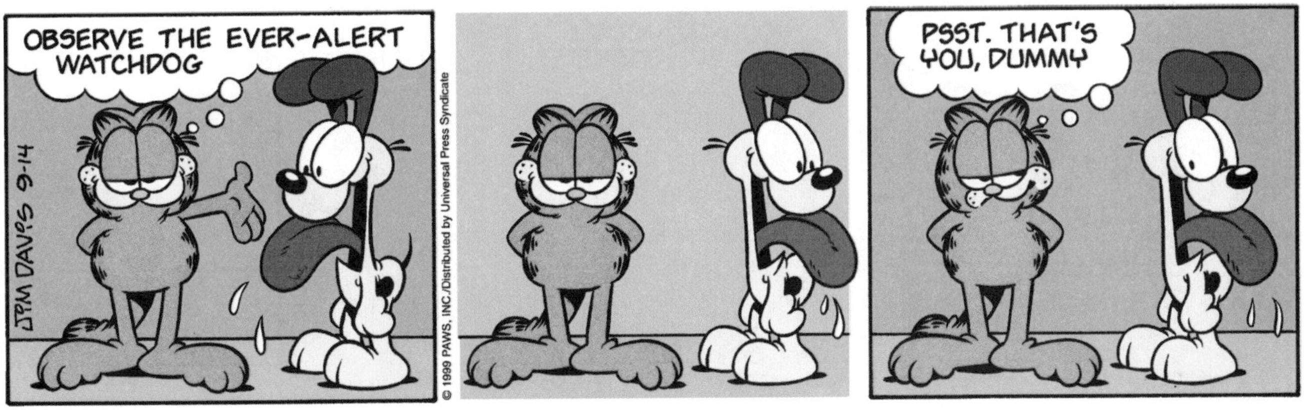
OBSERVE THE EVER-ALERT WATCHDOG
JIM DAVIS 9-14
PSST. THAT'S YOU, DUMMY



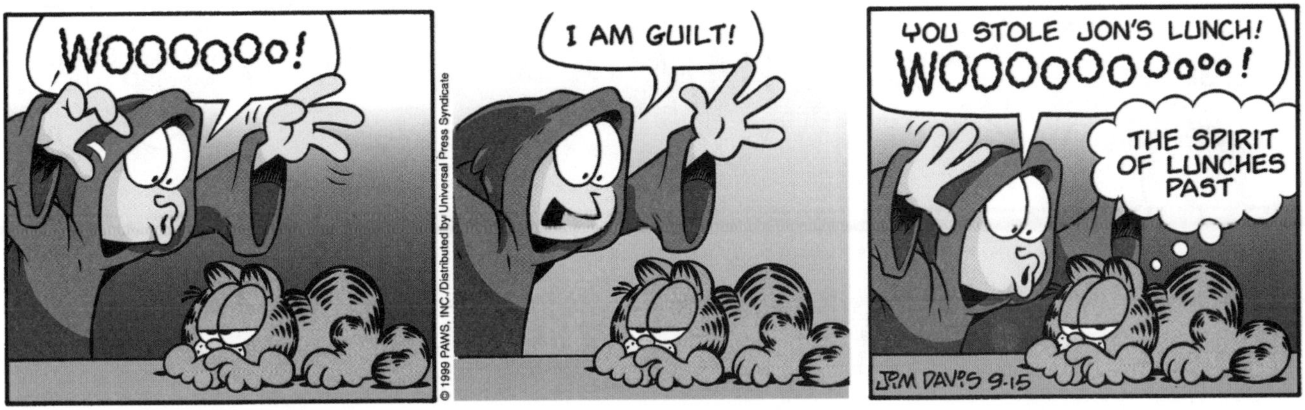
WOOOOOo!
I AM GUILT!
YOU STOLE JON'S LUNCH! WOOOOOOOoo!
THE SPIRIT OF LUNCHES PAST
JIM DAVIS 9-15

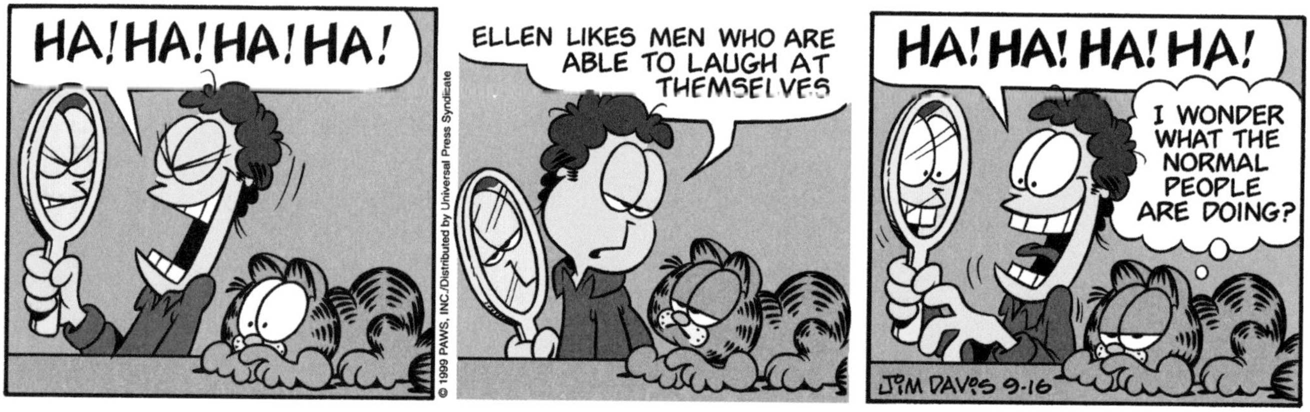
HA! HA! HA! HA!
ELLEN LIKES MEN WHO ARE ABLE TO LAUGH AT THEMSELVES
HA! HA! HA! HA!
I WONDER WHAT THE NORMAL PEOPLE ARE DOING?
© 1999 PAWS, INC./Distributed by Universal Press Syndicate
JIM DAVIS 9-16

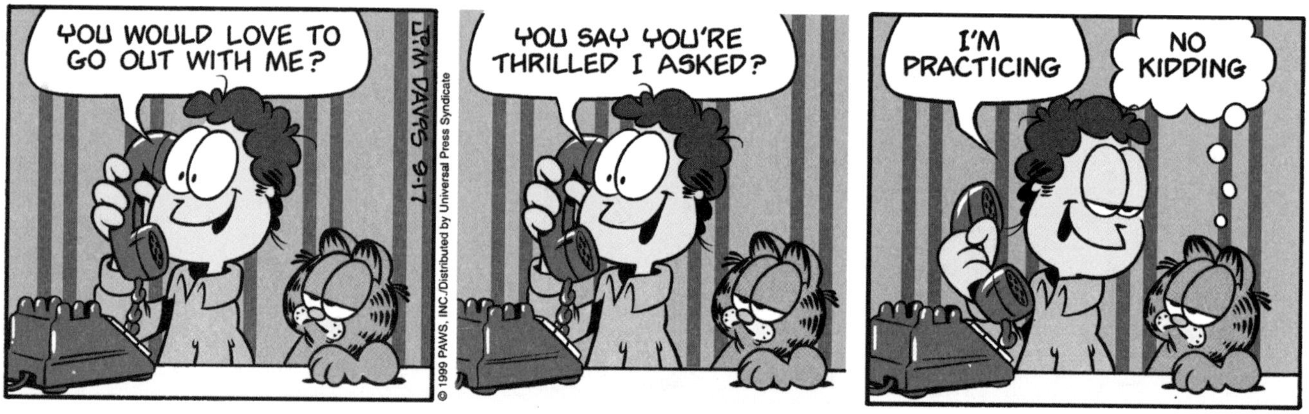
YOU WOULD LOVE TO GO OUT WITH ME?
JIM DAVIS 9-17
© 1999 PAWS, INC./Distributed by Universal Press Syndicate
YOU SAY YOU'RE THRILLED I ASKED?
I'M PRACTICING
NO KIDDING

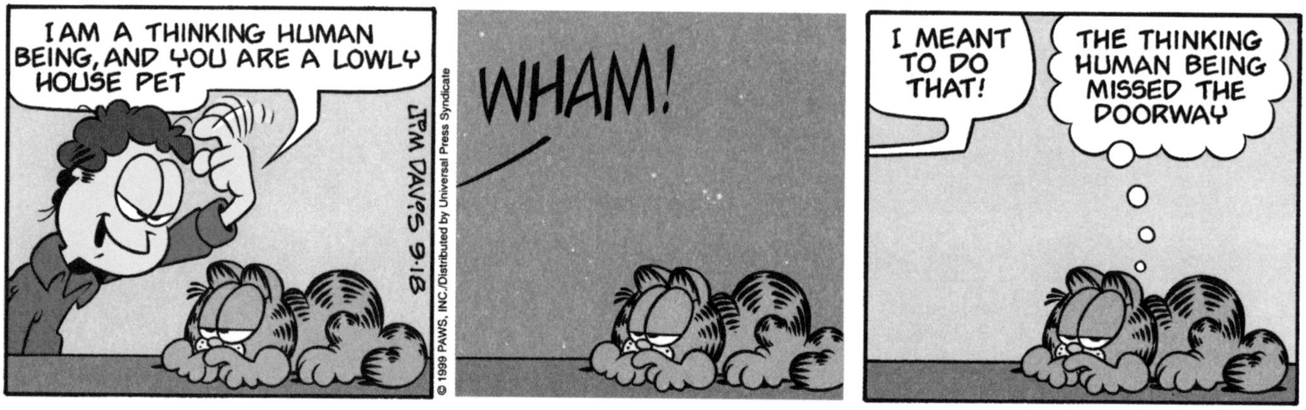
I AM A THINKING HUMAN BEING, AND YOU ARE A LOWLY HOUSE PET
JIM DAVIS 9-18
© 1999 PAWS, INC./Distributed by Universal Press Syndicate
WHAM!
I MEANT TO DO THAT!
THE THINKING HUMAN BEING MISSED THE DOORWAY

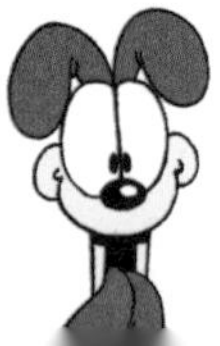

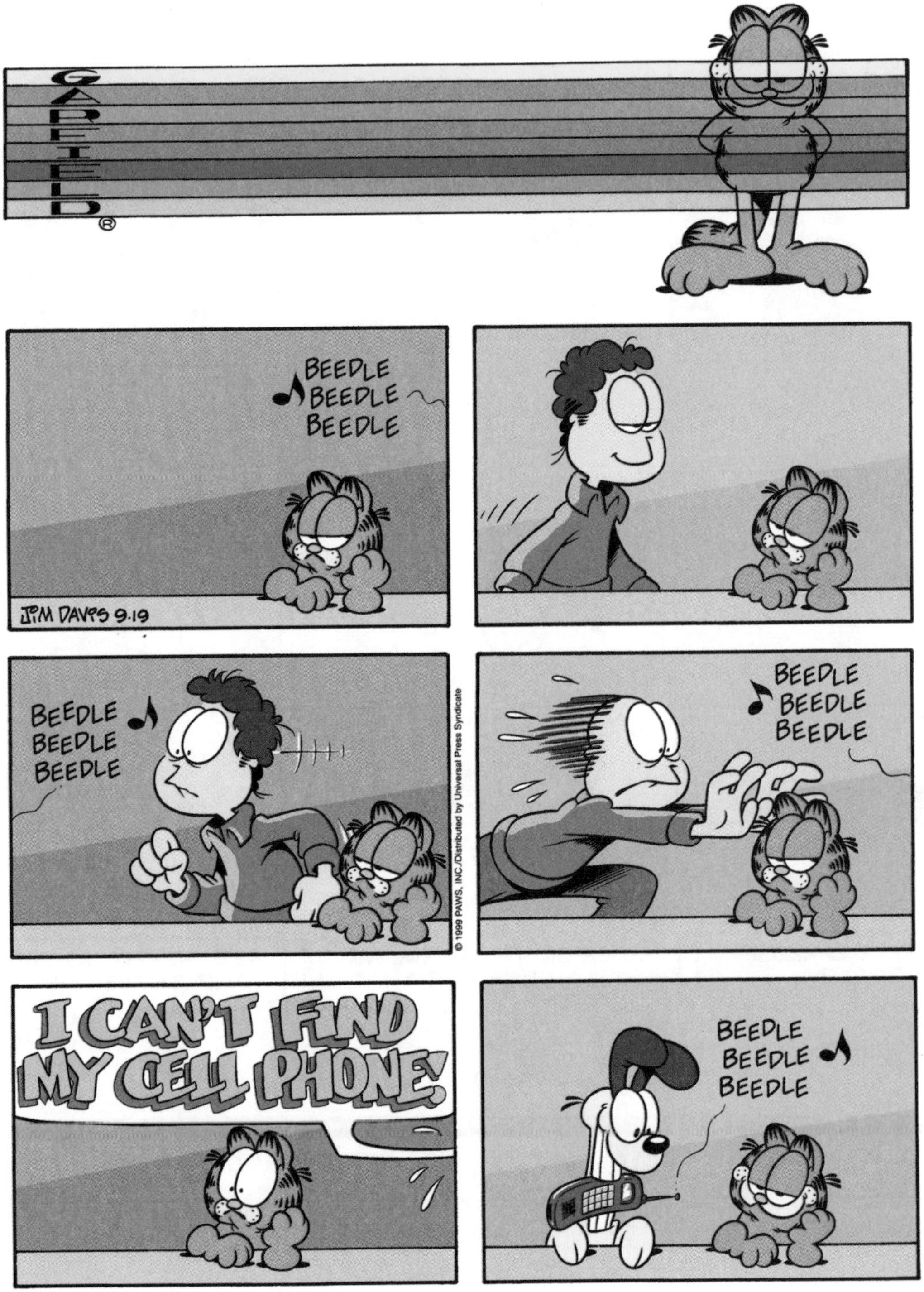
GARFIELD®
BEEDLE BEEDLE BEEDLE
JIM DAVIS 9.19
BEEDLE BEEDLE BEEDLE
© 1999 PAWS, INC./Distributed by Universal Press Syndicate
BEEDLE BEEDLE BEEDLE
I CAN'T FIND MY CELL PHONE!
BEEDLE BEEDLE BEEDLE

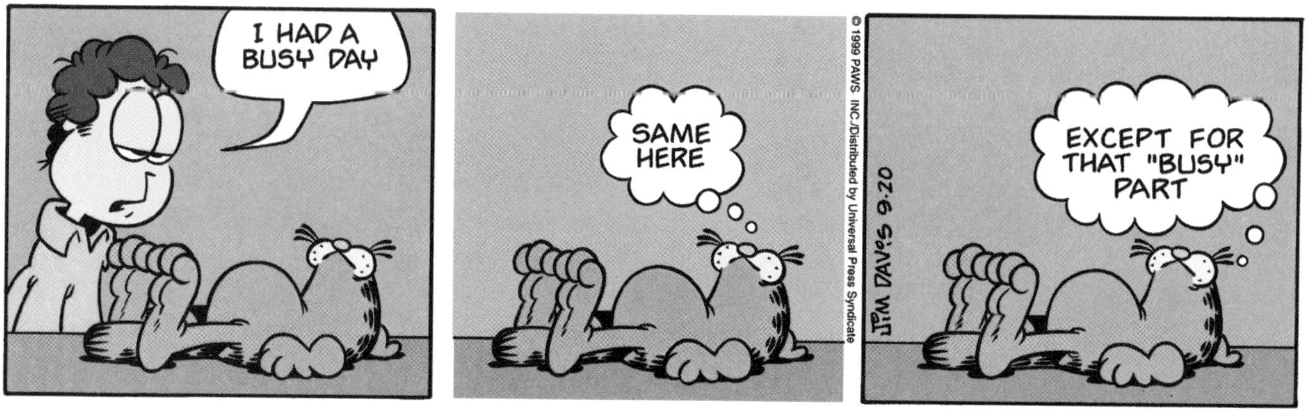
I HAD A BUSY DAY
SAME HERE
© 1999 PAWS, INC./Distributed by Universal Press Syndicate
JIM DAVIS 9·20
EXCEPT FOR THAT "BUSY" PART

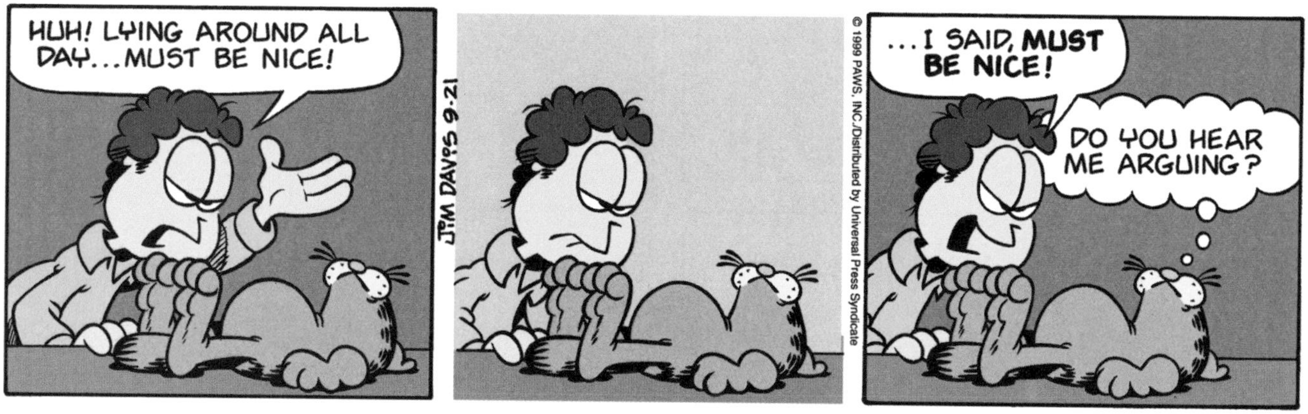
HUH! LYING AROUND ALL DAY...MUST BE NICE!
JIM DAVIS 9·21
© 1999 PAWS, INC./Distributed by Universal Press Syndicate
...I SAID, **MUST BE NICE!**
DO YOU HEAR ME ARGUING?

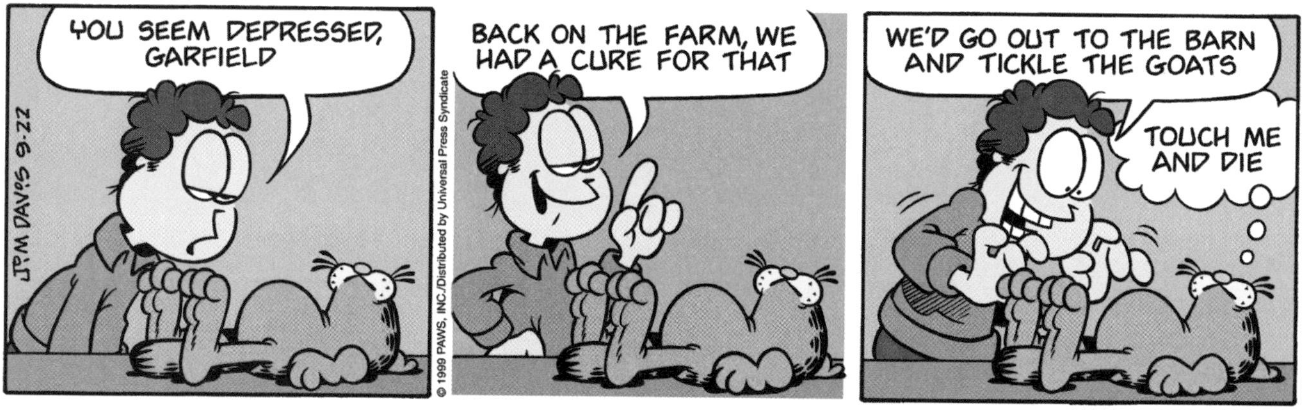
JIM DAVIS 9·22
YOU SEEM DEPRESSED, GARFIELD
© 1999 PAWS, INC./Distributed by Universal Press Syndicate
BACK ON THE FARM, WE HAD A CURE FOR THAT
WE'D GO OUT TO THE BARN AND TICKLE THE GOATS
TOUCH ME AND DIE

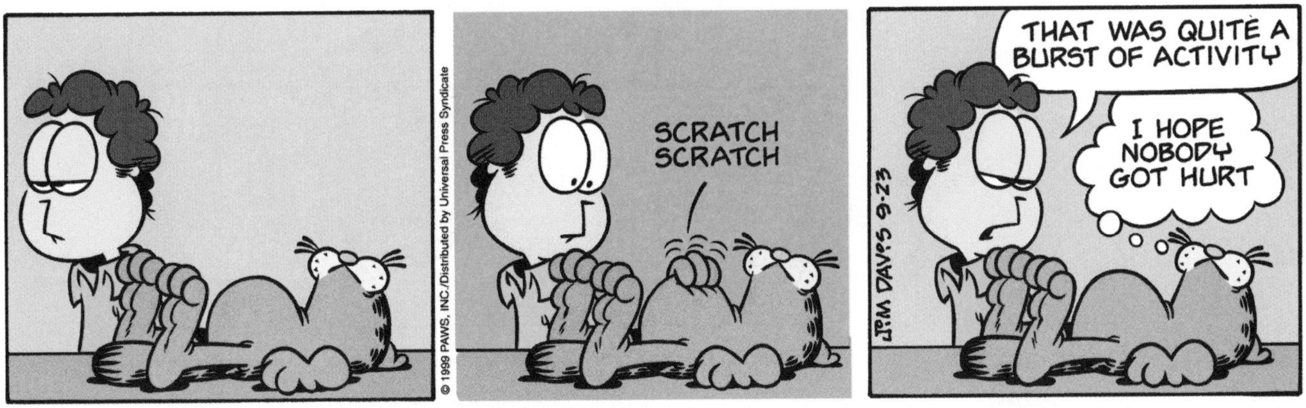
SCRATCH SCRATCH
THAT WAS QUITE A BURST OF ACTIVITY
I HOPE NOBODY GOT HURT
JIM DAVIS 9-23
© 1999 PAWS, INC./Distributed by Universal Press Syndicate

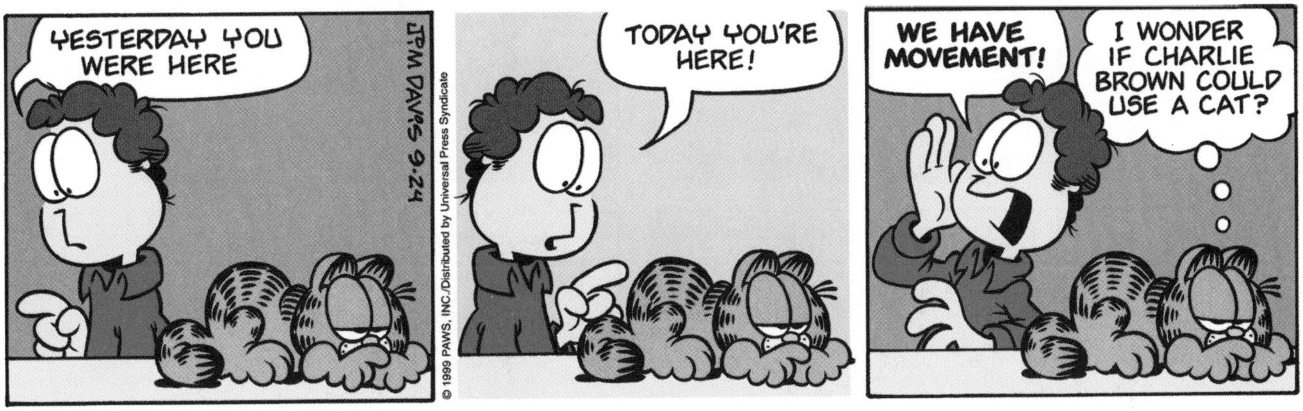
YESTERDAY YOU WERE HERE
TODAY YOU'RE HERE!
WE HAVE MOVEMENT!
I WONDER IF CHARLIE BROWN COULD USE A CAT?
JIM DAVIS 9-24
© 1999 PAWS, INC./Distributed by Universal Press Syndicate

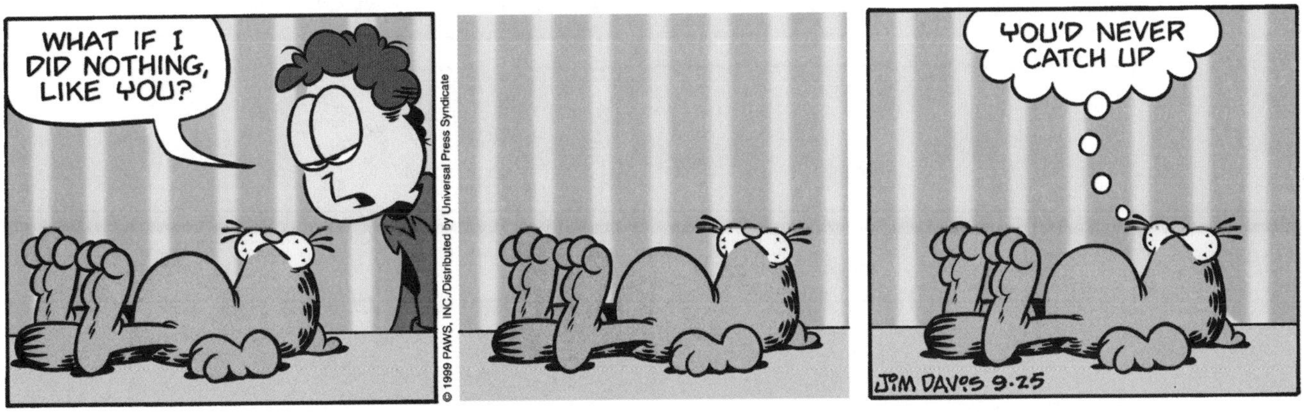
WHAT IF I DID NOTHING, LIKE YOU?
YOU'D NEVER CATCH UP
JIM DAVIS 9-25
© 1999 PAWS, INC./Distributed by Universal Press Syndicate

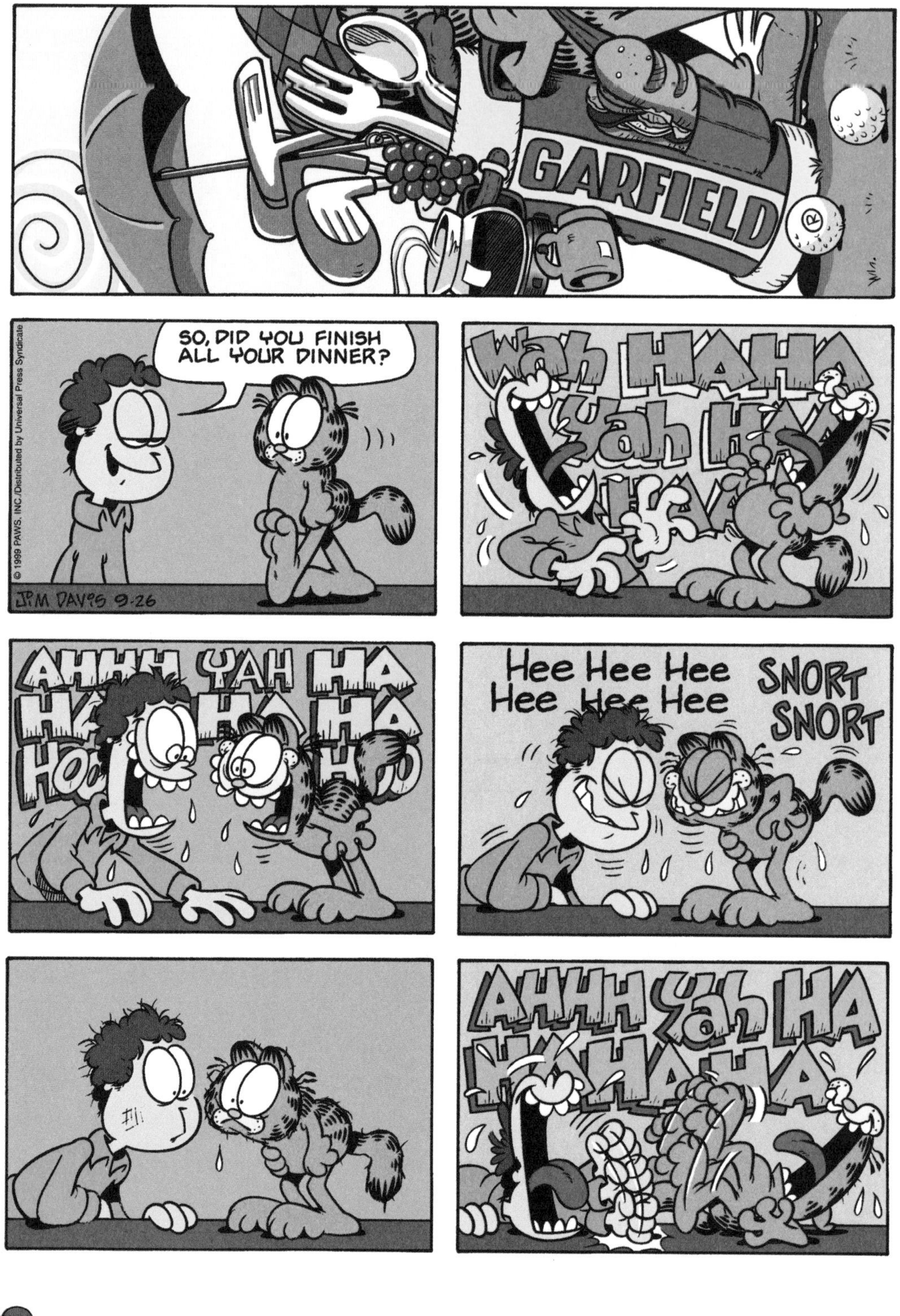
GARFIELD®
© 1999 PAWS. INC./Distributed by Universal Press Syndicate
JIM DAVIS 9-26
SO, DID YOU FINISH ALL YOUR DINNER?
WAH HAHA YAH HA HA
AHHH YAH HA HA HA HA HO
Hee Hee Hee Hee Hee Hee
SNORT SNORT
AHHH YAH HA HAHAHA

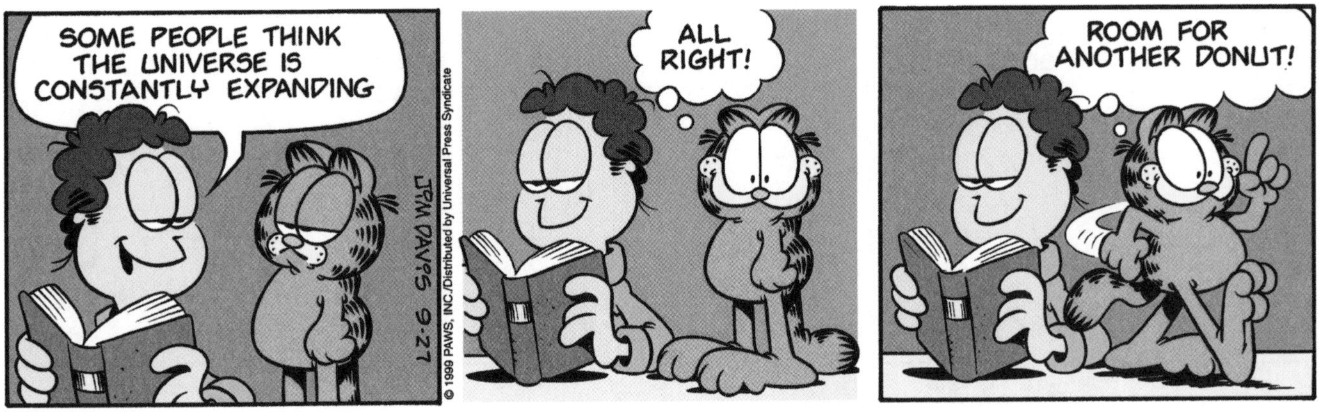
SOME PEOPLE THINK THE UNIVERSE IS CONSTANTLY EXPANDING
JIM DAVIS 9-27
© 1999 PAWS, INC./Distributed by Universal Press Syndicate
ALL RIGHT!
ROOM FOR ANOTHER DONUT!

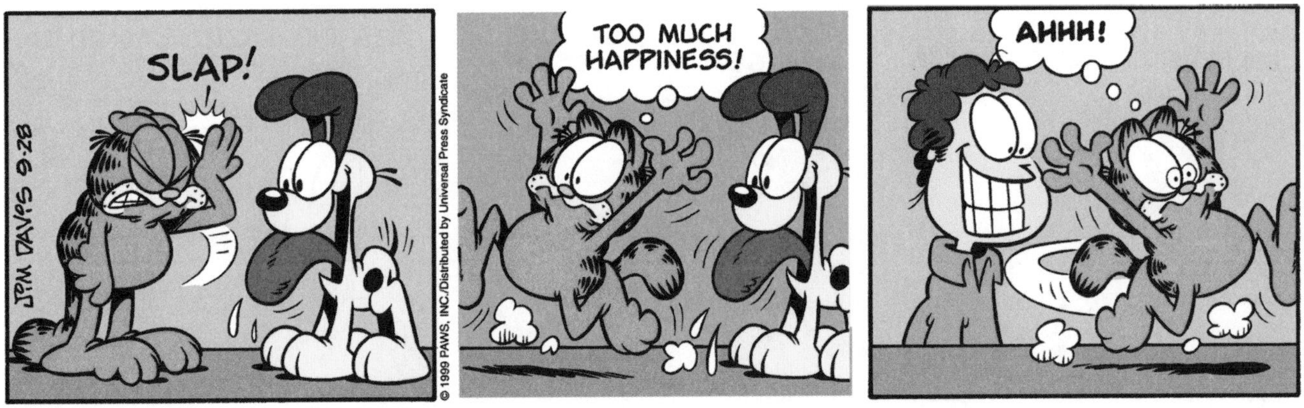
SLAP!
JIM DAVIS 9-28
© 1999 PAWS, INC./Distributed by Universal Press Syndicate
TOO MUCH HAPPINESS!
AHHH!

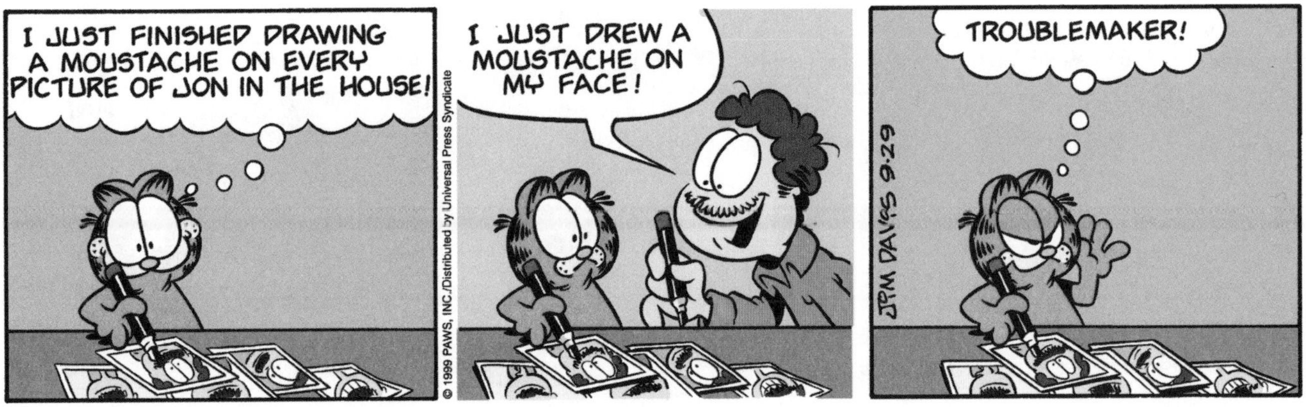
I JUST FINISHED DRAWING A MOUSTACHE ON EVERY PICTURE OF JON IN THE HOUSE!
© 1999 PAWS, INC./Distributed by Universal Press Syndicate
I JUST DREW A MOUSTACHE ON MY FACE!
JIM DAVIS 9-29
TROUBLEMAKER!

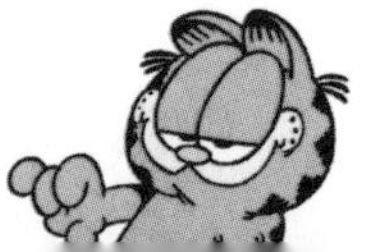

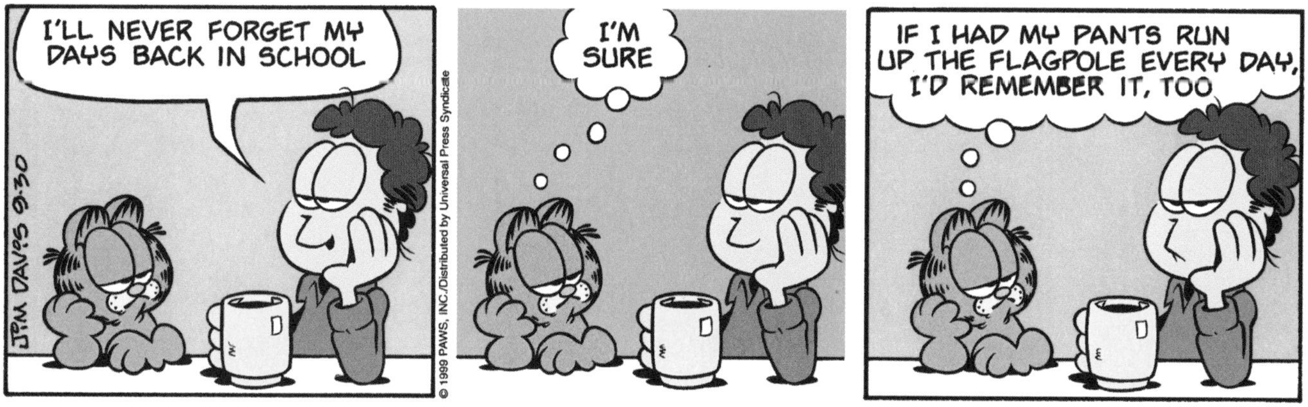
I'LL NEVER FORGET MY DAYS BACK IN SCHOOL
JIM DAVIS 9-30
© 1999 PAWS, INC./Distributed by Universal Press Syndicate
I'M SURE
IF I HAD MY PANTS RUN UP THE FLAGPOLE EVERY DAY, I'D REMEMBER IT, TOO

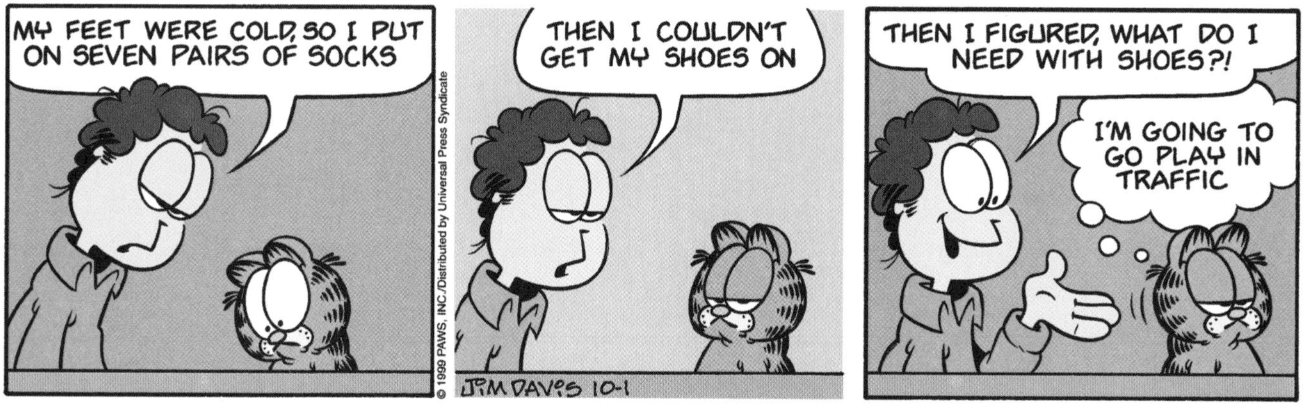
MY FEET WERE COLD, SO I PUT ON SEVEN PAIRS OF SOCKS
© 1999 PAWS, INC./Distributed by Universal Press Syndicate
THEN I COULDN'T GET MY SHOES ON
JIM DAVIS 10-1
THEN I FIGURED, WHAT DO I NEED WITH SHOES?!
I'M GOING TO GO PLAY IN TRAFFIC

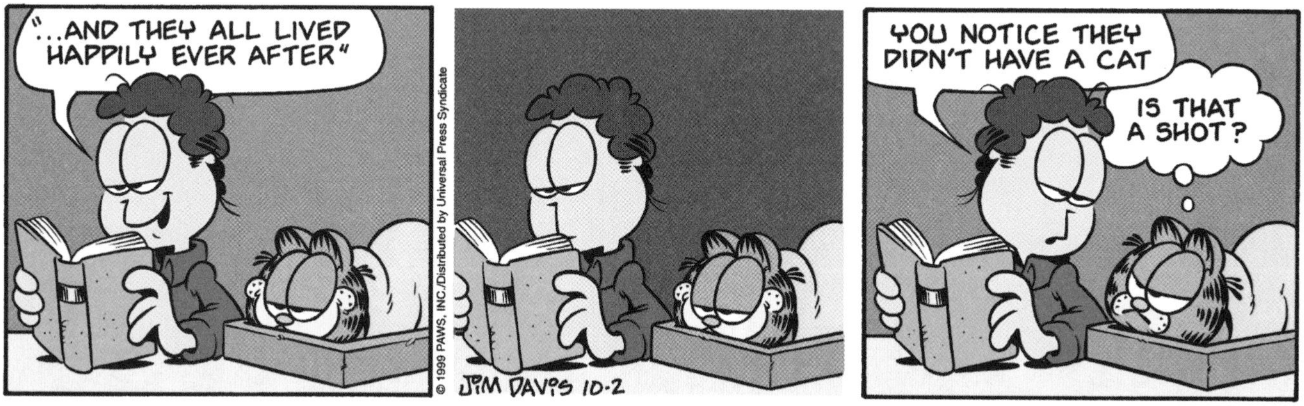
"...AND THEY ALL LIVED HAPPILY EVER AFTER"
© 1999 PAWS, INC./Distributed by Universal Press Syndicate
JIM DAVIS 10-2
YOU NOTICE THEY DIDN'T HAVE A CAT
IS THAT A SHOT?

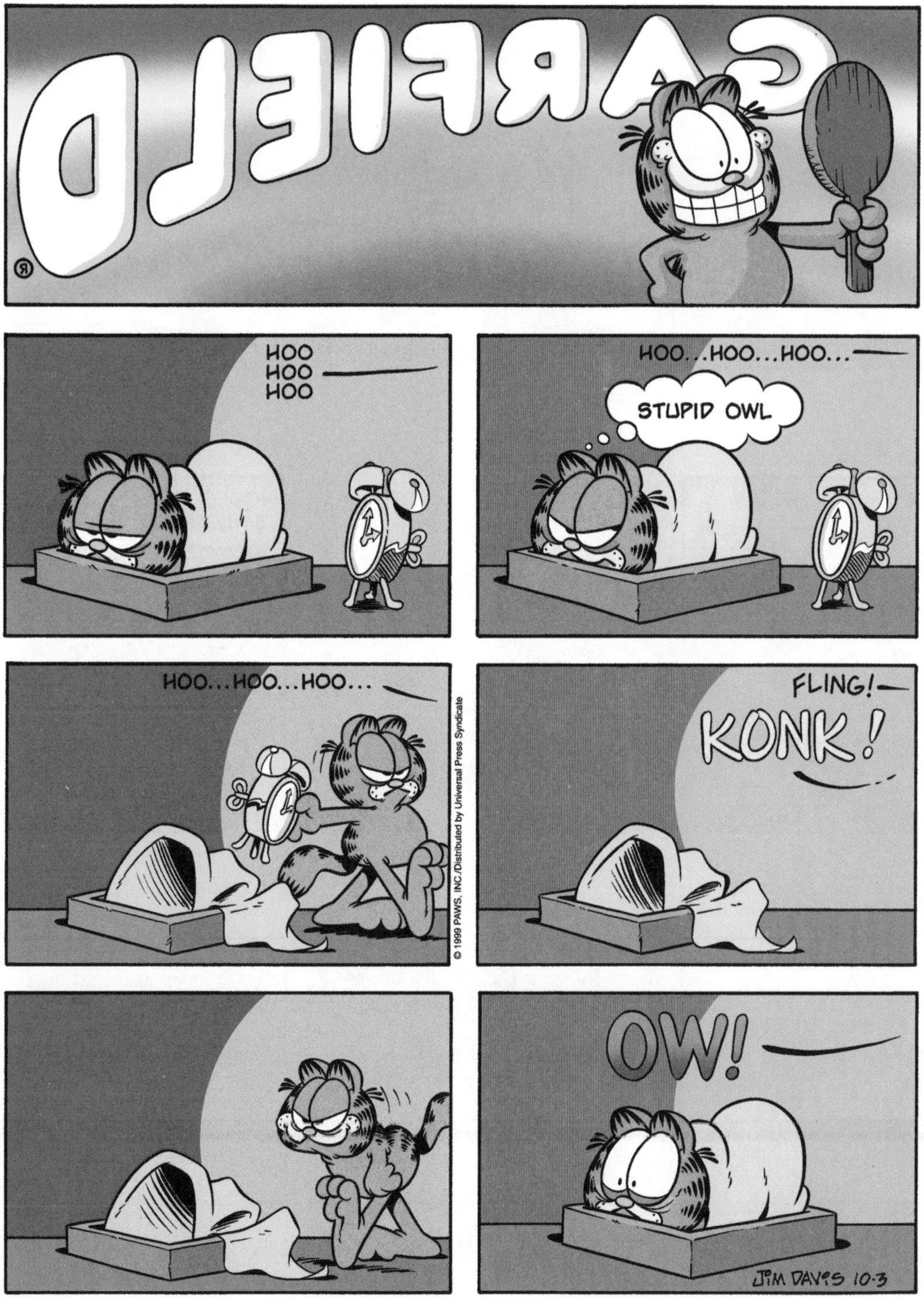

GARFIELD ®
HOO HOO HOO
HOO...HOO...HOO...
STUPID OWL
HOO...HOO...HOO...
FLING!
KONK!
OW!
© 1999 PAWS, INC./Distributed by Universal Press Syndicate
JIM DAVIS 10-3

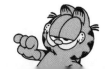

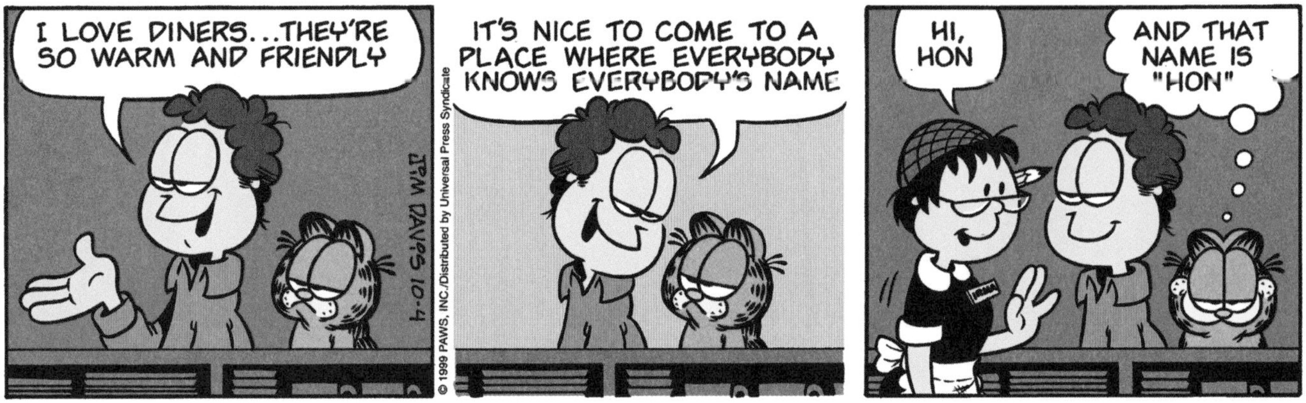
I LOVE DINERS...THEY'RE SO WARM AND FRIENDLY
JIM DAVIS 10-4
© 1999 PAWS, INC./Distributed by Universal Press Syndicate
IT'S NICE TO COME TO A PLACE WHERE EVERYBODY KNOWS EVERYBODY'S NAME
HI, HON
AND THAT NAME IS "HON"

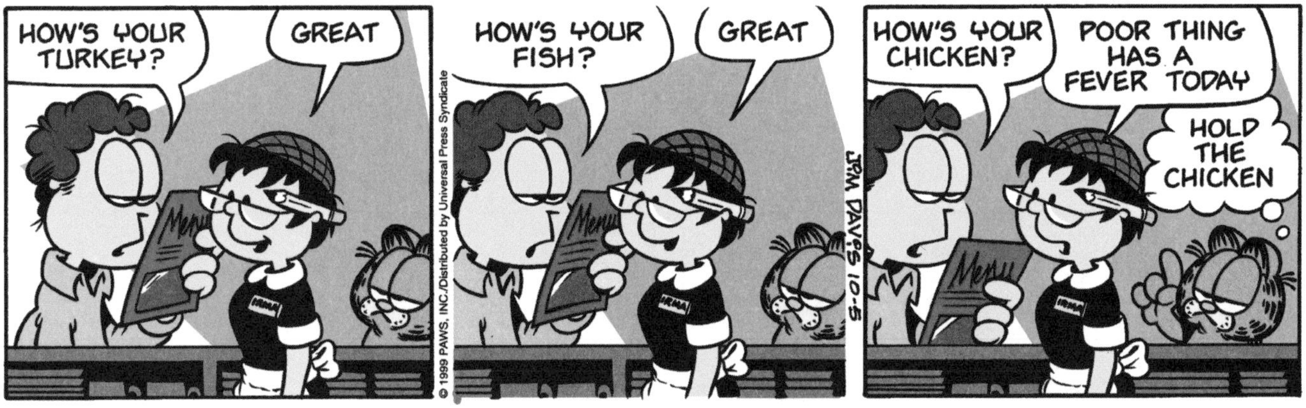
HOW'S YOUR TURKEY?
GREAT
Menu
© 1999 PAWS, INC./Distributed by Universal Press Syndicate
HOW'S YOUR FISH?
GREAT
Menu
JIM DAVIS 10-5
HOW'S YOUR CHICKEN?
POOR THING HAS A FEVER TODAY
HOLD THE CHICKEN
Menu

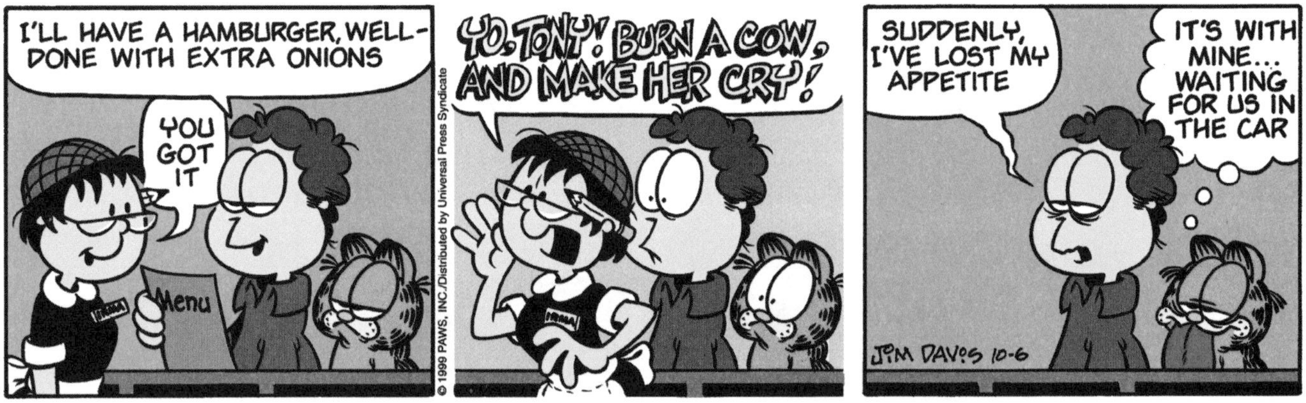
I'LL HAVE A HAMBURGER, WELL-DONE WITH EXTRA ONIONS
YOU GOT IT
Menu
© 1999 PAWS, INC./Distributed by Universal Press Syndicate
YO, TONY! BURN A COW, AND MAKE HER CRY!
SUDDENLY, I'VE LOST MY APPETITE
IT'S WITH MINE... WAITING FOR US IN THE CAR
JIM DAVIS 10-6

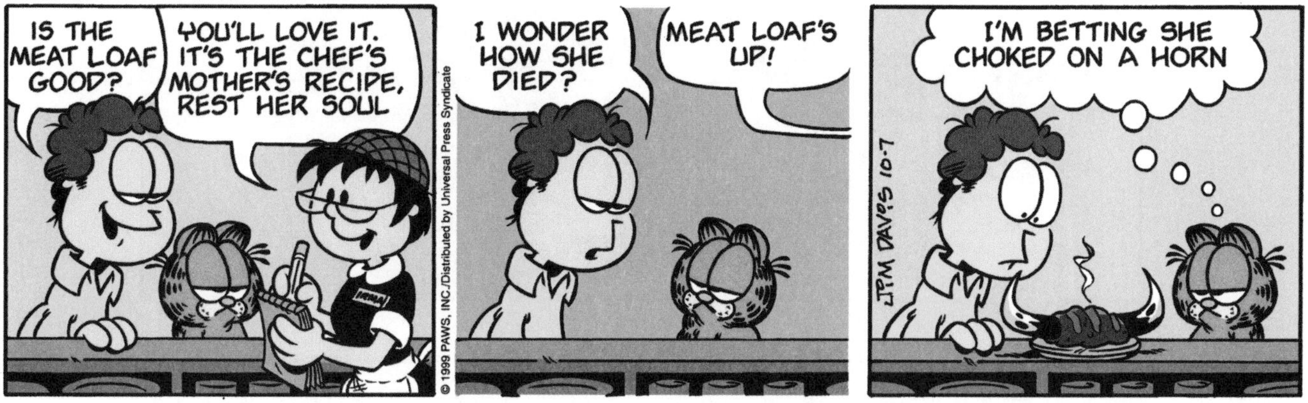
IS THE MEAT LOAF GOOD?
YOU'LL LOVE IT. IT'S THE CHEF'S MOTHER'S RECIPE, REST HER SOUL
© 1999 PAWS, INC./Distributed by Universal Press Syndicate
I WONDER HOW SHE DIED?
MEAT LOAF'S UP!
JIM DAVIS 10-7
I'M BETTING SHE CHOKED ON A HORN

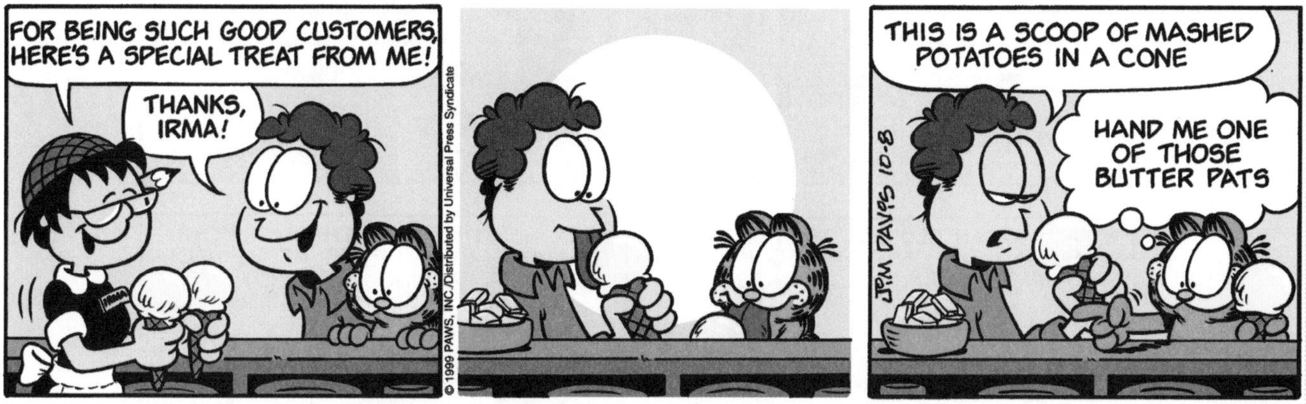
FOR BEING SUCH GOOD CUSTOMERS, HERE'S A SPECIAL TREAT FROM ME!
THANKS, IRMA!
© 1999 PAWS, INC./Distributed by Universal Press Syndicate
JIM DAVIS 10-8
THIS IS A SCOOP OF MASHED POTATOES IN A CONE
HAND ME ONE OF THOSE BUTTER PATS

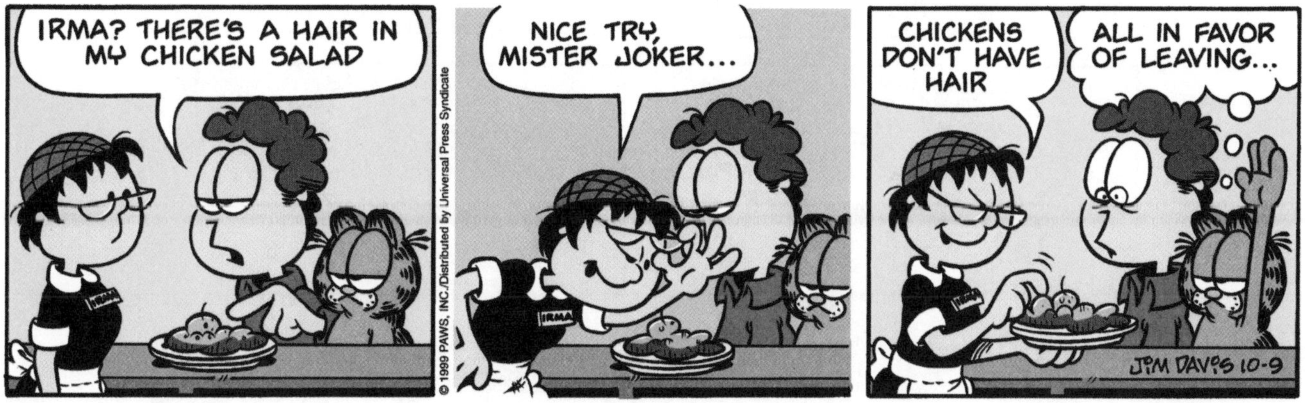
IRMA? THERE'S A HAIR IN MY CHICKEN SALAD
© 1999 PAWS, INC./Distributed by Universal Press Syndicate
NICE TRY, MISTER JOKER...
CHICKENS DON'T HAVE HAIR
ALL IN FAVOR OF LEAVING...
JIM DAVIS 10-9

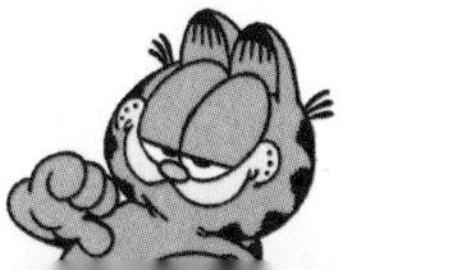

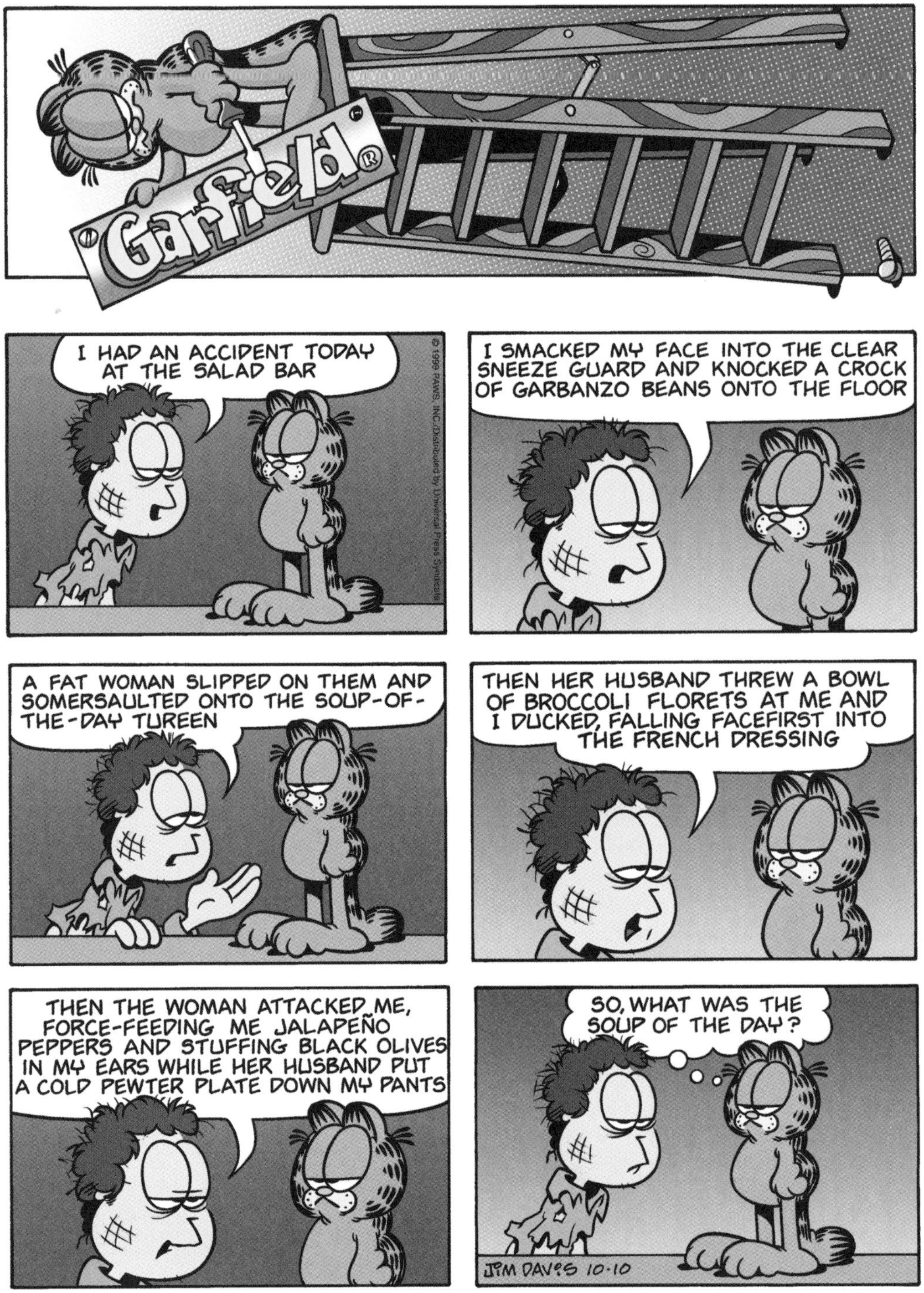
Garfield®
I HAD AN ACCIDENT TODAY AT THE SALAD BAR
© 1999 PAWS, INC./Distributed by Universal Press Syndicate
I SMACKED MY FACE INTO THE CLEAR SNEEZE GUARD AND KNOCKED A CROCK OF GARBANZO BEANS ONTO THE FLOOR
A FAT WOMAN SLIPPED ON THEM AND SOMERSAULTED ONTO THE SOUP-OF-THE-DAY TUREEN
THEN HER HUSBAND THREW A BOWL OF BROCCOLI FLORETS AT ME AND I DUCKED, FALLING FACEFIRST INTO THE FRENCH DRESSING
THEN THE WOMAN ATTACKED ME, FORCE-FEEDING ME JALAPEÑO PEPPERS AND STUFFING BLACK OLIVES IN MY EARS WHILE HER HUSBAND PUT A COLD PEWTER PLATE DOWN MY PANTS
SO, WHAT WAS THE SOUP OF THE DAY?
JIM DAVIS 10-10

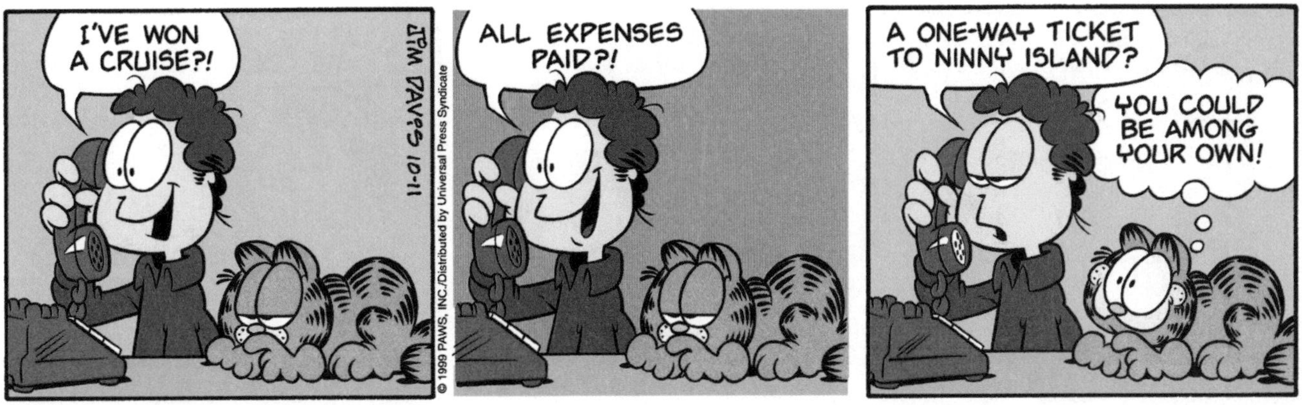
I'VE WON A CRUISE?!
JIM DAVIS 10-11
© 1999 PAWS, INC./Distributed by Universal Press Syndicate
ALL EXPENSES PAID?!
A ONE-WAY TICKET TO NINNY ISLAND?
YOU COULD BE AMONG YOUR OWN!

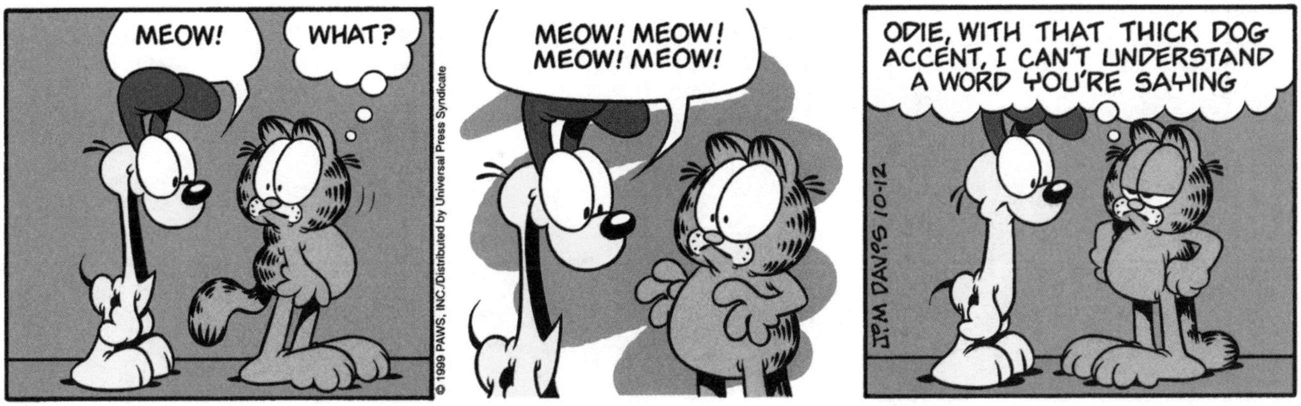
MEOW!
WHAT?
© 1999 PAWS, INC./Distributed by Universal Press Syndicate
MEOW! MEOW! MEOW! MEOW!
ODIE, WITH THAT THICK DOG ACCENT, I CAN'T UNDERSTAND A WORD YOU'RE SAYING
JIM DAVIS 10-12

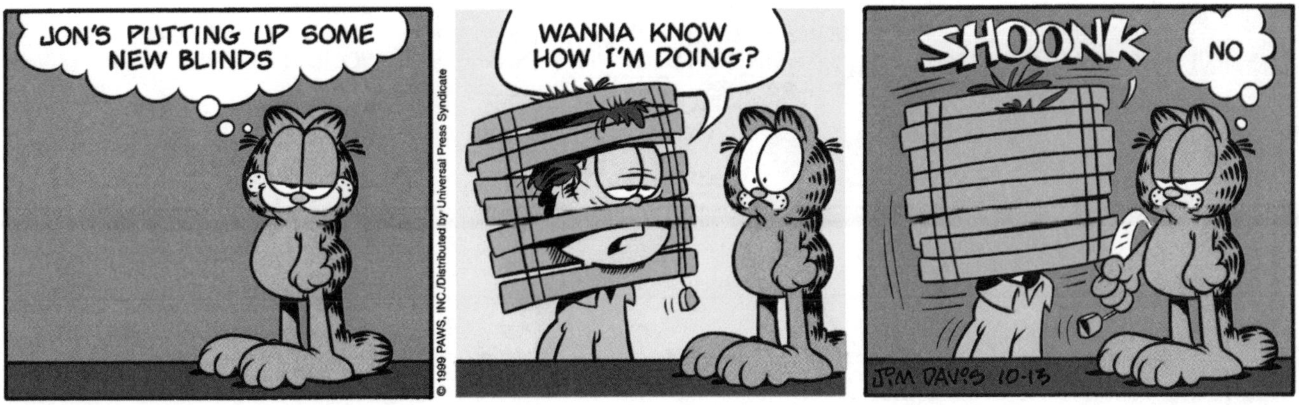
JON'S PUTTING UP SOME NEW BLINDS
© 1999 PAWS, INC./Distributed by Universal Press Syndicate
WANNA KNOW HOW I'M DOING?
SHOONK
NO
JIM DAVIS 10-13

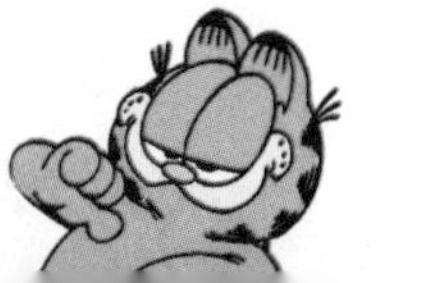

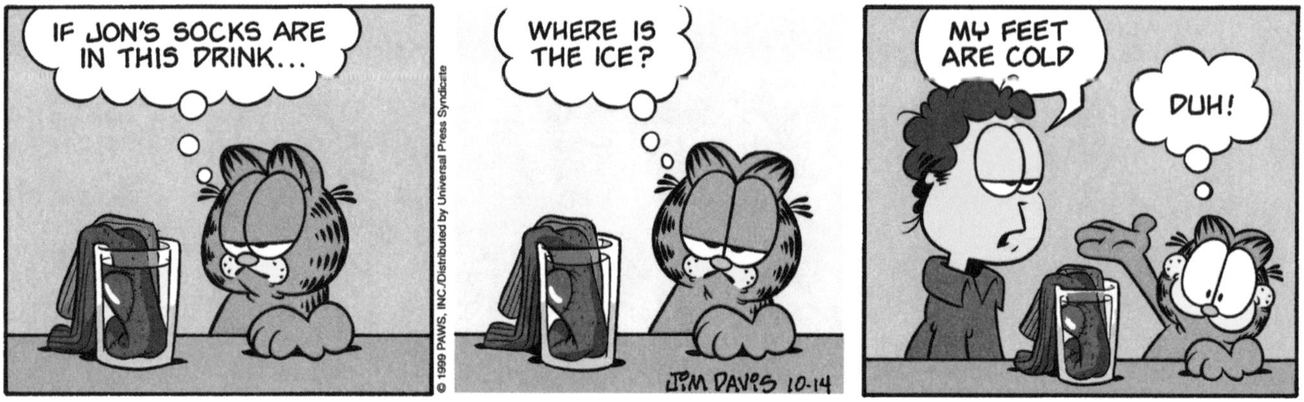
IF JON'S SOCKS ARE IN THIS DRINK...
WHERE IS THE ICE?
MY FEET ARE COLD
DUH!
JIM DAVIS 10-14
© 1999 PAWS, INC./Distributed by Universal Press Syndicate

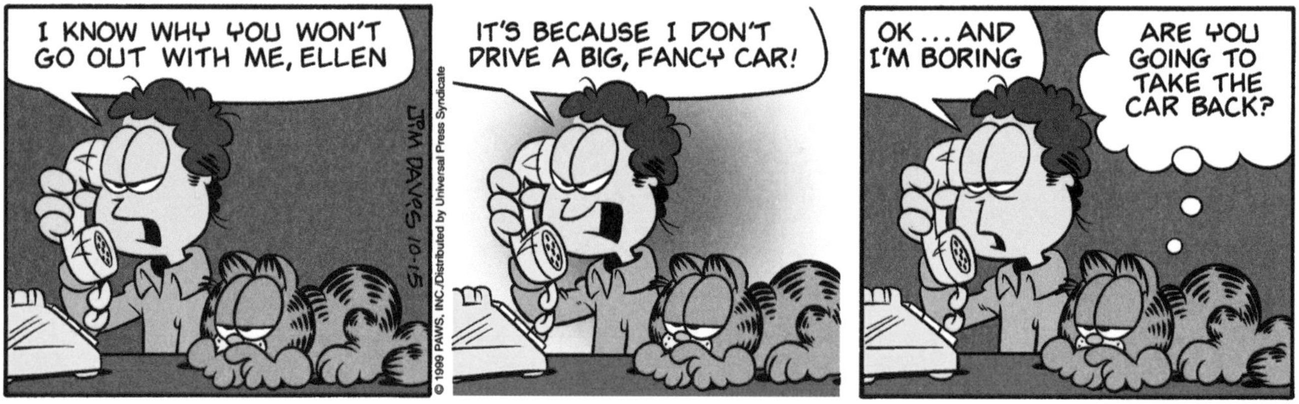
I KNOW WHY YOU WON'T GO OUT WITH ME, ELLEN
IT'S BECAUSE I DON'T DRIVE A BIG, FANCY CAR!
OK... AND I'M BORING
ARE YOU GOING TO TAKE THE CAR BACK?
JIM DAVIS 10-15
© 1999 PAWS, INC./Distributed by Universal Press Syndicate

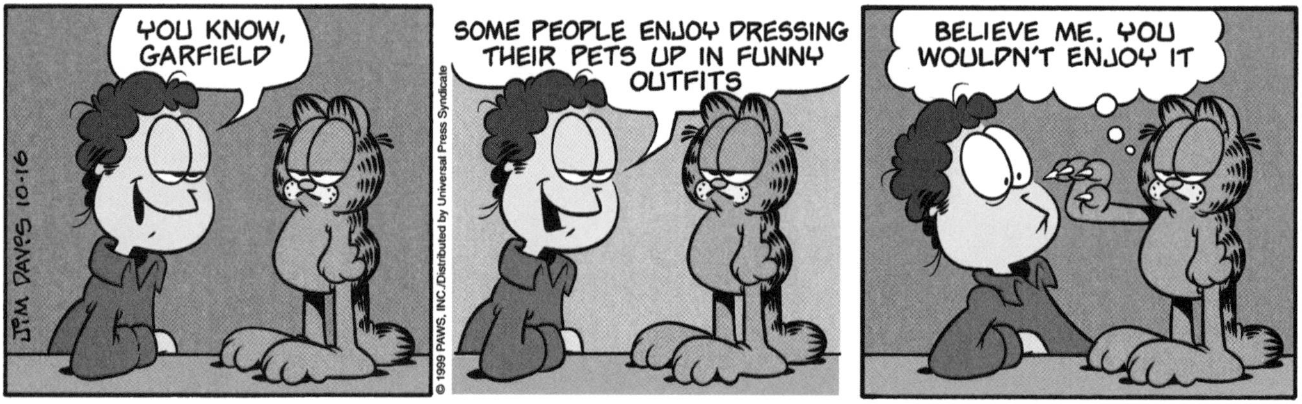
YOU KNOW, GARFIELD
SOME PEOPLE ENJOY DRESSING THEIR PETS UP IN FUNNY OUTFITS
BELIEVE ME. YOU WOULDN'T ENJOY IT
JIM DAVIS 10-16
© 1999 PAWS, INC./Distributed by Universal Press Syndicate

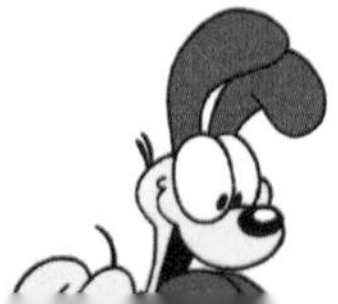

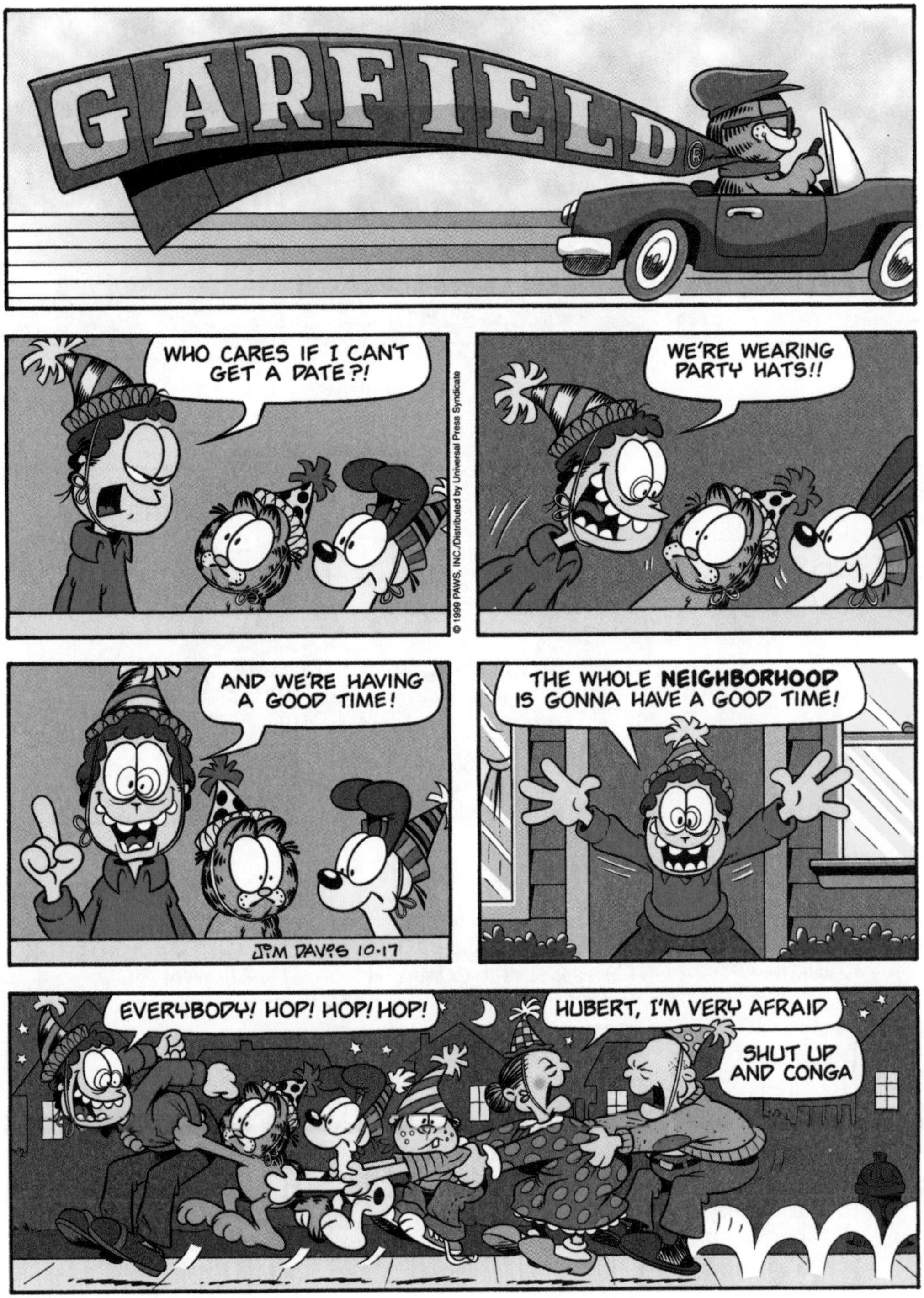
GARFIELD®
WHO CARES IF I CAN'T GET A DATE?!
© 1999 PAWS, INC./Distributed by Universal Press Syndicate
WE'RE WEARING PARTY HATS!!
AND WE'RE HAVING A GOOD TIME!
JIM DAVIS 10-17
THE WHOLE **NEIGHBORHOOD** IS GONNA HAVE A GOOD TIME!
EVERYBODY! HOP! HOP! HOP!
HUBERT, I'M VERY AFRAID
SHUT UP AND CONGA

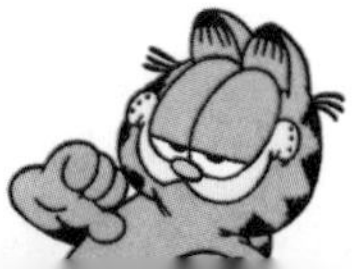

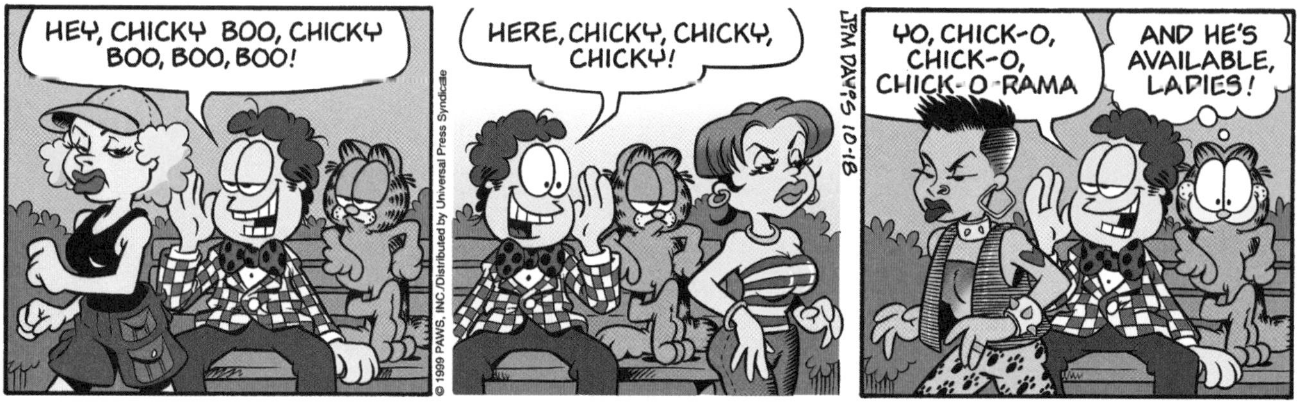
HEY, CHICKY BOO, CHICKY BOO, BOO, BOO!
HERE, CHICKY, CHICKY, CHICKY!
© 1999 PAWS, INC./Distributed by Universal Press Syndicate
JIM DAVIS 10-18
YO, CHICK-O, CHICK-O, CHICK-O-RAMA
AND HE'S AVAILABLE, LADIES!

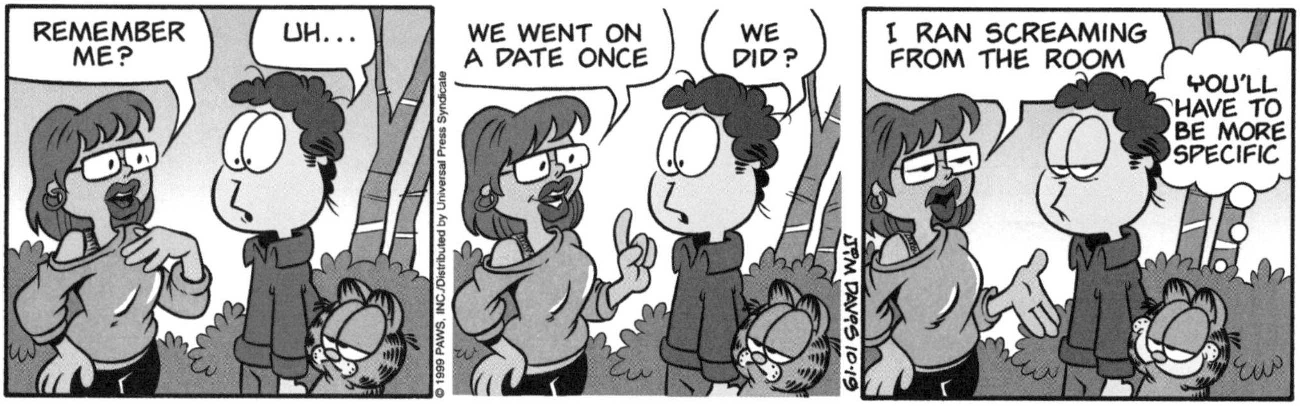
REMEMBER ME?
UH...
© 1999 PAWS, INC./Distributed by Universal Press Syndicate
WE WENT ON A DATE ONCE
WE DID?
JIM DAVIS 10-19
I RAN SCREAMING FROM THE ROOM
YOU'LL HAVE TO BE MORE SPECIFIC

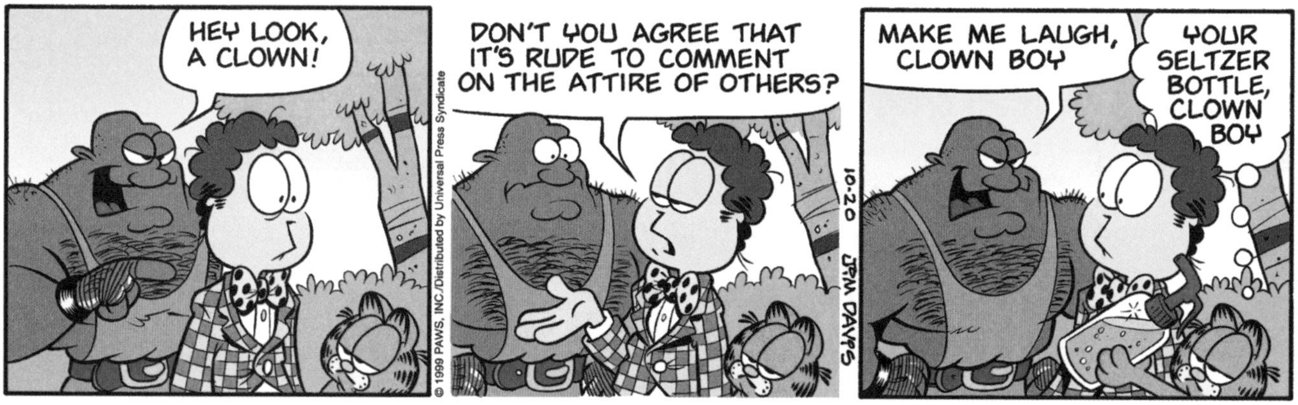
HEY LOOK, A CLOWN!
© 1999 PAWS, INC./Distributed by Universal Press Syndicate
DON'T YOU AGREE THAT IT'S RUDE TO COMMENT ON THE ATTIRE OF OTHERS?
10-20 JIM DAVIS
MAKE ME LAUGH, CLOWN BOY
YOUR SELTZER BOTTLE, CLOWN BOY



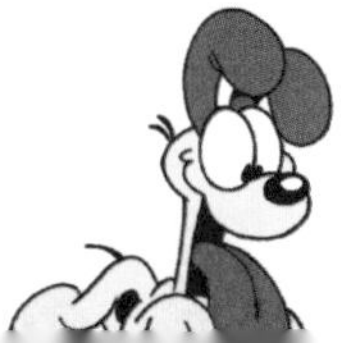

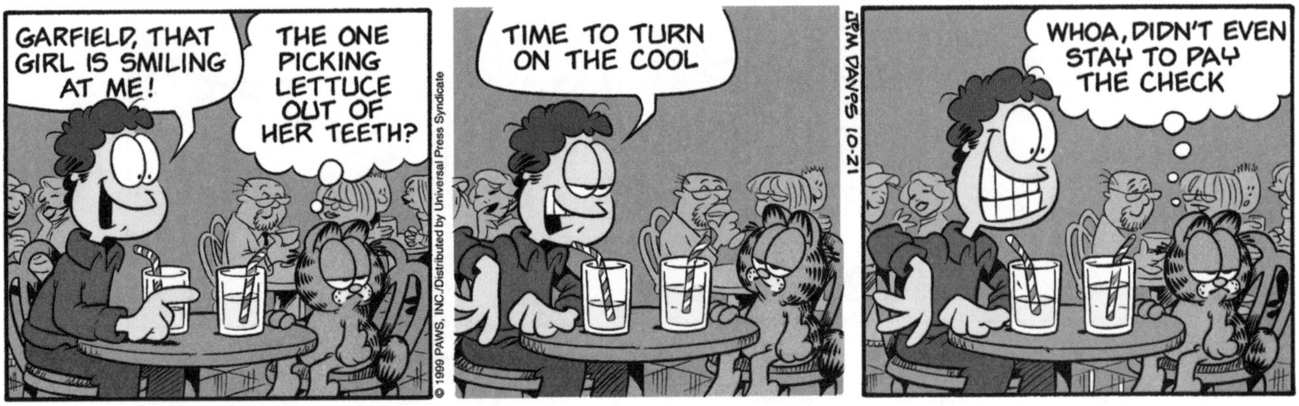
GARFIELD, THAT GIRL IS SMILING AT ME!
THE ONE PICKING LETTUCE OUT OF HER TEETH?
© 1999 PAWS, INC./Distributed by Universal Press Syndicate
TIME TO TURN ON THE COOL
JIM DAVIS 10-21
WHOA, DIDN'T EVEN STAY TO PAY THE CHECK

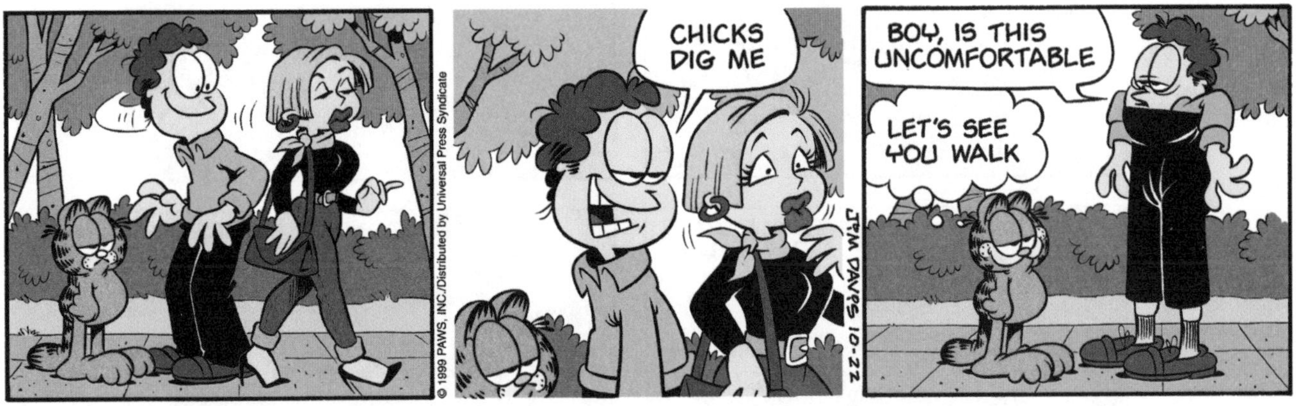
© 1999 PAWS, INC./Distributed by Universal Press Syndicate
CHICKS DIG ME
JIM DAVIS 10-22
BOY, IS THIS UNCOMFORTABLE
LET'S SEE YOU WALK

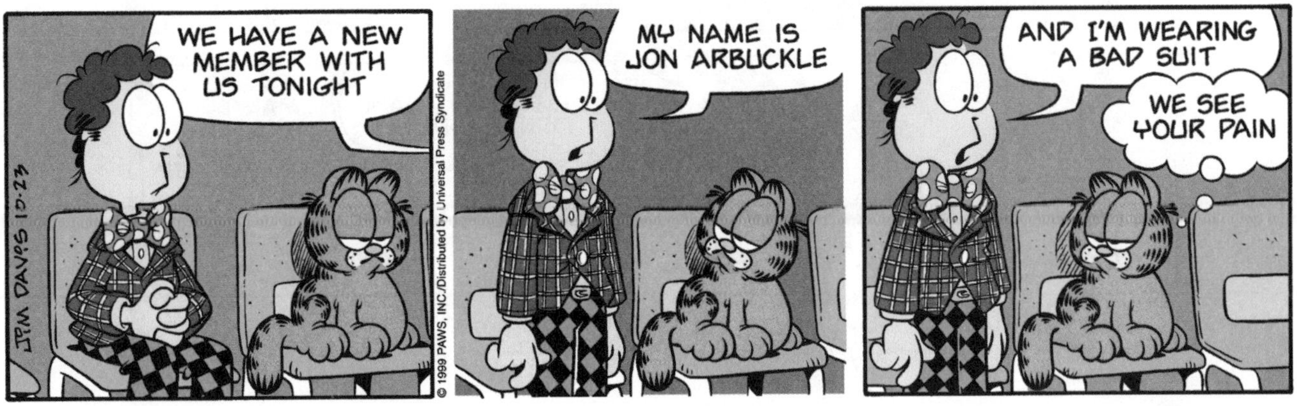
WE HAVE A NEW MEMBER WITH US TONIGHT
JIM DAVIS 10-23
© 1999 PAWS, INC./Distributed by Universal Press Syndicate
MY NAME IS JON ARBUCKLE
AND I'M WEARING A BAD SUIT
WE SEE YOUR PAIN

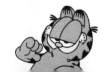

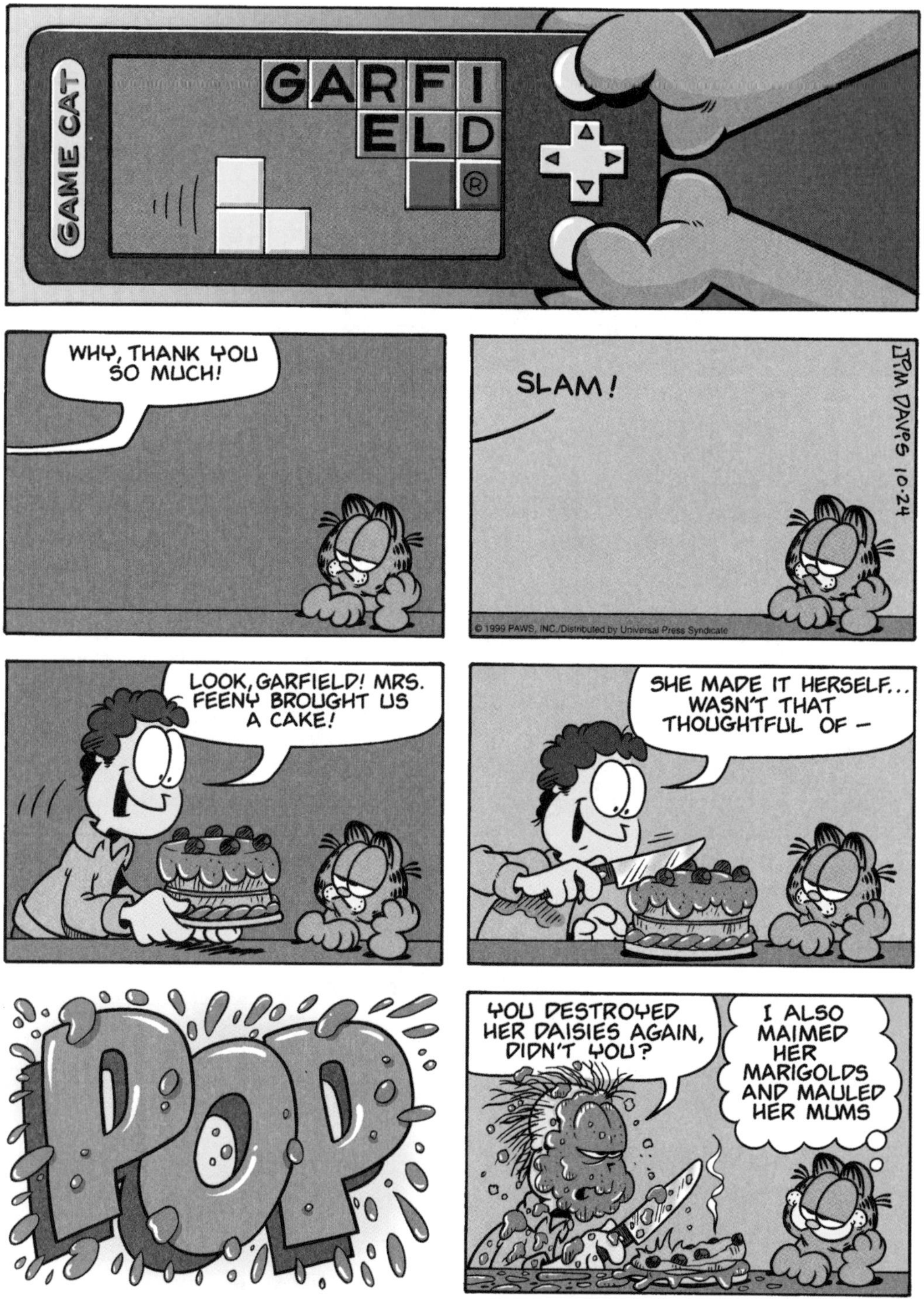
GAME CAT
GARFIELD®
WHY, THANK YOU SO MUCH!
SLAM!
JPM DAVPS 10·24
© 1999 PAWS, INC./Distributed by Universal Press Syndicate
LOOK, GARFIELD! MRS. FEENY BROUGHT US A CAKE!
SHE MADE IT HERSELF... WASN'T THAT THOUGHTFUL OF –
POP
YOU DESTROYED HER DAISIES AGAIN, DIDN'T YOU?
I ALSO MAIMED HER MARIGOLDS AND MAULED HER MUMS

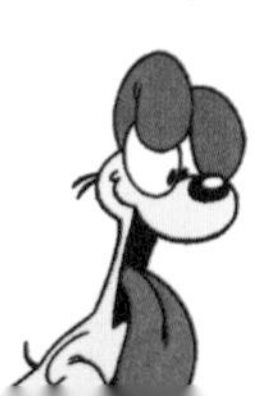

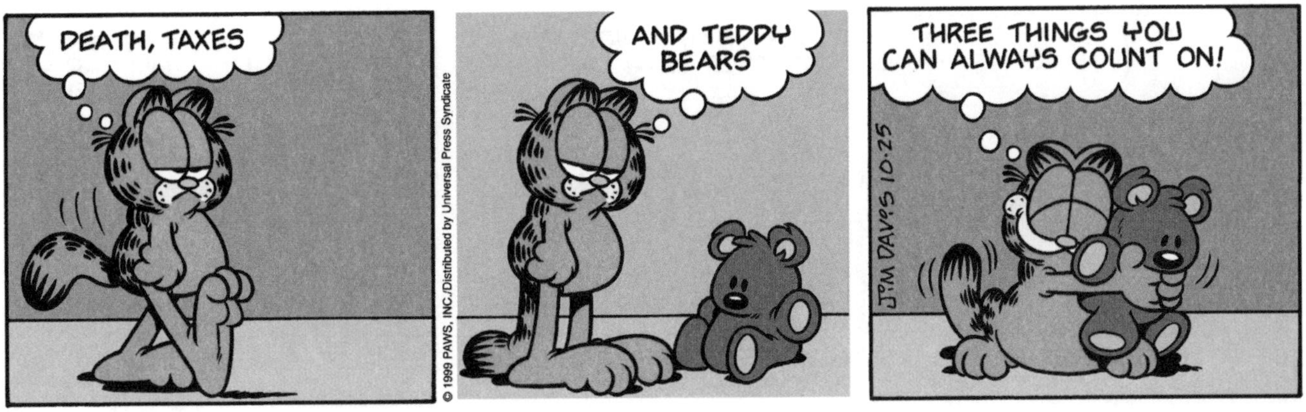
DEATH, TAXES
AND TEDDY BEARS
THREE THINGS YOU CAN ALWAYS COUNT ON!
JIM DAVIS 10-25
© 1999 PAWS, INC./Distributed by Universal Press Syndicate

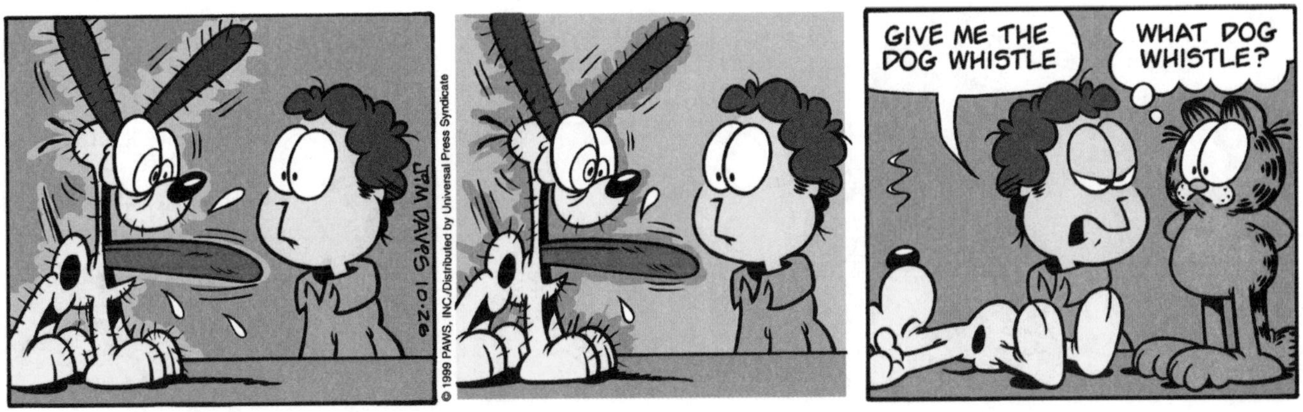
JIM DAVIS 10-26
© 1999 PAWS, INC./Distributed by Universal Press Syndicate
GIVE ME THE DOG WHISTLE
WHAT DOG WHISTLE?

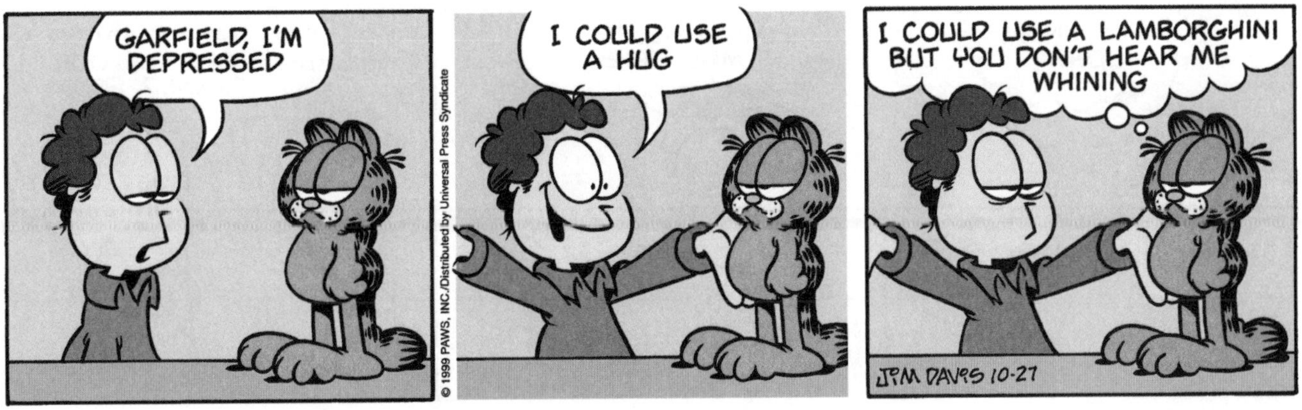
GARFIELD, I'M DEPRESSED
© 1999 PAWS, INC./Distributed by Universal Press Syndicate
I COULD USE A HUG
I COULD USE A LAMBORGHINI BUT YOU DON'T HEAR ME WHINING
JIM DAVIS 10-27

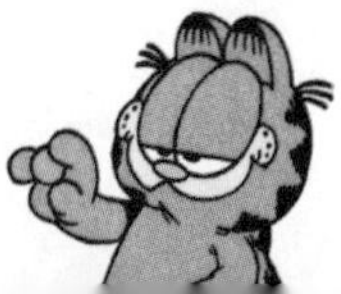

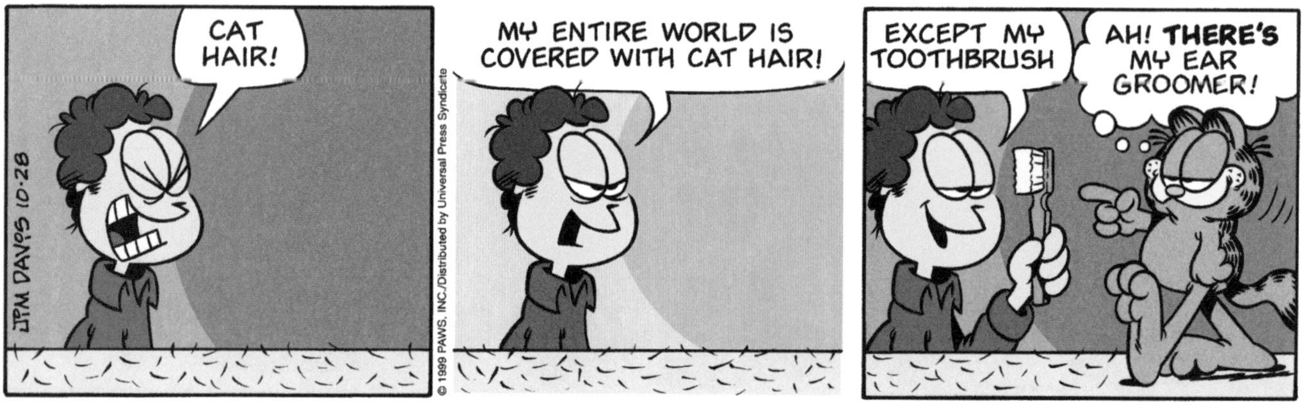
CAT HAIR!
JIM DAVIS 10-28
© 1999 PAWS, INC./Distributed by Universal Press Syndicate
MY ENTIRE WORLD IS COVERED WITH CAT HAIR!
EXCEPT MY TOOTHBRUSH
AH! **THERE'S** MY EAR GROOMER!

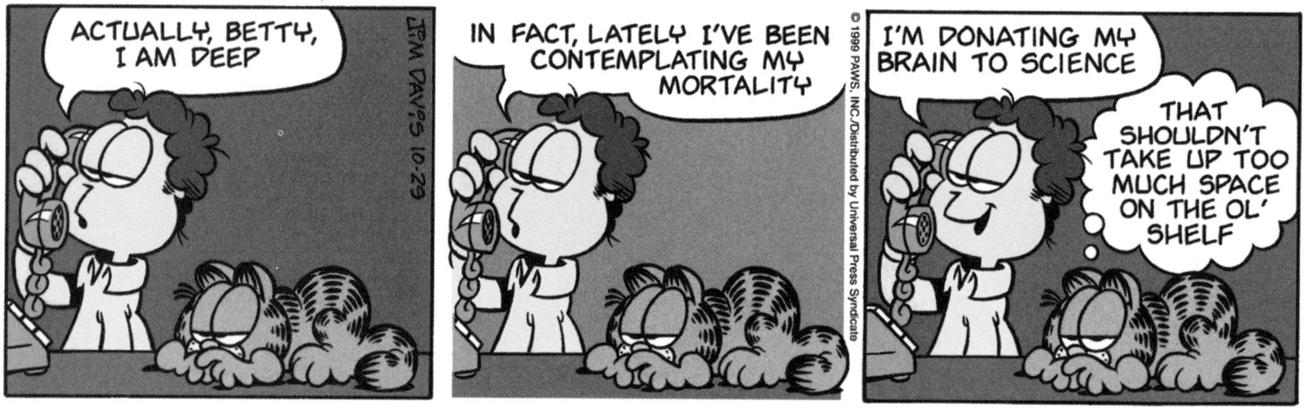
ACTUALLY, BETTY, I AM DEEP
JIM DAVIS 10-29
IN FACT, LATELY I'VE BEEN CONTEMPLATING MY MORTALITY
© 1999 PAWS, INC./Distributed by Universal Press Syndicate
I'M DONATING MY BRAIN TO SCIENCE
THAT SHOULDN'T TAKE UP TOO MUCH SPACE ON THE OL' SHELF

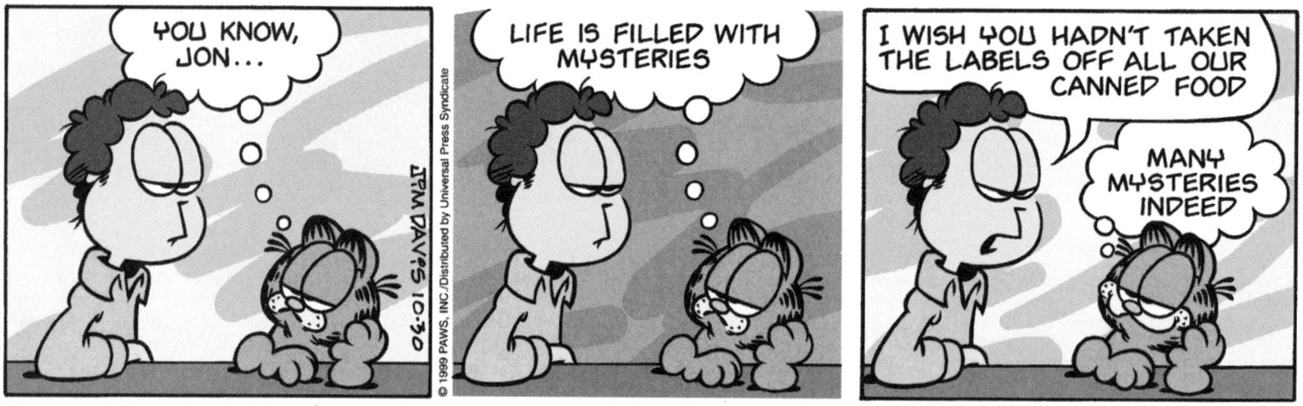
YOU KNOW, JON...
JIM DAVIS 10-30
© 1999 PAWS, INC./Distributed by Universal Press Syndicate
LIFE IS FILLED WITH MYSTERIES
I WISH YOU HADN'T TAKEN THE LABELS OFF ALL OUR CANNED FOOD
MANY MYSTERIES INDEED



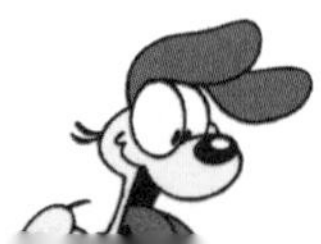

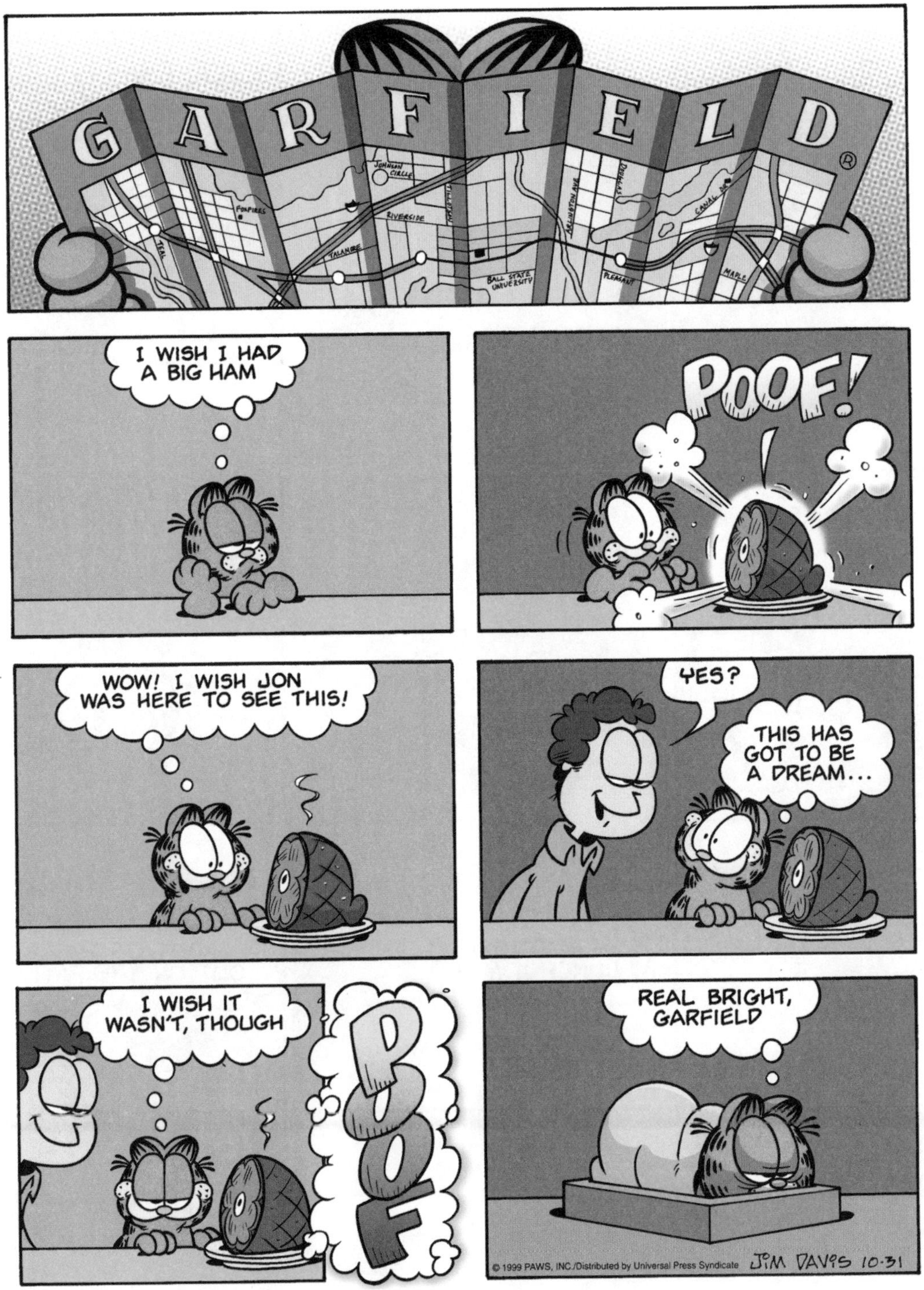
GARFIELD®
I WISH I HAD A BIG HAM
POOF!
WOW! I WISH JON WAS HERE TO SEE THIS!
YES?
THIS HAS GOT TO BE A DREAM...
I WISH IT WASN'T, THOUGH
POOF
REAL BRIGHT, GARFIELD
© 1999 PAWS, INC./Distributed by Universal Press Syndicate
JIM DAVIS 10-31

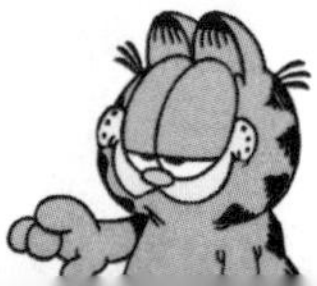

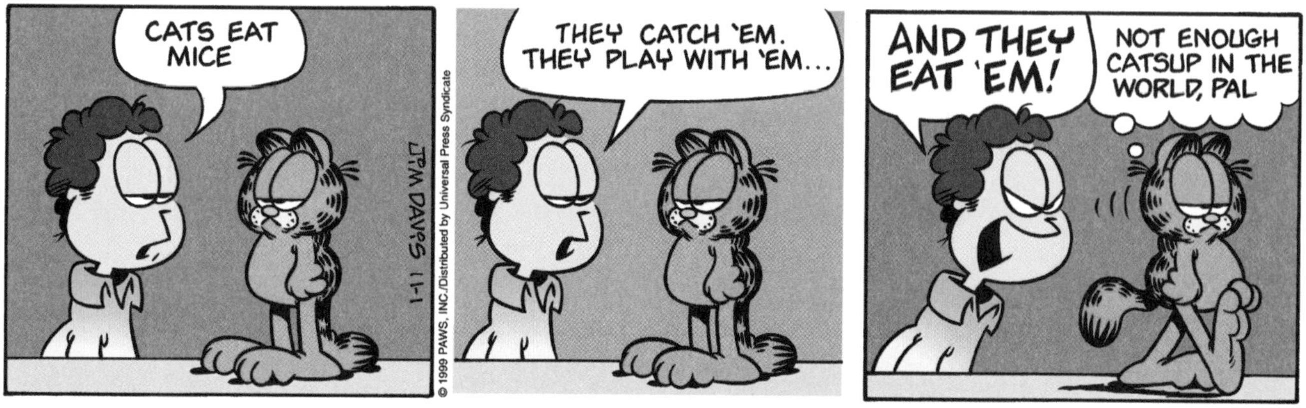
CATS EAT MICE
JIM DAVIS 11-1
© 1999 PAWS, INC./Distributed by Universal Press Syndicate
THEY CATCH 'EM. THEY PLAY WITH 'EM...
AND THEY EAT 'EM!
NOT ENOUGH CATSUP IN THE WORLD, PAL

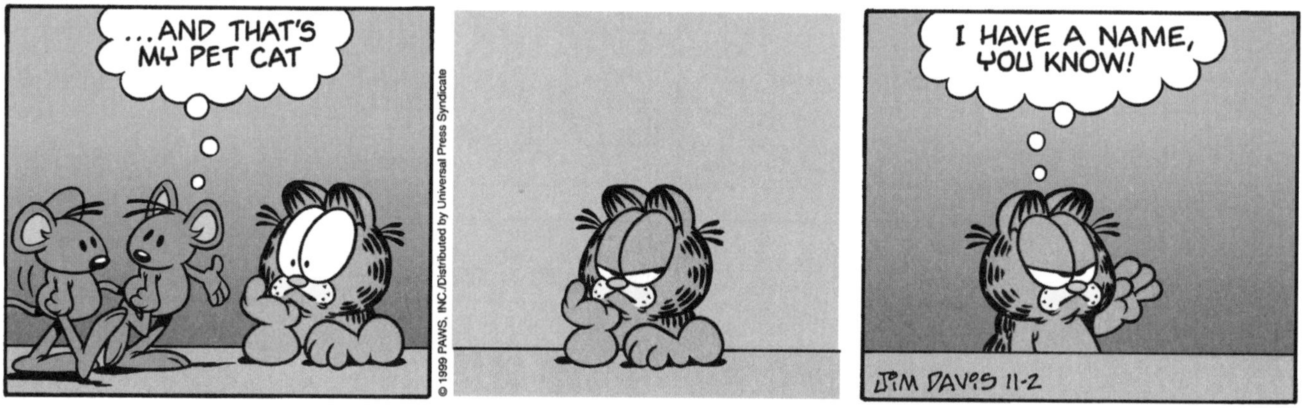
...AND THAT'S MY PET CAT
© 1999 PAWS, INC./Distributed by Universal Press Syndicate
I HAVE A NAME, YOU KNOW!
JIM DAVIS 11-2

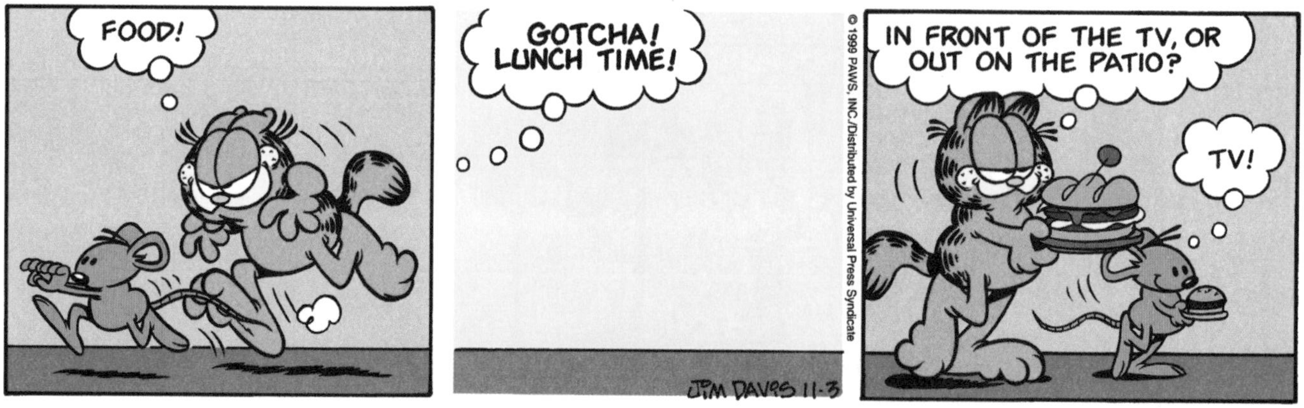
FOOD!
GOTCHA! LUNCH TIME!
JIM DAVIS 11-3
© 1999 PAWS, INC./Distributed by Universal Press Syndicate
IN FRONT OF THE TV, OR OUT ON THE PATIO?
TV!



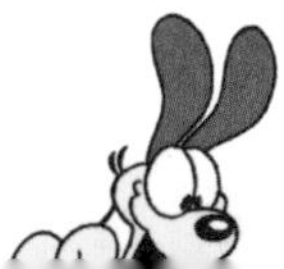

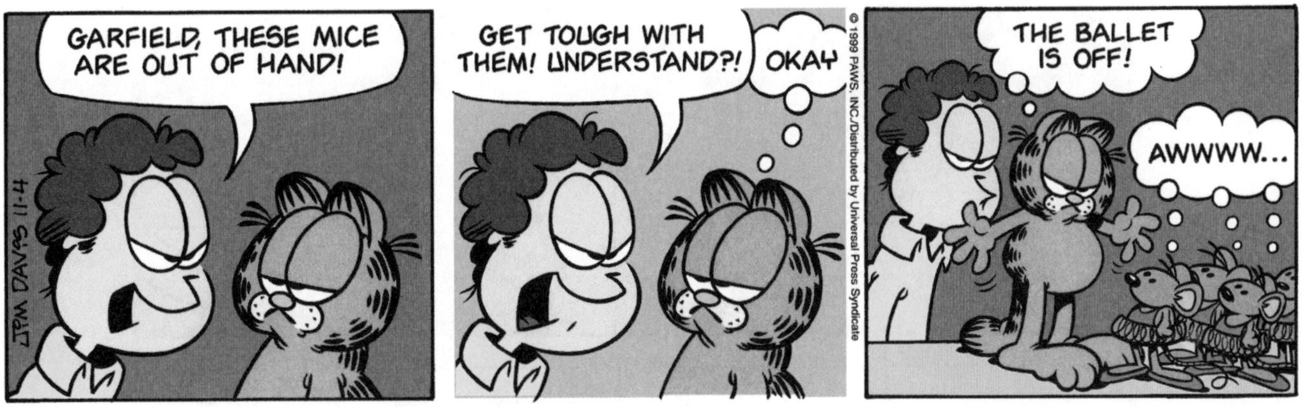
JPM DAVIS 11-4
GARFIELD, THESE MICE ARE OUT OF HAND!
GET TOUGH WITH THEM! UNDERSTAND?!
OKAY
© 1999 PAWS, INC./Distributed by Universal Press Syndicate
THE BALLET IS OFF!
AWWWW...

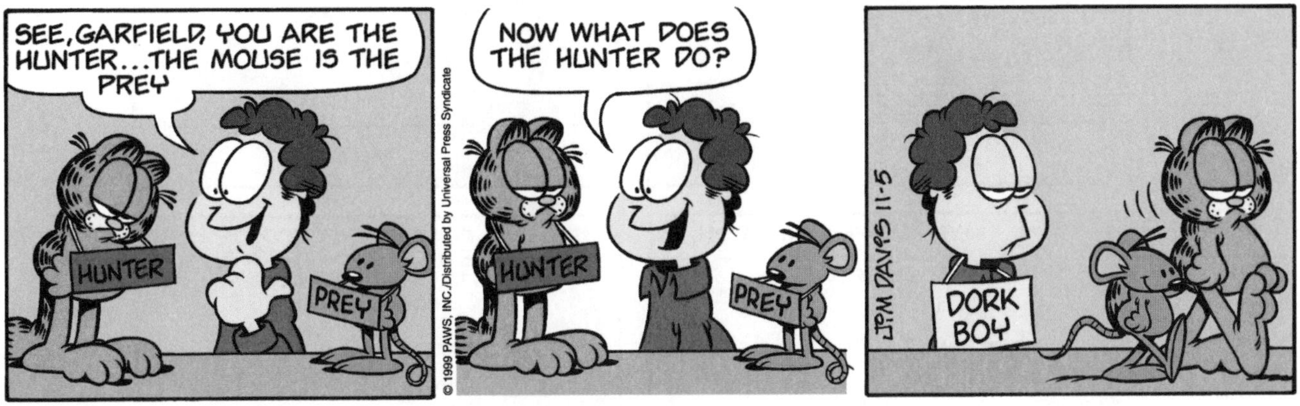
SEE, GARFIELD, YOU ARE THE HUNTER...THE MOUSE IS THE PREY
HUNTER
PREY
© 1999 PAWS, INC./Distributed by Universal Press Syndicate
NOW WHAT DOES THE HUNTER DO?
HUNTER
PREY
JPM DAVIS 11-5
DORK BOY

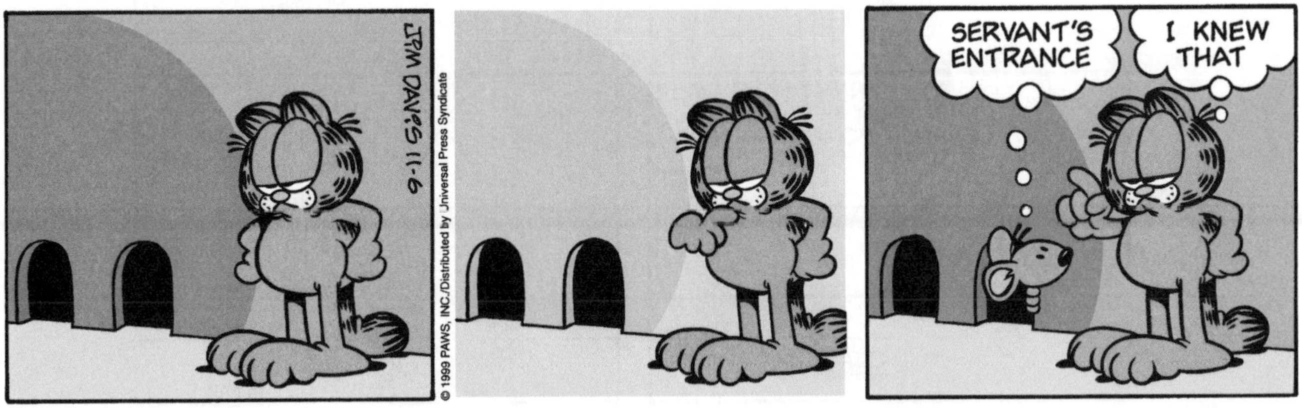
JPM DAVIS 11-6
© 1999 PAWS, INC./Distributed by Universal Press Syndicate
SERVANT'S ENTRANCE
I KNEW THAT

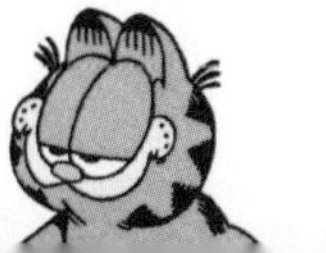

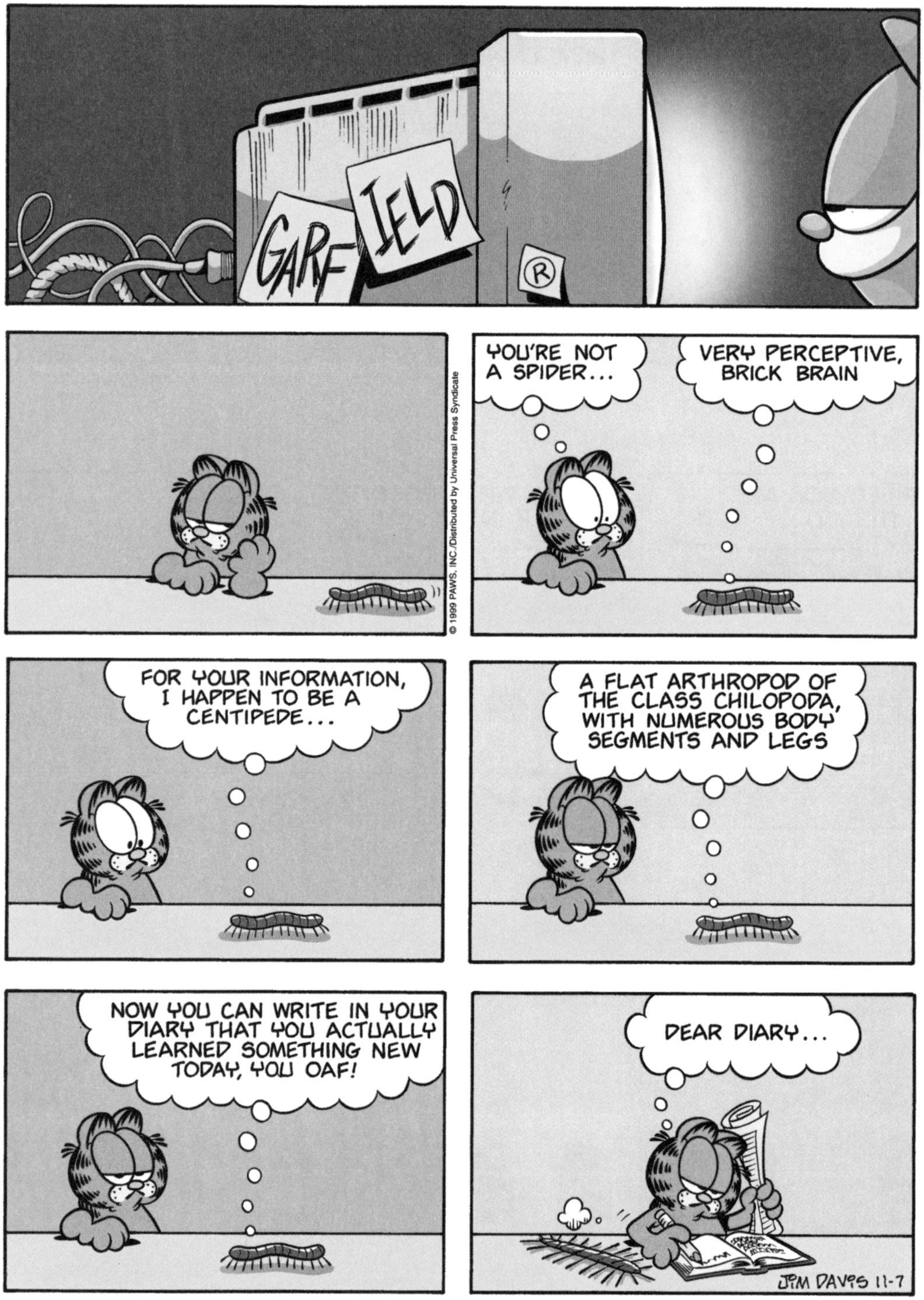
GARF
IELD
®
YOU'RE NOT A SPIDER...
VERY PERCEPTIVE, BRICK BRAIN
FOR YOUR INFORMATION, I HAPPEN TO BE A CENTIPEDE...
A FLAT ARTHROPOD OF THE CLASS CHILOPODA, WITH NUMEROUS BODY SEGMENTS AND LEGS
NOW YOU CAN WRITE IN YOUR DIARY THAT YOU ACTUALLY LEARNED SOMETHING NEW TODAY, YOU OAF!
DEAR DIARY...
JIM DAVIS 11-7





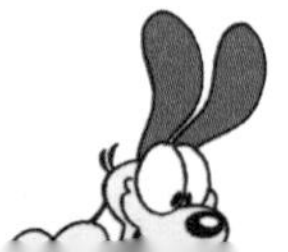

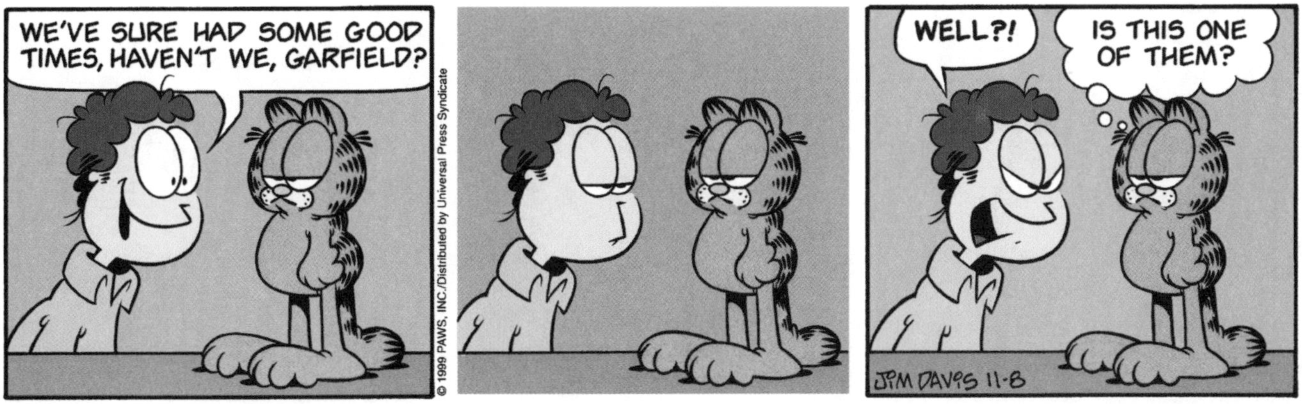
WE'VE SURE HAD SOME GOOD TIMES, HAVEN'T WE, GARFIELD?
© 1999 PAWS, INC./Distributed by Universal Press Syndicate
WELL?!
IS THIS ONE OF THEM?
JIM DAVIS 11-8

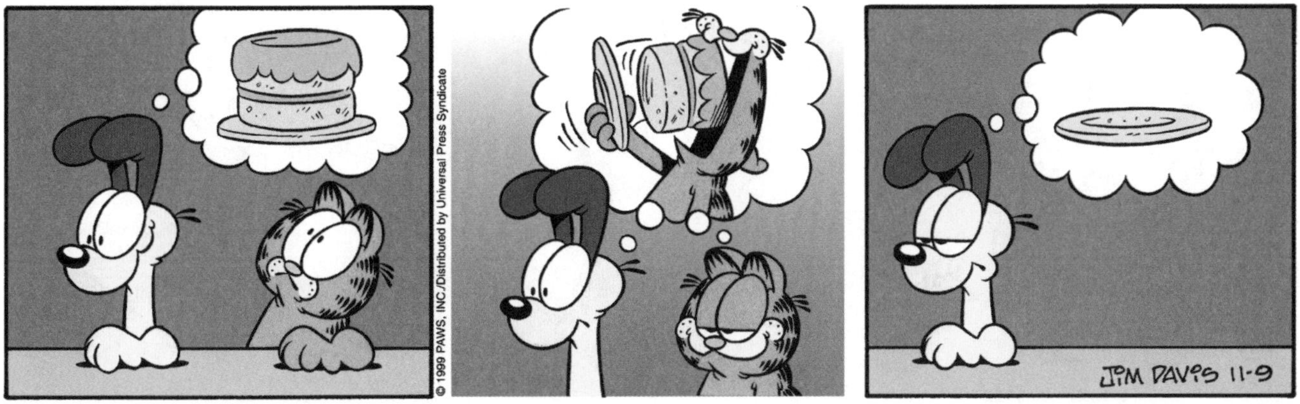
© 1999 PAWS, INC./Distributed by Universal Press Syndicate
JIM DAVIS 11-9

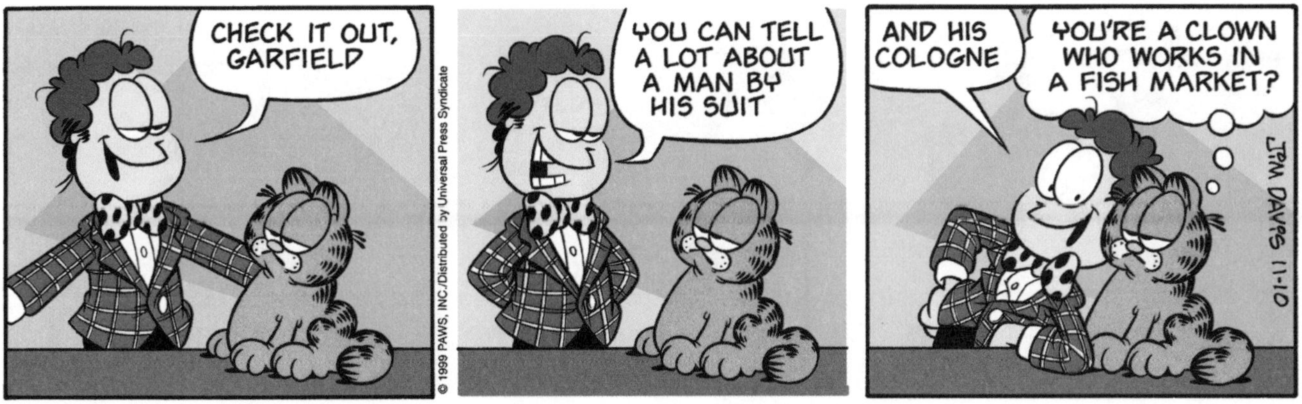
CHECK IT OUT, GARFIELD
© 1999 PAWS, INC./Distributed by Universal Press Syndicate
YOU CAN TELL A LOT ABOUT A MAN BY HIS SUIT
AND HIS COLOGNE
YOU'RE A CLOWN WHO WORKS IN A FISH MARKET?
JIM DAVIS 11-10

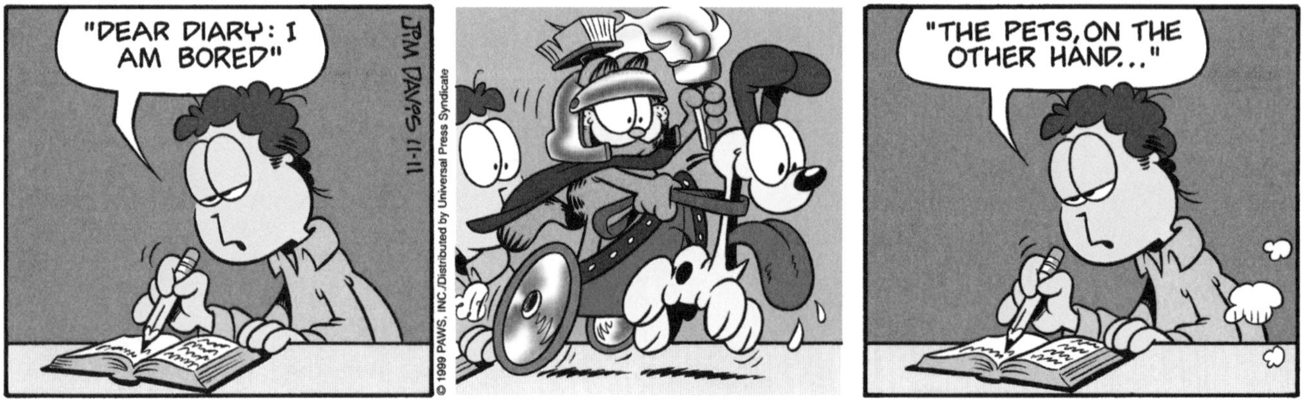
"DEAR DIARY: I AM BORED"
JIM DAVIS 11-11
© 1999 PAWS, INC./Distributed by Universal Press Syndicate
"THE PETS, ON THE OTHER HAND..."

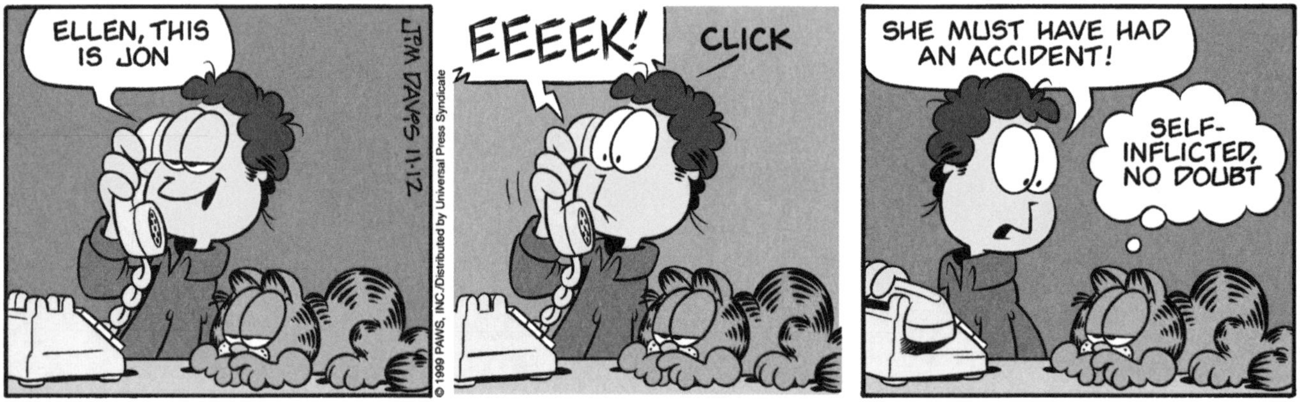
ELLEN, THIS IS JON
JIM DAVIS 11-12
© 1999 PAWS, INC./Distributed by Universal Press Syndicate
EEEEK!
CLICK
SHE MUST HAVE HAD AN ACCIDENT!
SELF-INFLICTED, NO DOUBT

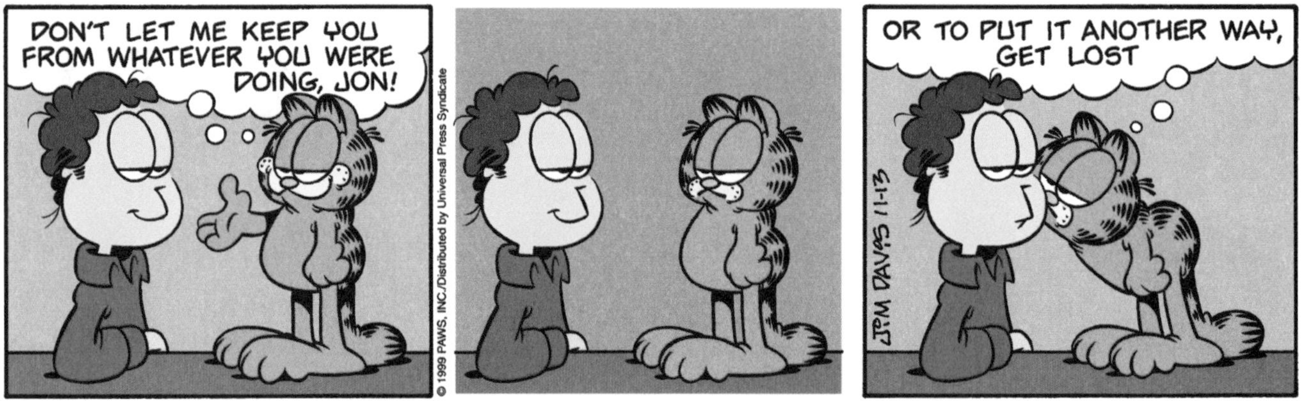
DON'T LET ME KEEP YOU FROM WHATEVER YOU WERE DOING, JON!
© 1999 PAWS, INC./Distributed by Universal Press Syndicate
JIM DAVIS 11-13
OR TO PUT IT ANOTHER WAY, GET LOST

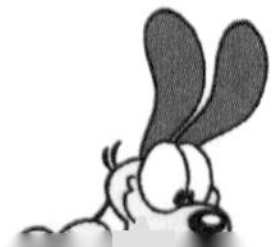

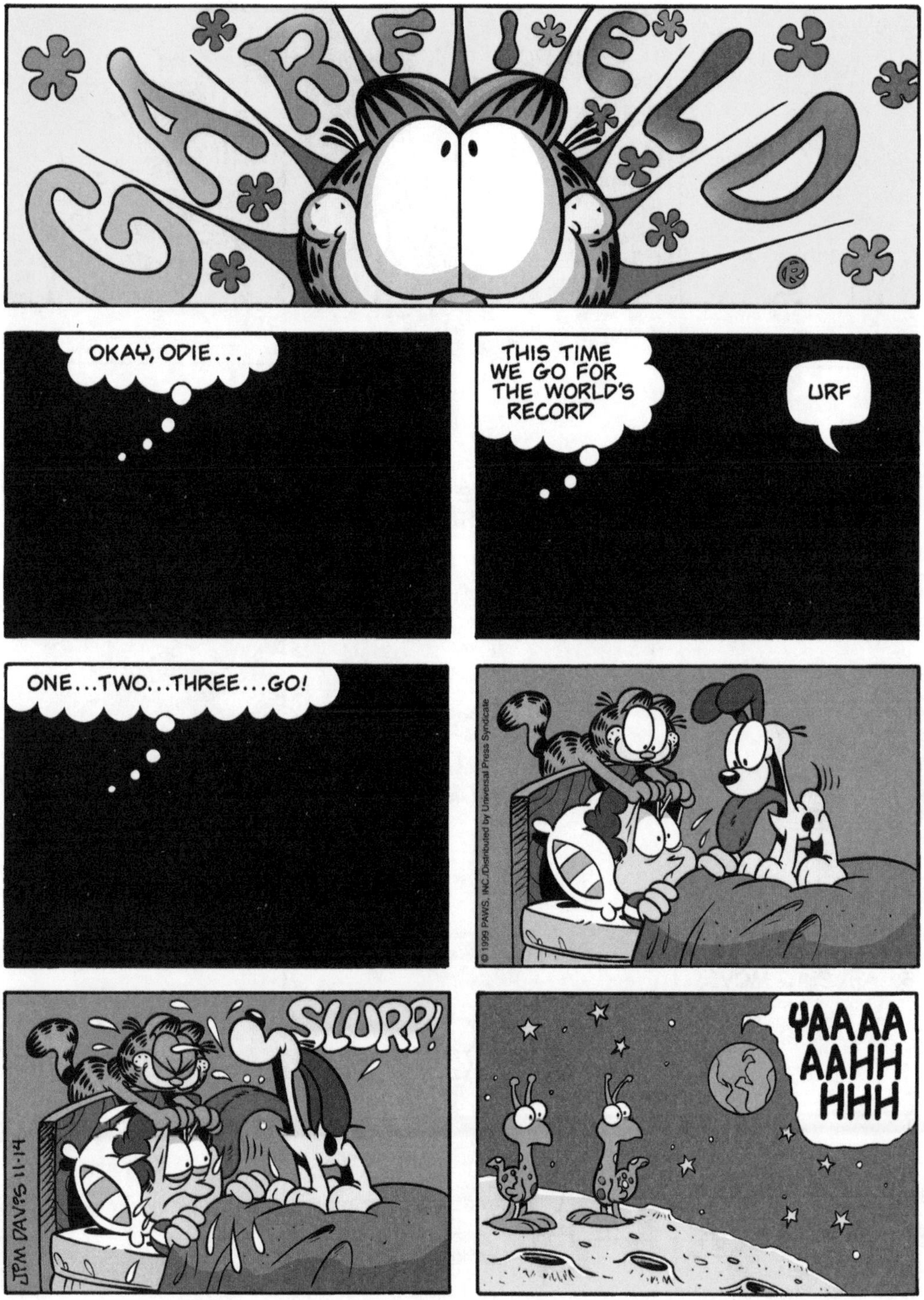
GARFIELD
OKAY, ODIE...
THIS TIME WE GO FOR THE WORLD'S RECORD
URF
ONE...TWO...THREE...GO!
© 1999 PAWS, INC./Distributed by Universal Press Syndicate
SLURP!
JIM DAVIS 11-14
YAAAAAAHHHHH

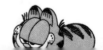

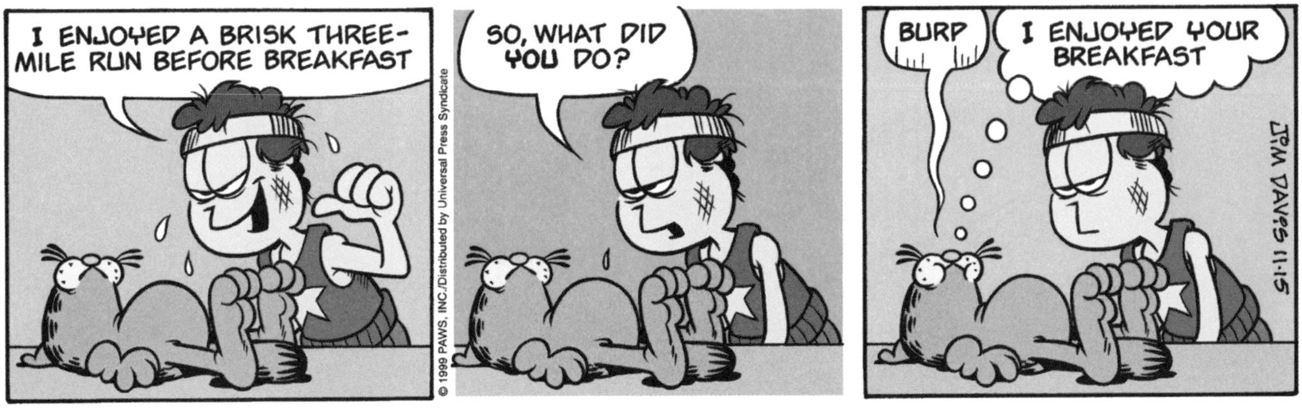
I ENJOYED A BRISK THREE-MILE RUN BEFORE BREAKFAST
SO, WHAT DID YOU DO?
BURP
I ENJOYED YOUR BREAKFAST
© 1999 PAWS, INC./Distributed by Universal Press Syndicate
JIM DAVIS 11-15

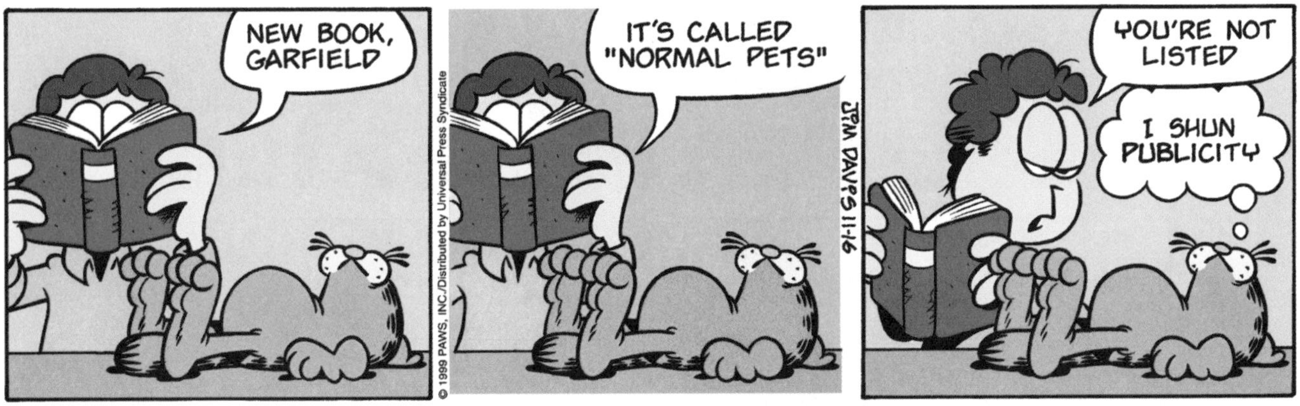
NEW BOOK, GARFIELD
IT'S CALLED "NORMAL PETS"
YOU'RE NOT LISTED
I SHUN PUBLICITY
© 1999 PAWS, INC./Distributed by Universal Press Syndicate
JIM DAVIS 11-16

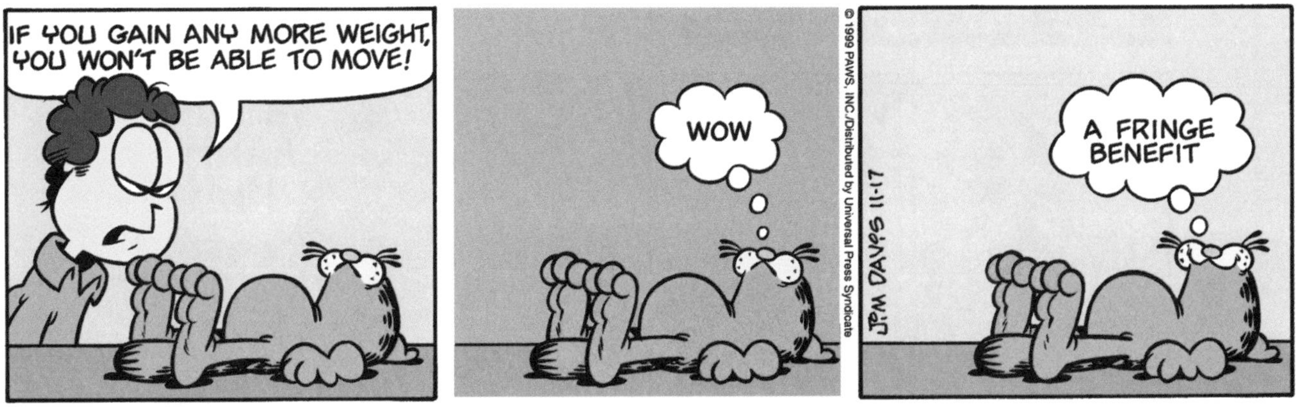
IF YOU GAIN ANY MORE WEIGHT, YOU WON'T BE ABLE TO MOVE!
WOW
A FRINGE BENEFIT
© 1999 PAWS, INC./Distributed by Universal Press Syndicate
JIM DAVIS 11-17

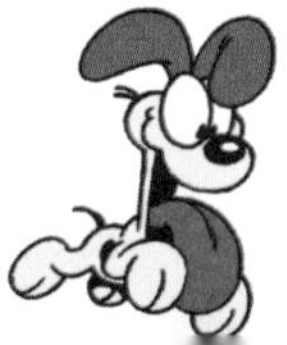

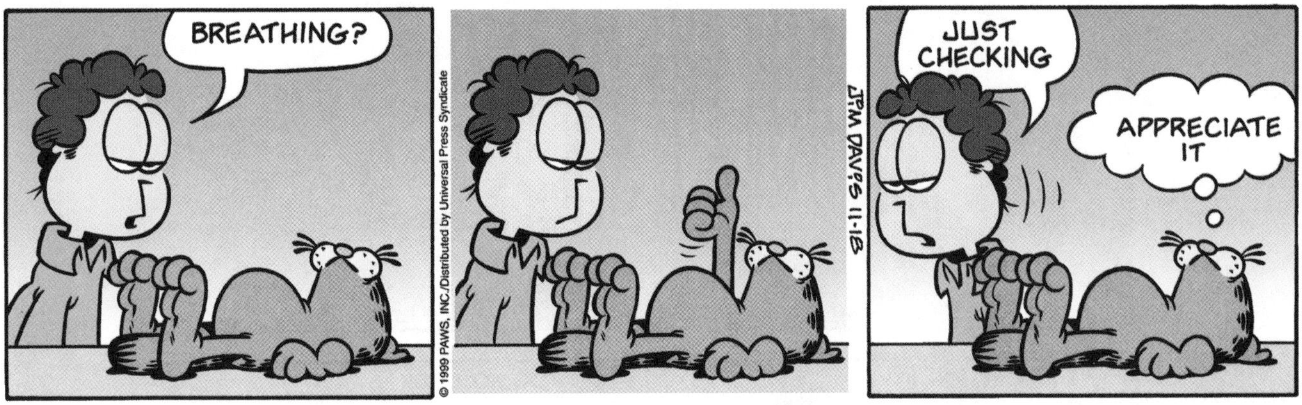
BREATHING?
© 1999 PAWS, INC./Distributed by Universal Press Syndicate
JIM DAVIS 11-18
JUST CHECKING
APPRECIATE IT

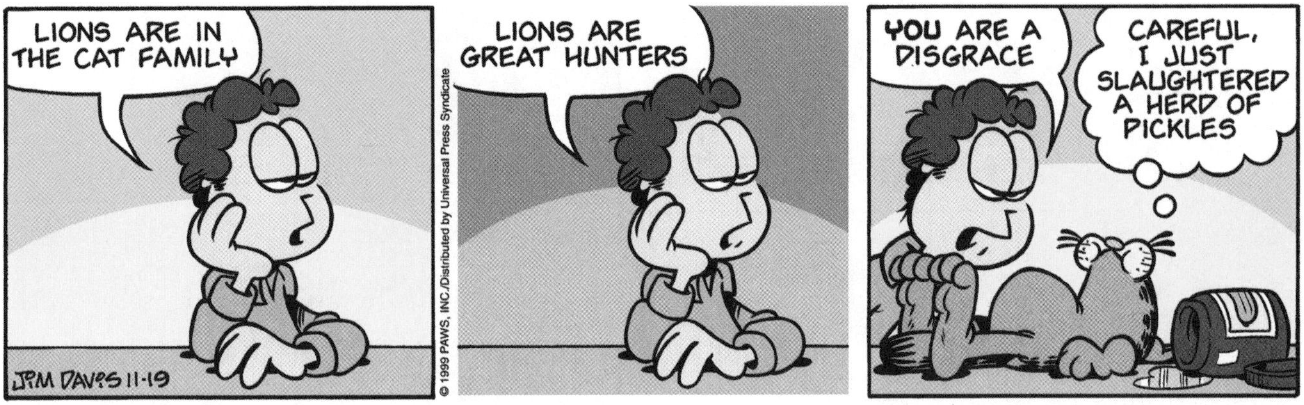
LIONS ARE IN THE CAT FAMILY
JIM DAVIS 11-19
© 1999 PAWS, INC./Distributed by Universal Press Syndicate
LIONS ARE GREAT HUNTERS
YOU ARE A DISGRACE
CAREFUL, I JUST SLAUGHTERED A HERD OF PICKLES

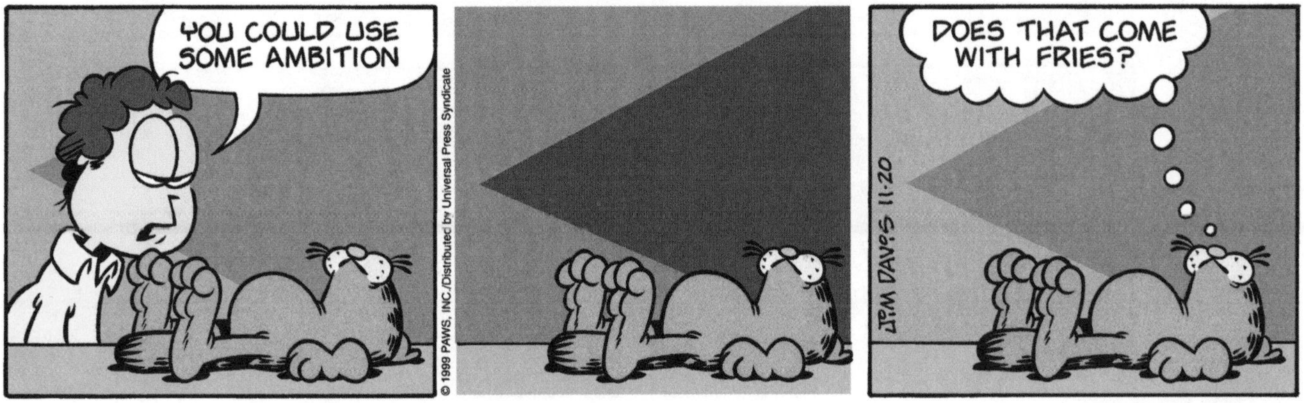
YOU COULD USE SOME AMBITION
© 1999 PAWS, INC./Distributed by Universal Press Syndicate
JIM DAVIS 11-20
DOES THAT COME WITH FRIES?

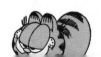

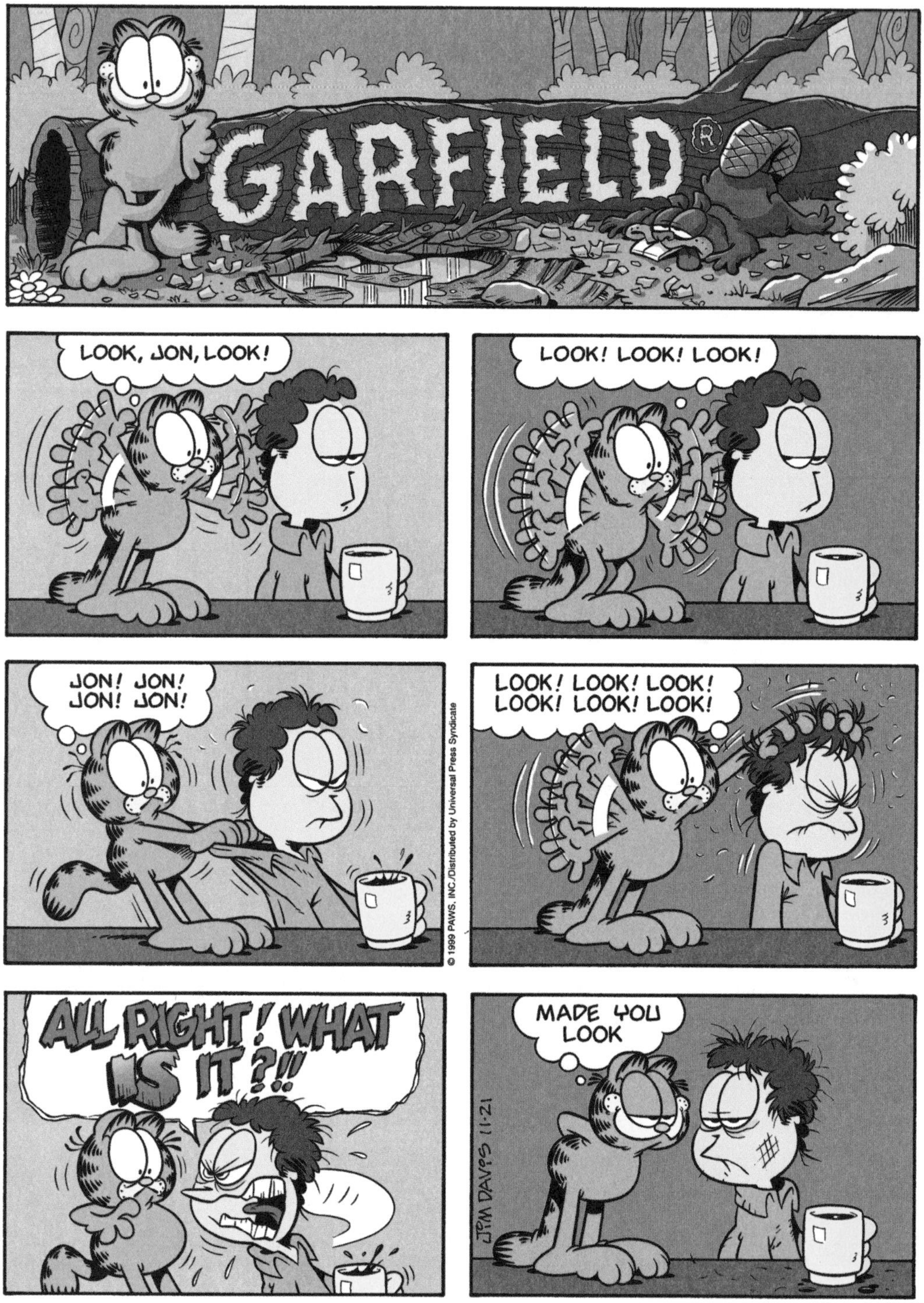
GARFIELD®
LOOK, JON, LOOK!
LOOK! LOOK! LOOK!
JON! JON! JON! JON!
LOOK! LOOK! LOOK! LOOK! LOOK! LOOK!
© 1999 PAWS, INC./Distributed by Universal Press Syndicate
ALL RIGHT! WHAT IS IT?!!
JIM DAVIS 11-21
MADE YOU LOOK

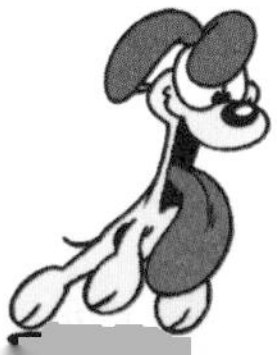

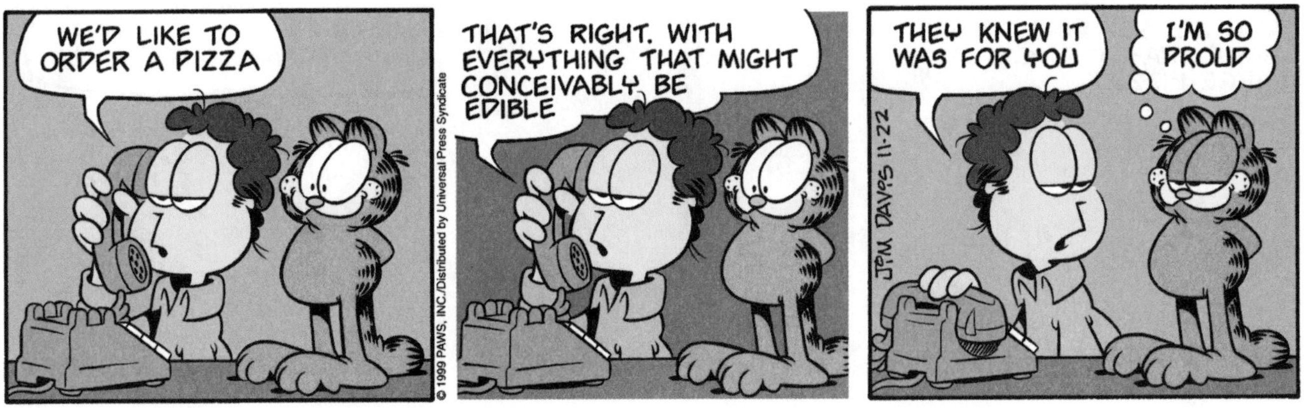
WE'D LIKE TO ORDER A PIZZA
© 1999 PAWS, INC./Distributed by Universal Press Syndicate
THAT'S RIGHT. WITH EVERYTHING THAT MIGHT CONCEIVABLY BE EDIBLE
JIM DAVIS 11-22
THEY KNEW IT WAS FOR YOU
I'M SO PROUD

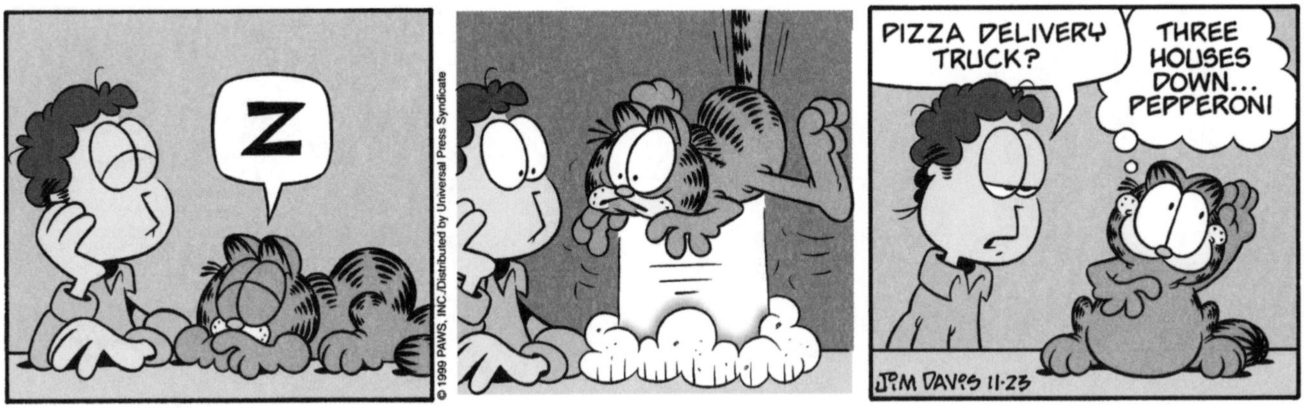
Z
© 1999 PAWS, INC./Distributed by Universal Press Syndicate
PIZZA DELIVERY TRUCK?
THREE HOUSES DOWN... PEPPERONI
JIM DAVIS 11-23

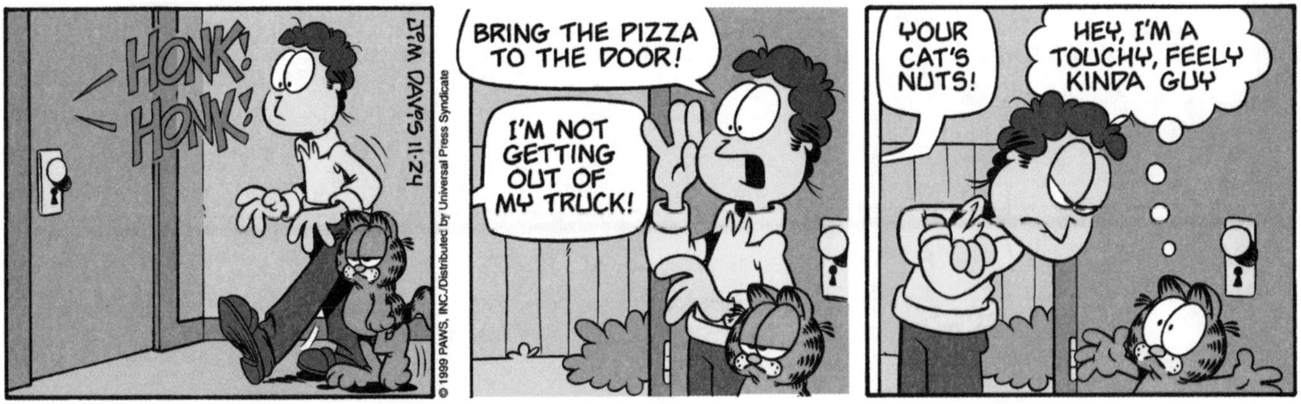
HONK! HONK!
JIM DAVIS 11-24
© 1999 PAWS, INC./Distributed by Universal Press Syndicate
BRING THE PIZZA TO THE DOOR!
I'M NOT GETTING OUT OF MY TRUCK!
YOUR CAT'S NUTS!
HEY, I'M A TOUCHY, FEELY KINDA GUY

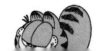

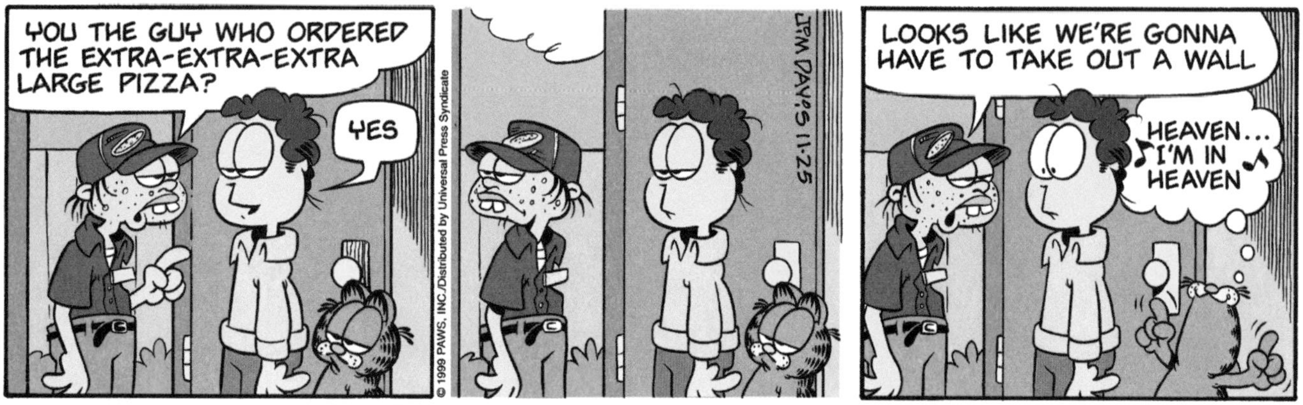
YOU THE GUY WHO ORDERED THE EXTRA-EXTRA-EXTRA LARGE PIZZA?
YES
© 1999 PAWS, INC./Distributed by Universal Press Syndicate
JIM DAVIS 11-25
LOOKS LIKE WE'RE GONNA HAVE TO TAKE OUT A WALL
HEAVEN... I'M IN HEAVEN

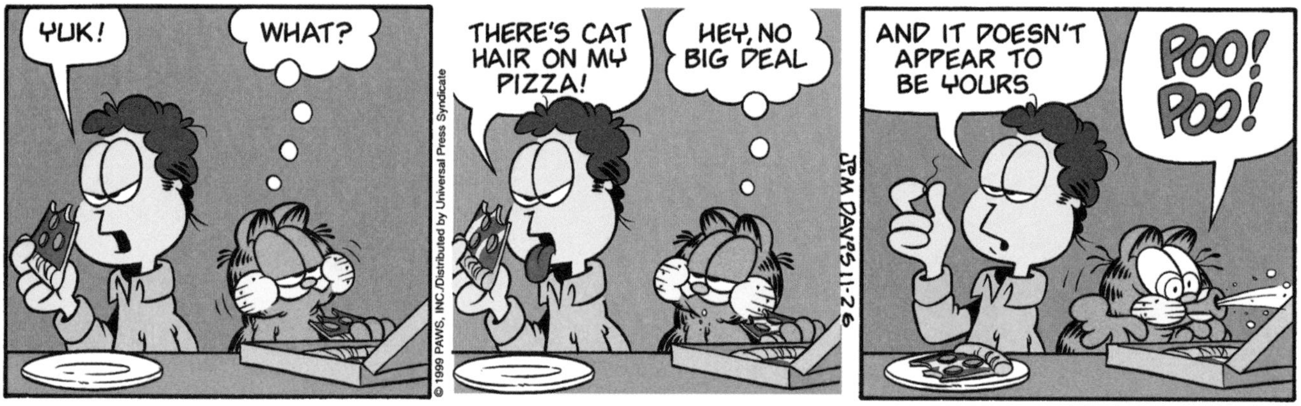
YUK!
WHAT?
© 1999 PAWS, INC./Distributed by Universal Press Syndicate
THERE'S CAT HAIR ON MY PIZZA!
HEY, NO BIG DEAL
JIM DAVIS 11-26
AND IT DOESN'T APPEAR TO BE YOURS
POO! POO!

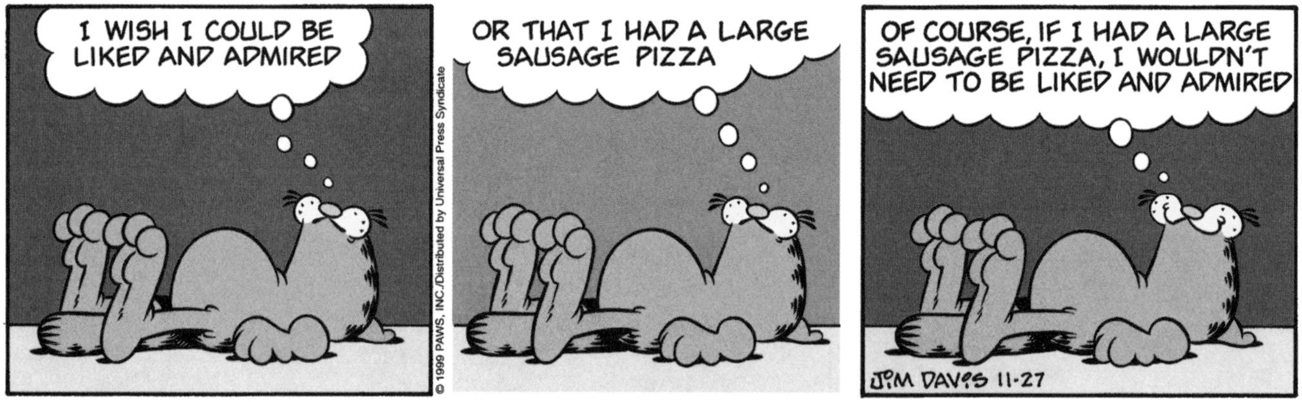
I WISH I COULD BE LIKED AND ADMIRED
© 1999 PAWS, INC./Distributed by Universal Press Syndicate
OR THAT I HAD A LARGE SAUSAGE PIZZA
OF COURSE, IF I HAD A LARGE SAUSAGE PIZZA, I WOULDN'T NEED TO BE LIKED AND ADMIRED
JIM DAVIS 11-27



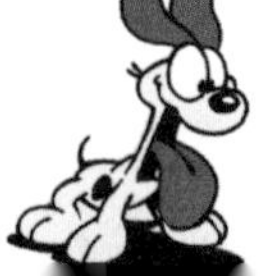

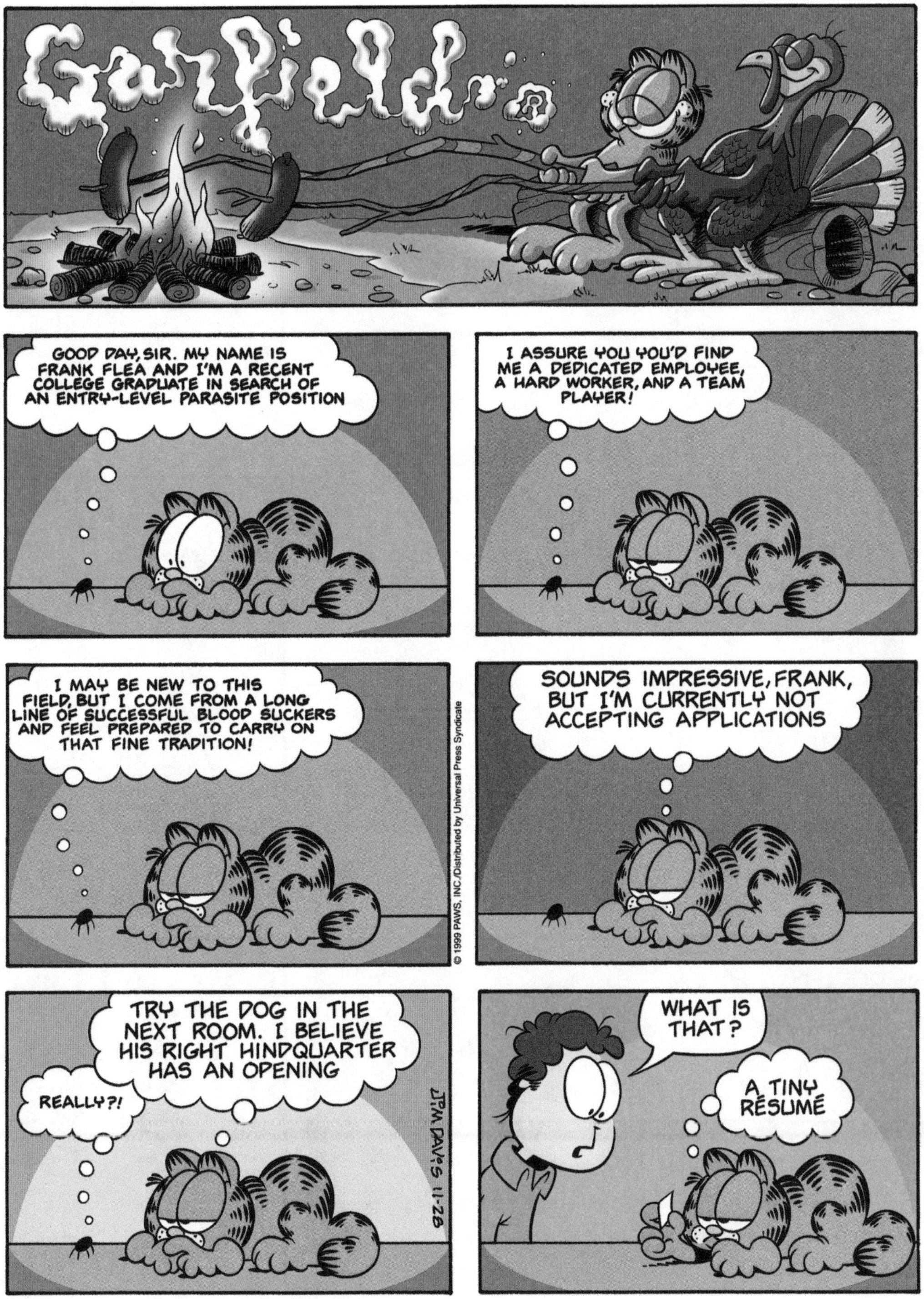
GARFIELD®
GOOD DAY, SIR. MY NAME IS FRANK FLEA AND I'M A RECENT COLLEGE GRADUATE IN SEARCH OF AN ENTRY-LEVEL PARASITE POSITION
I ASSURE YOU YOU'D FIND ME A DEDICATED EMPLOYEE, A HARD WORKER, AND A TEAM PLAYER!
I MAY BE NEW TO THIS FIELD, BUT I COME FROM A LONG LINE OF SUCCESSFUL BLOOD SUCKERS AND FEEL PREPARED TO CARRY ON THAT FINE TRADITION!
SOUNDS IMPRESSIVE, FRANK, BUT I'M CURRENTLY NOT ACCEPTING APPLICATIONS
TRY THE DOG IN THE NEXT ROOM. I BELIEVE HIS RIGHT HINDQUARTER HAS AN OPENING
REALLY?!
JIM DAVIS 11-28
WHAT IS THAT?
A TINY RÉSUMÉ

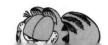

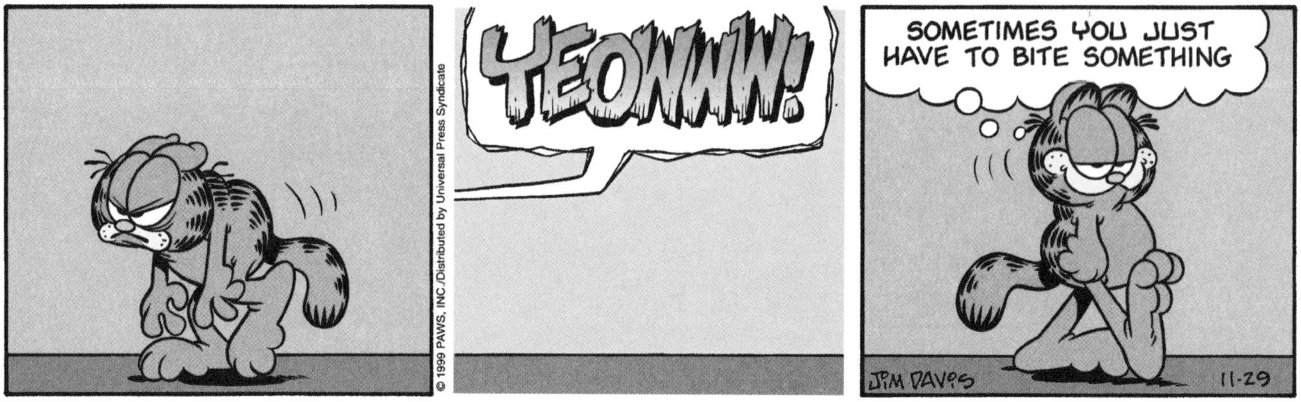
YEOWWW!
SOMETIMES YOU JUST HAVE TO BITE SOMETHING
© 1999 PAWS, INC./Distributed by Universal Press Syndicate
JIM DAVIS 11-29

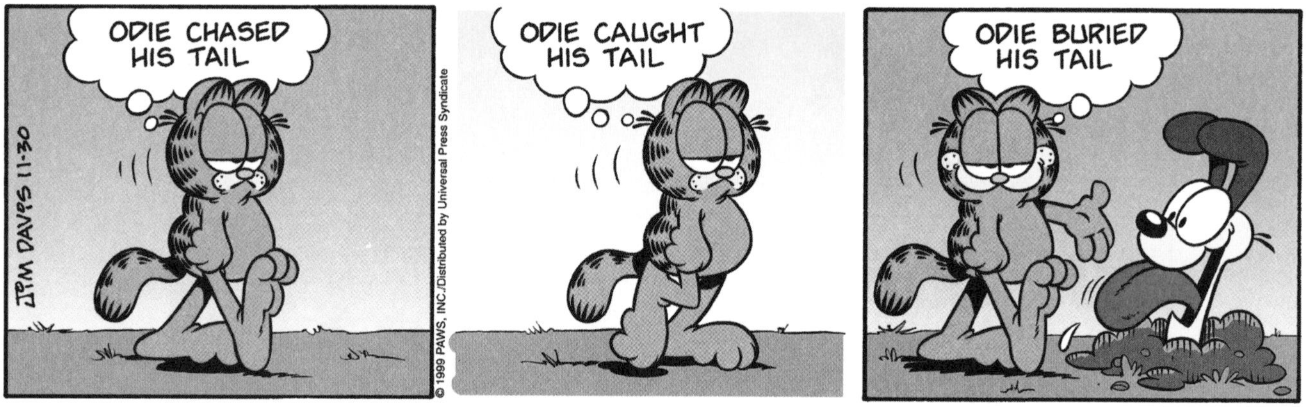
JIM DAVIS 11-30
ODIE CHASED HIS TAIL
ODIE CAUGHT HIS TAIL
ODIE BURIED HIS TAIL
© 1999 PAWS, INC./Distributed by Universal Press Syndicate

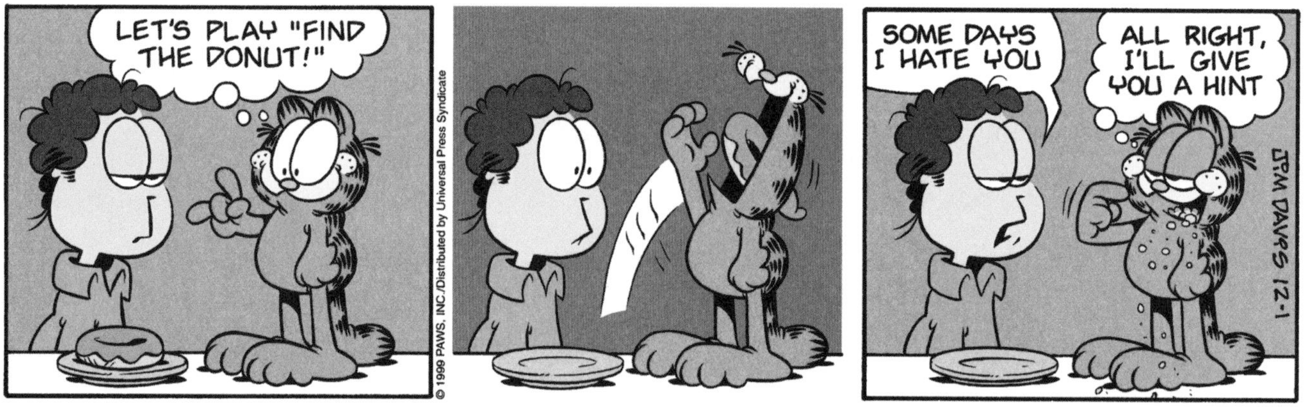
LET'S PLAY "FIND THE DONUT!"
SOME DAYS I HATE YOU
ALL RIGHT, I'LL GIVE YOU A HINT
JIM DAVIS 12-1
© 1999 PAWS, INC./Distributed by Universal Press Syndicate



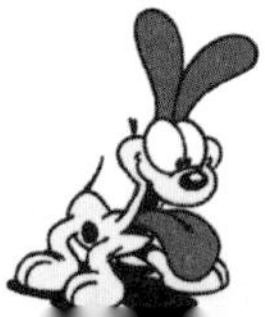

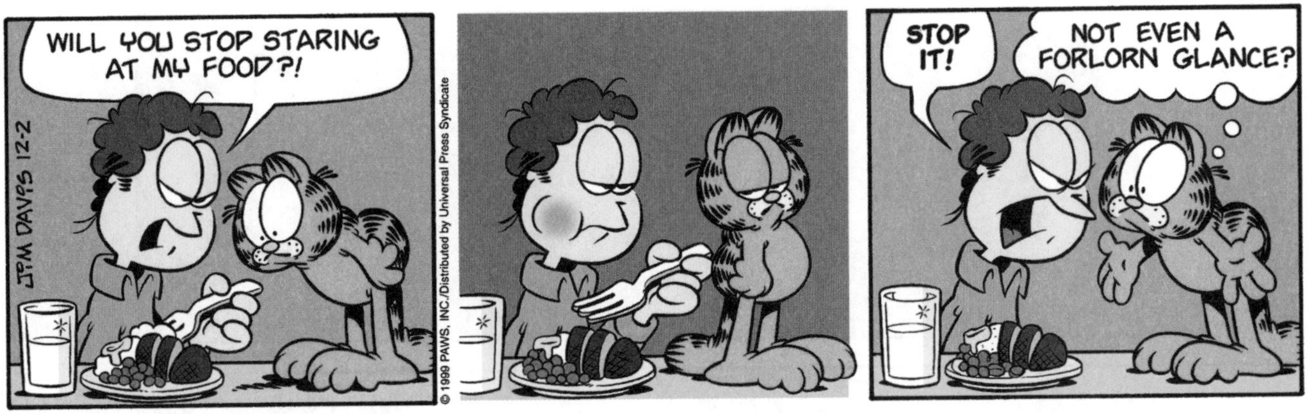
WILL YOU STOP STARING AT MY FOOD?!
JIM DAVIS 12-2
© 1999 PAWS, INC./Distributed by Universal Press Syndicate
STOP IT!
NOT EVEN A FORLORN GLANCE?

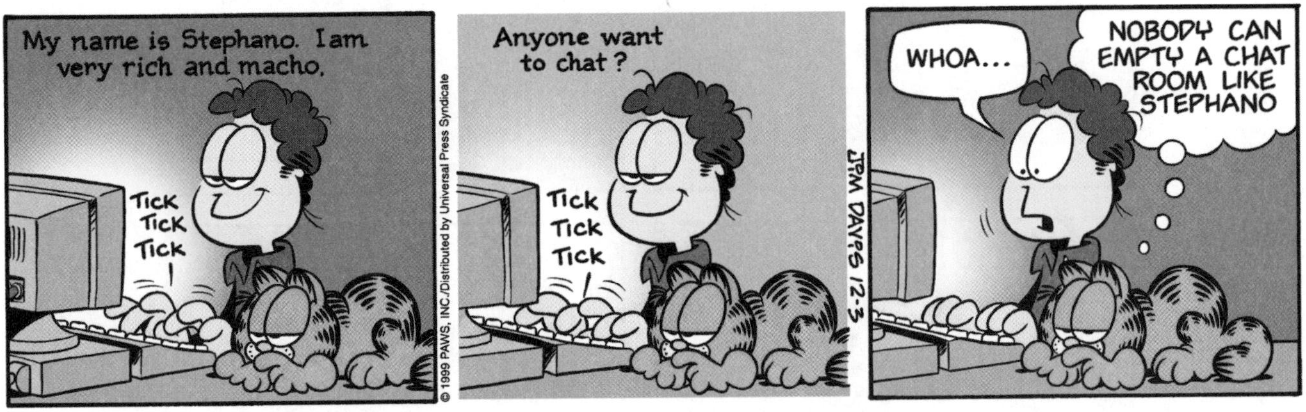
My name is Stephano. I am very rich and macho.
Tick Tick Tick
© 1999 PAWS, INC./Distributed by Universal Press Syndicate
Anyone want to chat?
Tick Tick Tick
JIM DAVIS 12-3
WHOA...
NOBODY CAN EMPTY A CHAT ROOM LIKE STEPHANO

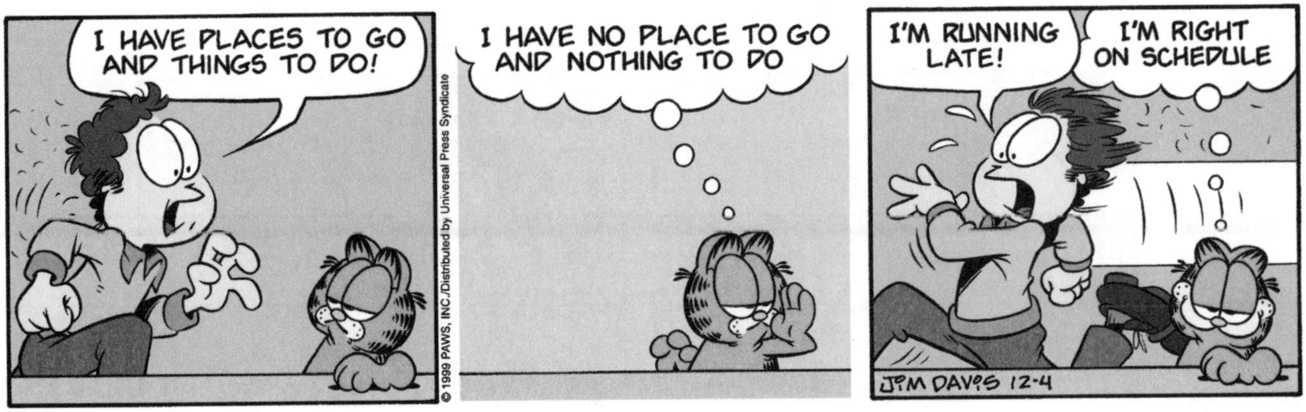
I HAVE PLACES TO GO AND THINGS TO DO!
© 1999 PAWS, INC./Distributed by Universal Press Syndicate
I HAVE NO PLACE TO GO AND NOTHING TO DO
I'M RUNNING LATE!
I'M RIGHT ON SCHEDULE
JIM DAVIS 12-4

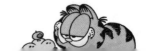

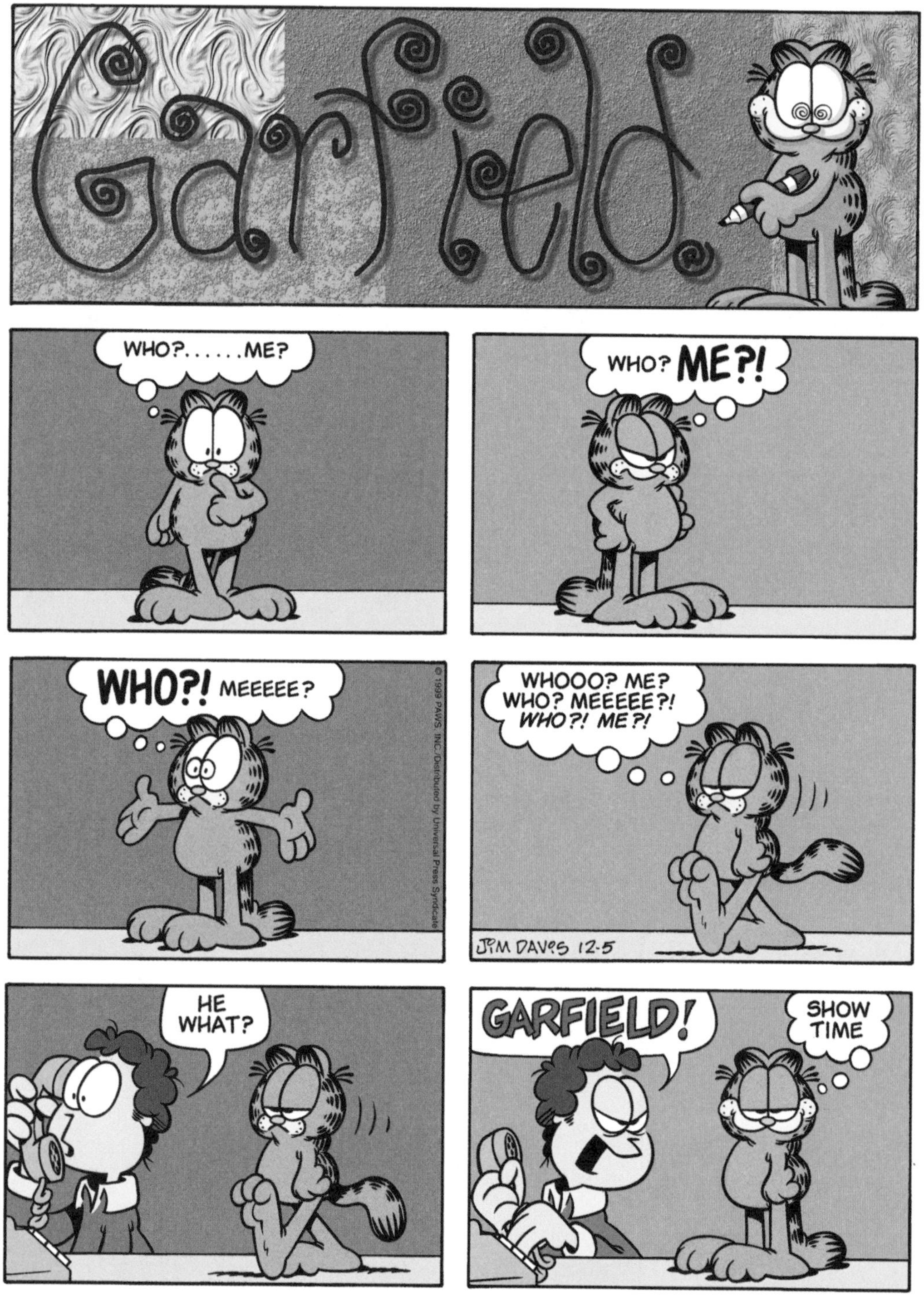
Garfield
WHO?......ME?
WHO? ME?!
WHO?! MEEEEE?
© 1999 PAWS, INC./Distributed by Universal Press Syndicate
WHOOO? ME?
WHO? MEEEEE?!
WHO?! ME?!
JIM DAVIS 12-5
HE WHAT?
GARFIELD!
SHOW TIME

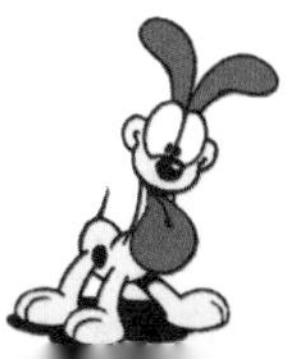

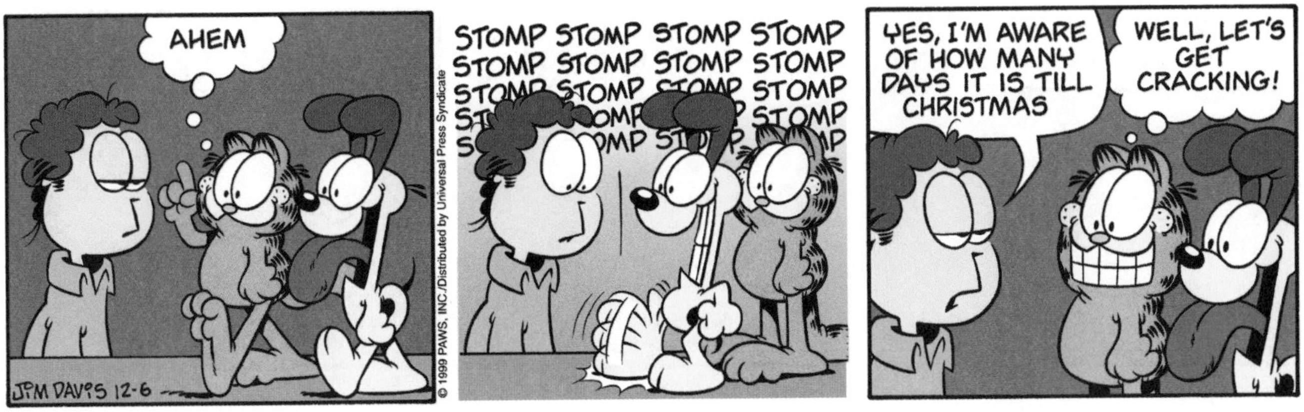
AHEM
JIM DAVIS 12-6
© 1999 PAWS, INC./Distributed by Universal Press Syndicate
STOMP STOMP STOMP STOMP
STOMP STOMP STOMP STOMP
STOMP STOMP STOMP STOMP
STOMP STOMP STOMP STOMP
STOMP STOMP STOMP STOMP
YES, I'M AWARE OF HOW MANY DAYS IT IS TILL CHRISTMAS
WELL, LET'S GET CRACKING!

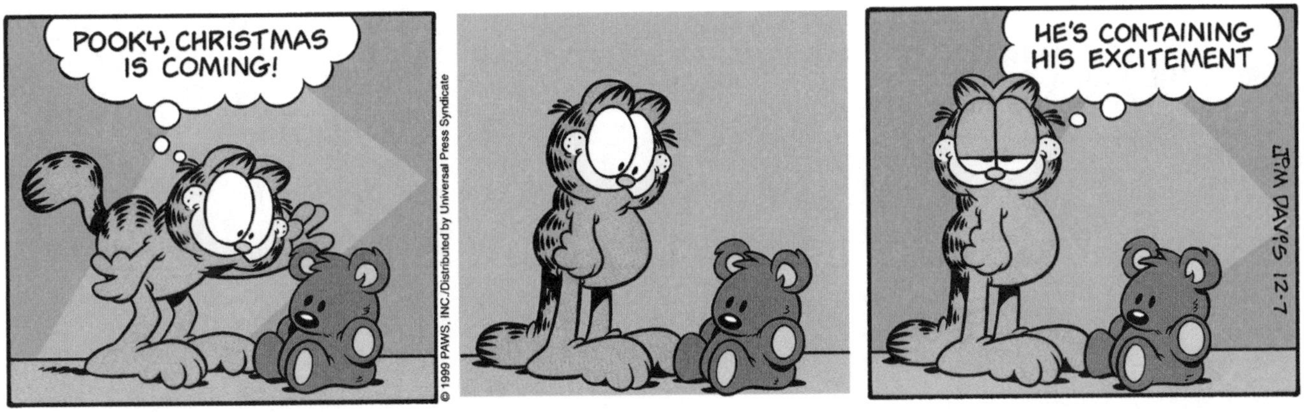
POOKY, CHRISTMAS IS COMING!
© 1999 PAWS, INC./Distributed by Universal Press Syndicate
HE'S CONTAINING HIS EXCITEMENT
JIM DAVIS 12-7

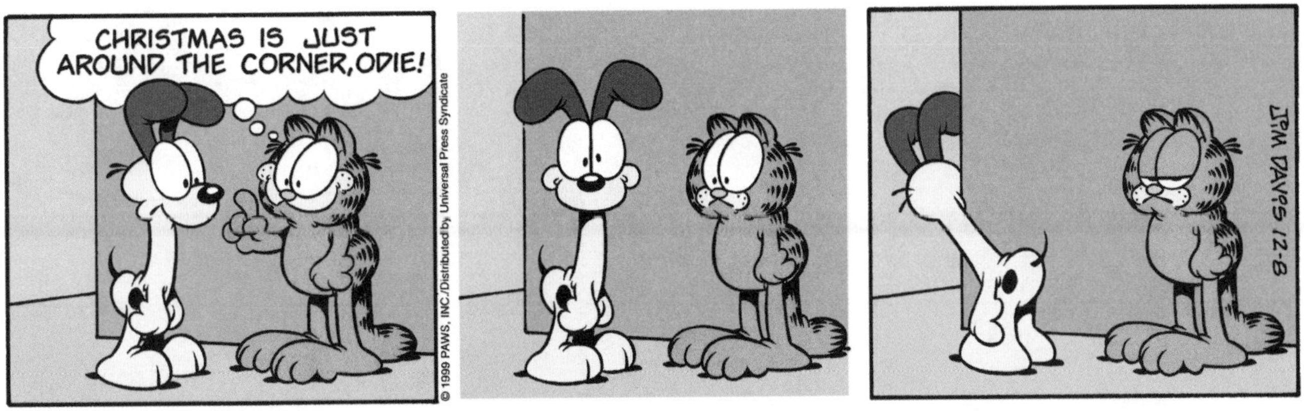
CHRISTMAS IS JUST AROUND THE CORNER, ODIE!
© 1999 PAWS, INC./Distributed by Universal Press Syndicate
JIM DAVIS 12-8

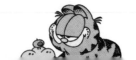

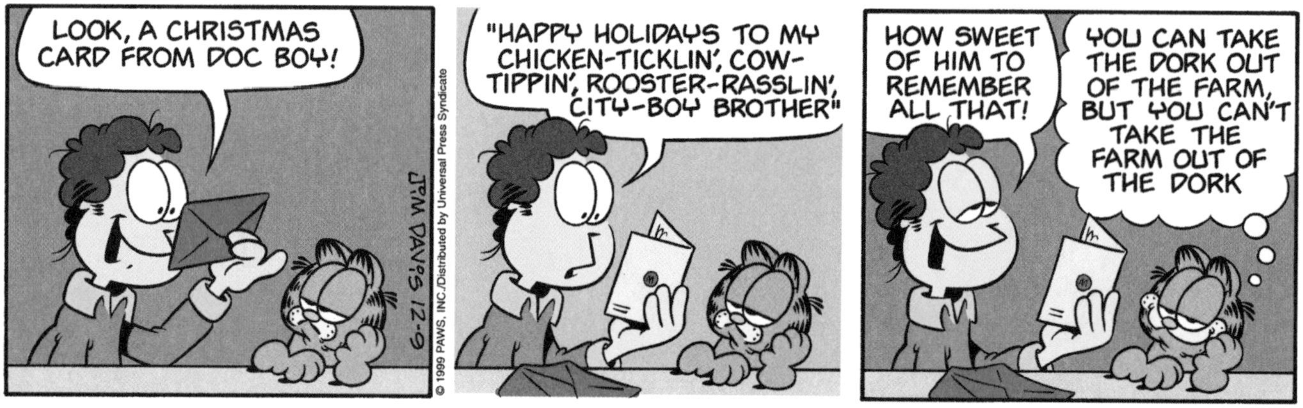
LOOK, A CHRISTMAS CARD FROM DOC BOY!
JPM DAVPS 12-9
© 1999 PAWS, INC./Distributed by Universal Press Syndicate
"HAPPY HOLIDAYS TO MY CHICKEN-TICKLIN', COW-TIPPIN', ROOSTER-RASSLIN', CITY-BOY BROTHER"
HOW SWEET OF HIM TO REMEMBER ALL THAT!
YOU CAN TAKE THE DORK OUT OF THE FARM, BUT YOU CAN'T TAKE THE FARM OUT OF THE DORK

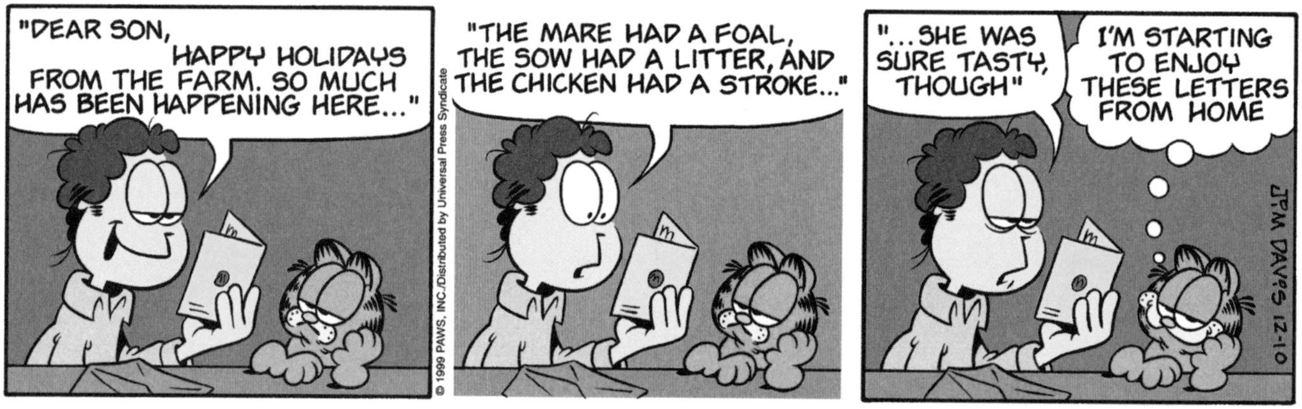
"DEAR SON, HAPPY HOLIDAYS FROM THE FARM. SO MUCH HAS BEEN HAPPENING HERE..."
© 1999 PAWS, INC./Distributed by Universal Press Syndicate
"THE MARE HAD A FOAL, THE SOW HAD A LITTER, AND THE CHICKEN HAD A STROKE..."
"...SHE WAS SURE TASTY, THOUGH"
I'M STARTING TO ENJOY THESE LETTERS FROM HOME
JPM DAVPS 12-10

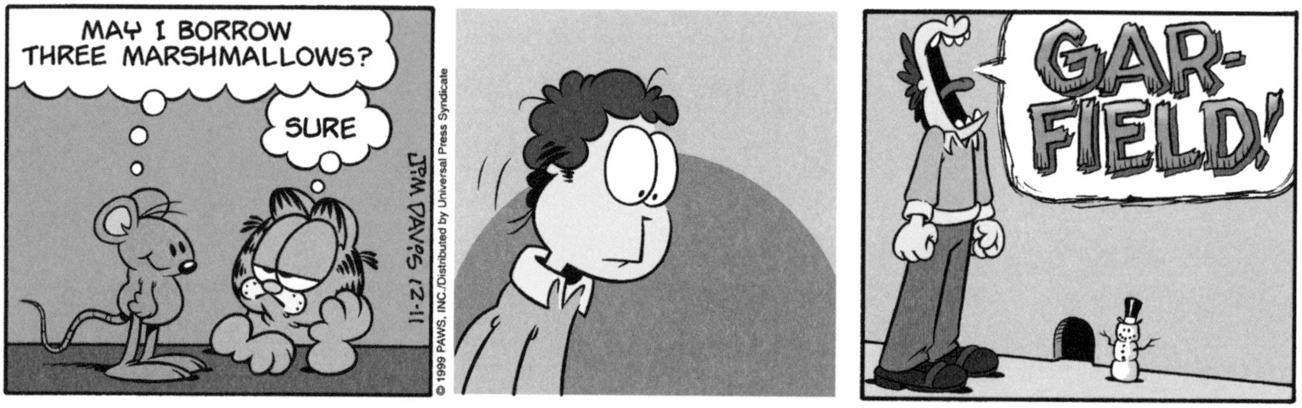
MAY I BORROW THREE MARSHMALLOWS?
SURE
JPM DAVPS 12-11
© 1999 PAWS, INC./Distributed by Universal Press Syndicate
GAR-FIELD!

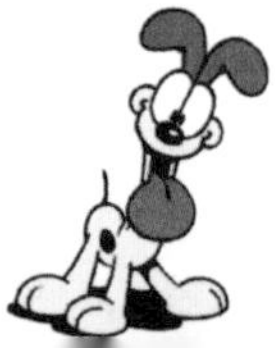

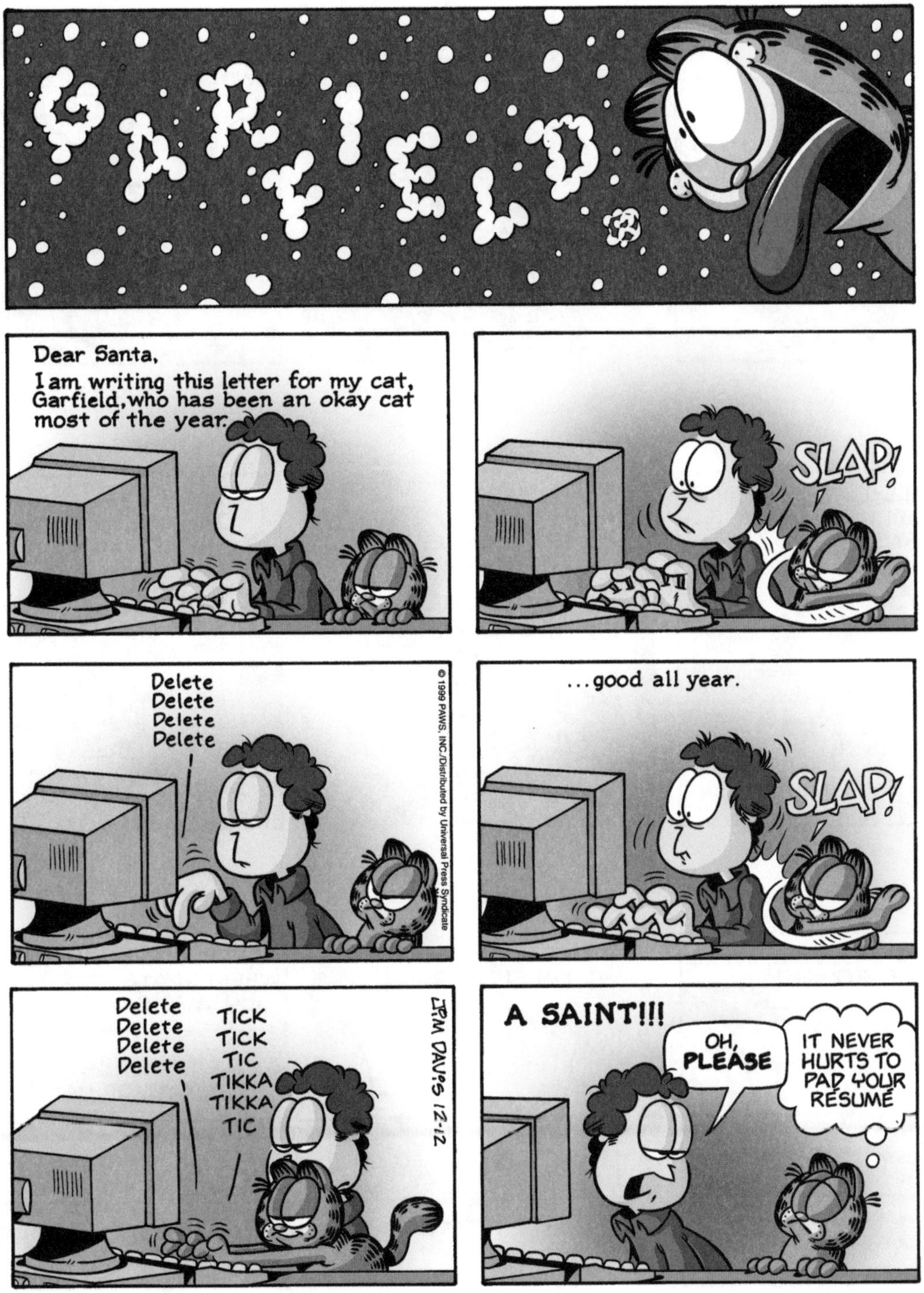
GARFIELD
Dear Santa,
I am writing this letter for my cat, Garfield, who has been an okay cat most of the year.
SLAP!
Delete
Delete
Delete
Delete
© 1999 PAWS, INC./Distributed by Universal Press Syndicate
...good all year.
SLAP!
Delete
Delete
Delete
Delete
TICK
TICK
TIC
TIKKA
TIKKA
TIC
JPM DAVIS 12-12
A SAINT!!!
OH, PLEASE
IT NEVER HURTS TO PAD YOUR RESUMÉ

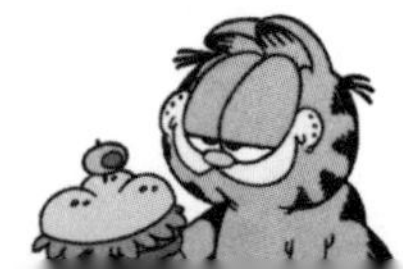

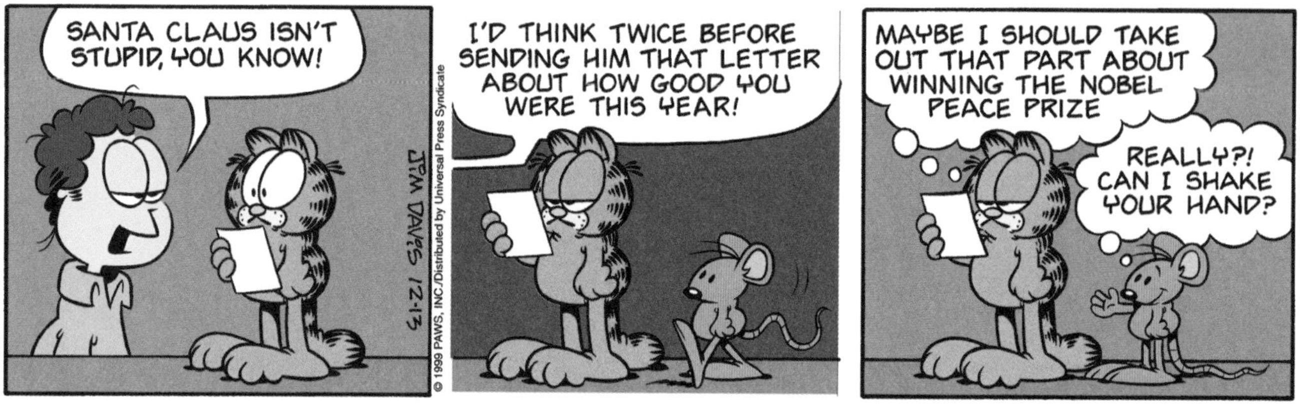
SANTA CLAUS ISN'T STUPID, YOU KNOW!
JIM DAVIS 12-13
© 1999 PAWS, INC./Distributed by Universal Press Syndicate
I'D THINK TWICE BEFORE SENDING HIM THAT LETTER ABOUT HOW GOOD YOU WERE THIS YEAR!
MAYBE I SHOULD TAKE OUT THAT PART ABOUT WINNING THE NOBEL PEACE PRIZE
REALLY?! CAN I SHAKE YOUR HAND?

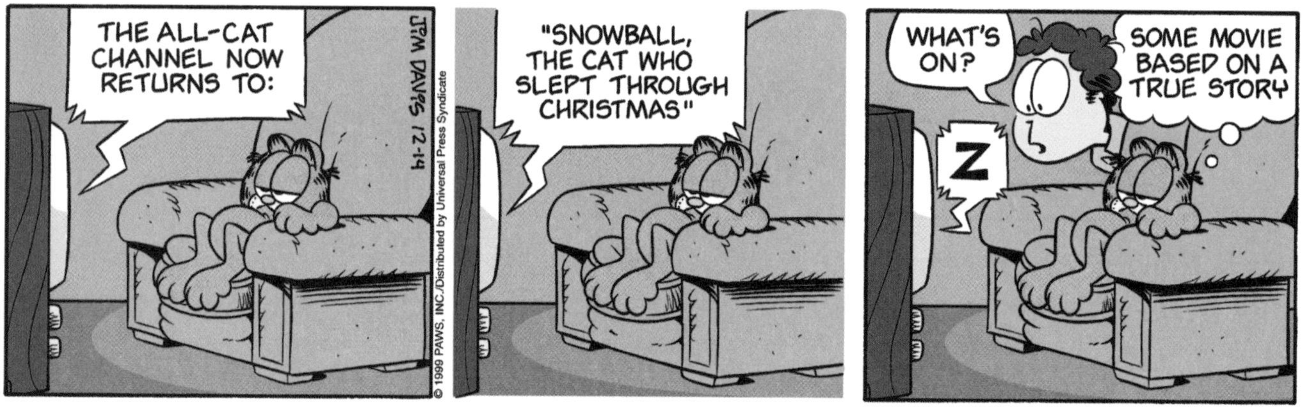
THE ALL-CAT CHANNEL NOW RETURNS TO:
JIM DAVIS 12-14
© 1999 PAWS, INC./Distributed by Universal Press Syndicate
"SNOWBALL, THE CAT WHO SLEPT THROUGH CHRISTMAS"
WHAT'S ON?
SOME MOVIE BASED ON A TRUE STORY
Z

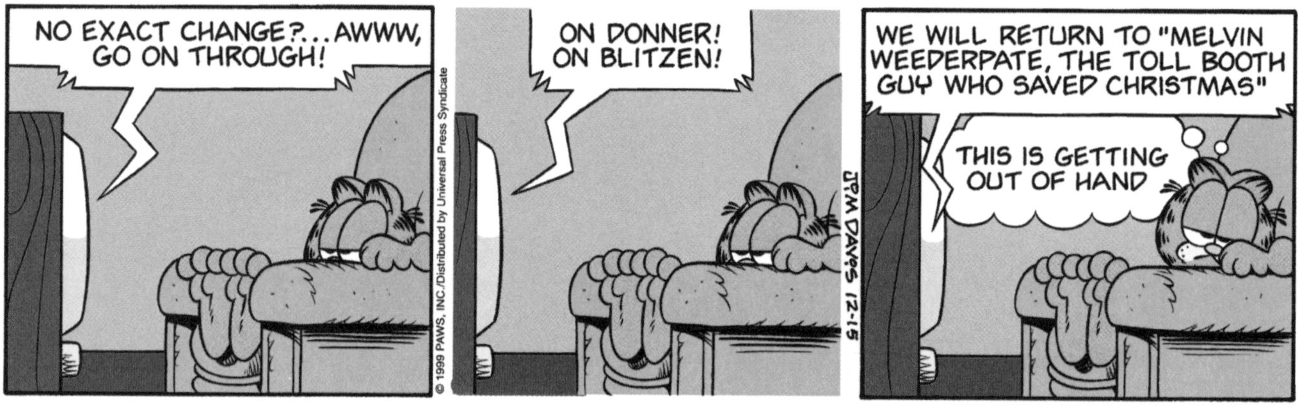
NO EXACT CHANGE?... AWWW, GO ON THROUGH!
© 1999 PAWS, INC./Distributed by Universal Press Syndicate
ON DONNER! ON BLITZEN!
JIM DAVIS 12-15
WE WILL RETURN TO "MELVIN WEEDERPATE, THE TOLL BOOTH GUY WHO SAVED CHRISTMAS"
THIS IS GETTING OUT OF HAND



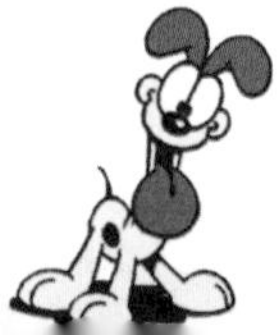

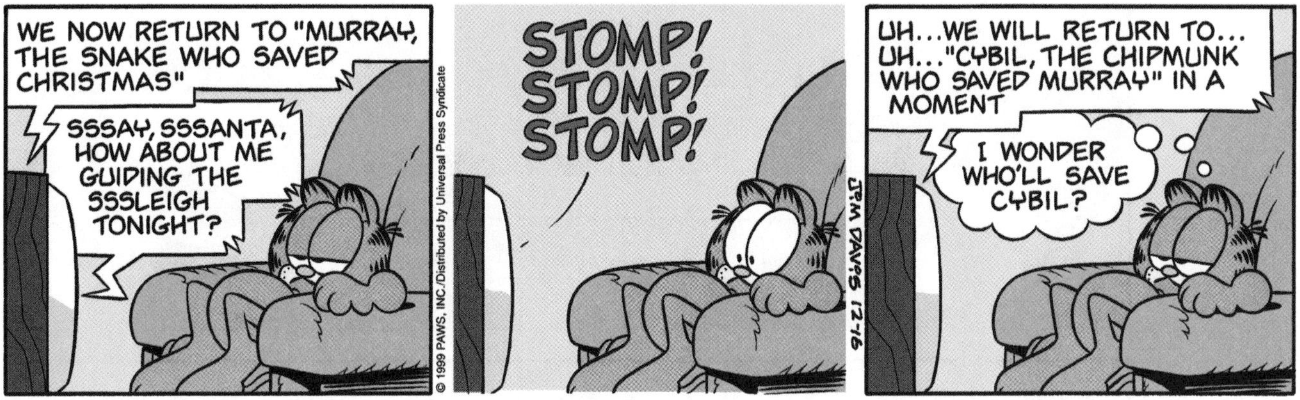
WE NOW RETURN TO "MURRAY, THE SNAKE WHO SAVED CHRISTMAS"
SSSAY, SSSANTA, HOW ABOUT ME GUIDING THE SSSLEIGH TONIGHT?
© 1999 PAWS, INC./Distributed by Universal Press Syndicate
STOMP! STOMP! STOMP!
JIM DAVIS 12-16
UH...WE WILL RETURN TO... UH..."CYBIL, THE CHIPMUNK WHO SAVED MURRAY" IN A MOMENT
I WONDER WHO'LL SAVE CYBIL?

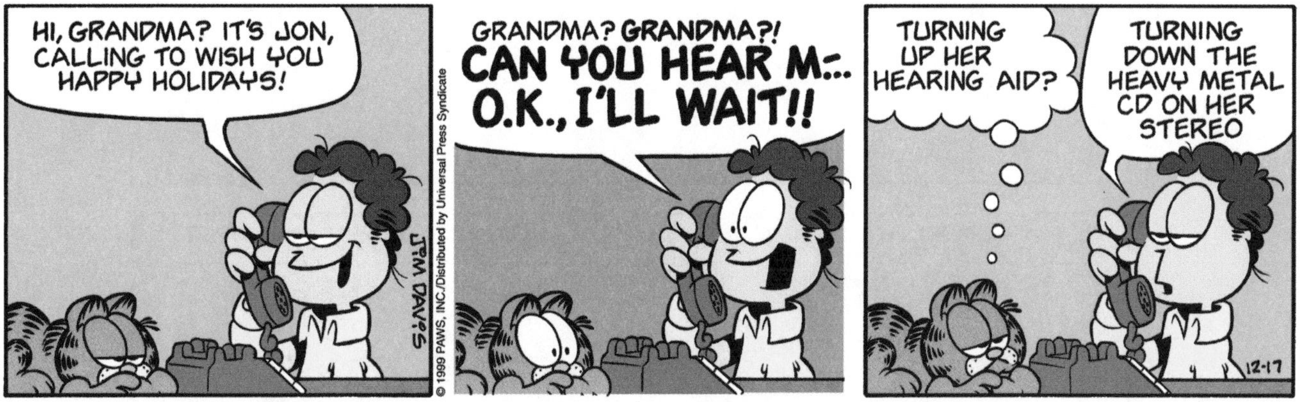
HI, GRANDMA? IT'S JON, CALLING TO WISH YOU HAPPY HOLIDAYS!
JIM DAVIS
© 1999 PAWS, INC./Distributed by Universal Press Syndicate
GRANDMA? GRANDMA?! CAN YOU HEAR M-... O.K., I'LL WAIT!!
TURNING UP HER HEARING AID?
TURNING DOWN THE HEAVY METAL CD ON HER STEREO
12-17

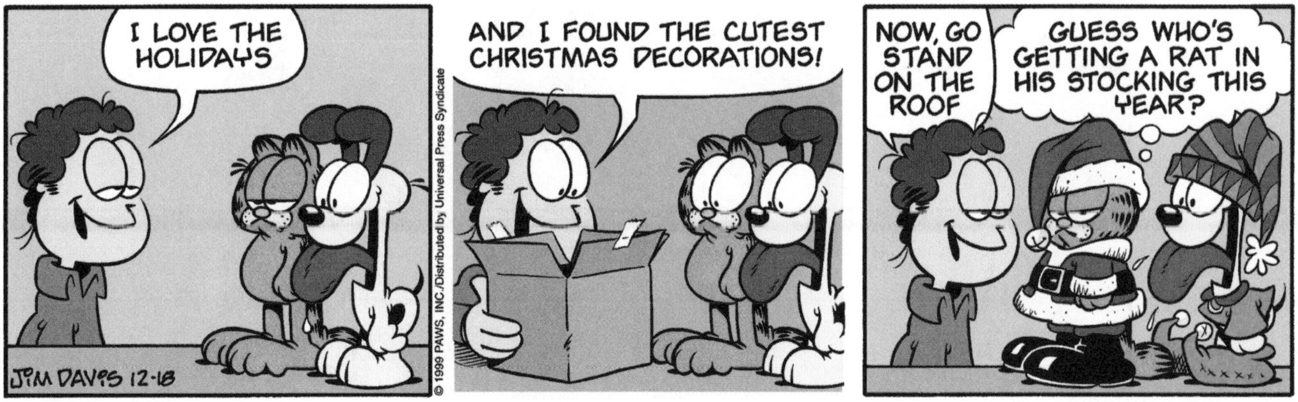
I LOVE THE HOLIDAYS
JIM DAVIS 12-18
© 1999 PAWS, INC./Distributed by Universal Press Syndicate
AND I FOUND THE CUTEST CHRISTMAS DECORATIONS!
NOW, GO STAND ON THE ROOF
GUESS WHO'S GETTING A RAT IN HIS STOCKING THIS YEAR?

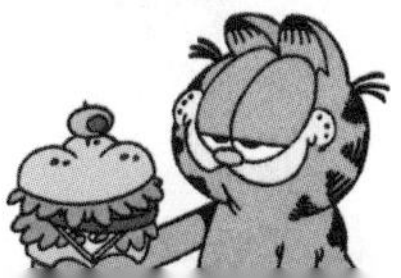

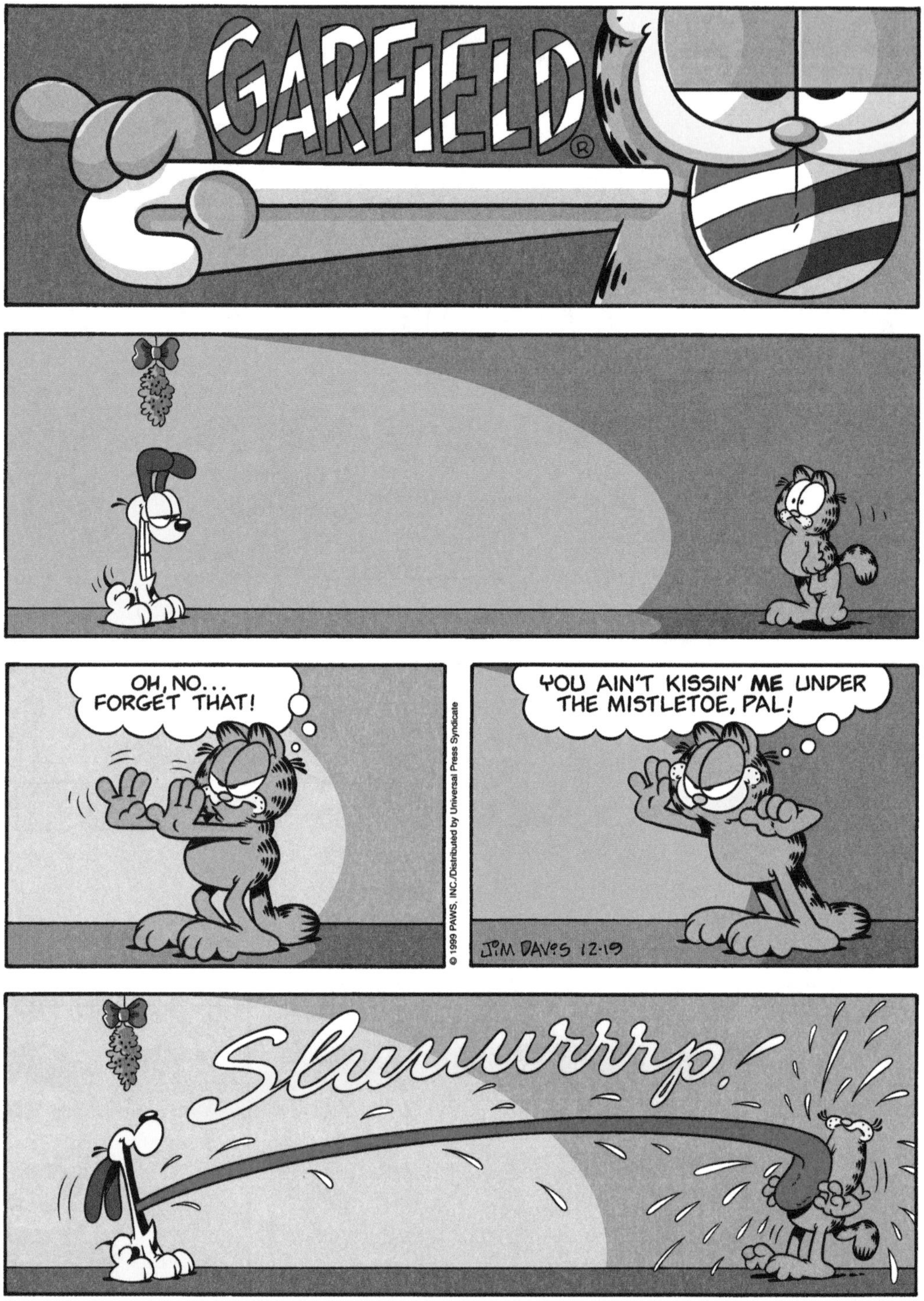
GARFIELD®
OH, NO... FORGET THAT!
YOU AIN'T KISSIN' ME UNDER THE MISTLETOE, PAL!
© 1999 PAWS, INC./Distributed by Universal Press Syndicate
JIM DAVIS 12-19
Sluuurrrp!

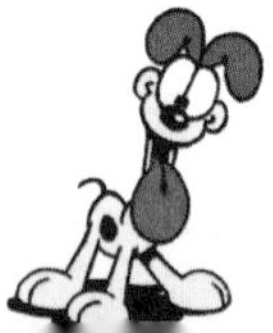

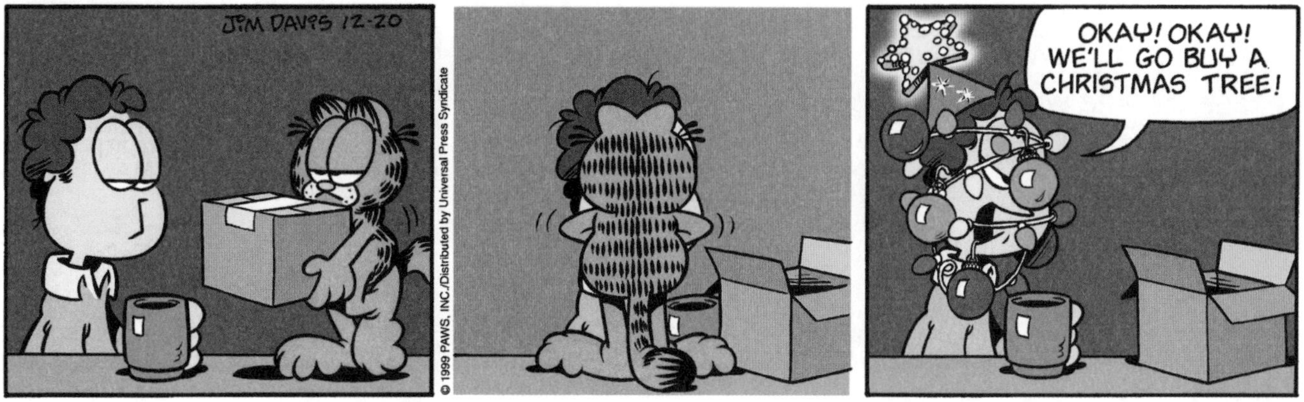
JIM DAVIS 12-20
© 1999 PAWS, INC./Distributed by Universal Press Syndicate
OKAY! OKAY! WE'LL GO BUY A CHRISTMAS TREE!

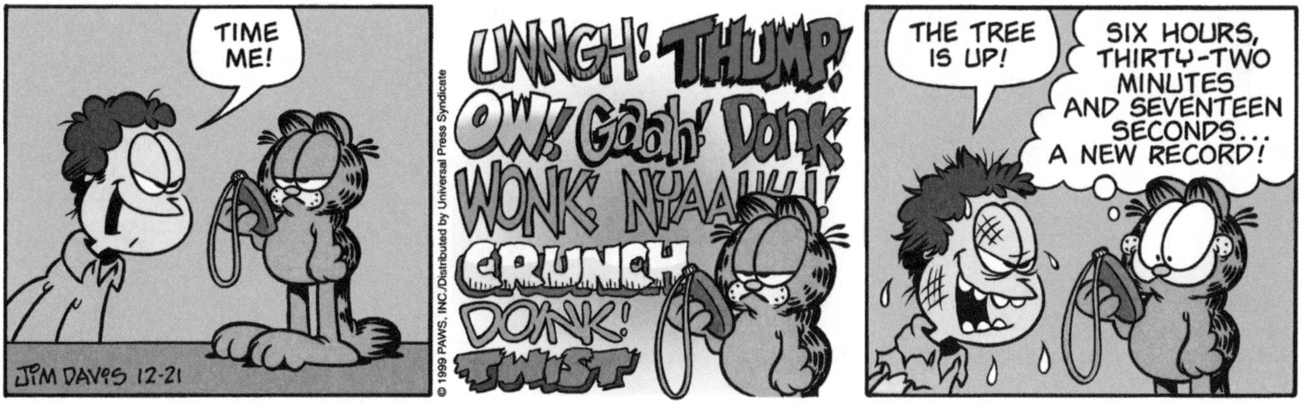
TIME ME!
JIM DAVIS 12-21
© 1999 PAWS, INC./Distributed by Universal Press Syndicate
UNNGH! THUMP!
OW! Gaah! Donk!
WONK! NYAA
CRUNCH
DONK!
TWIST
THE TREE IS UP!
SIX HOURS, THIRTY-TWO MINUTES AND SEVENTEEN SECONDS... A NEW RECORD!

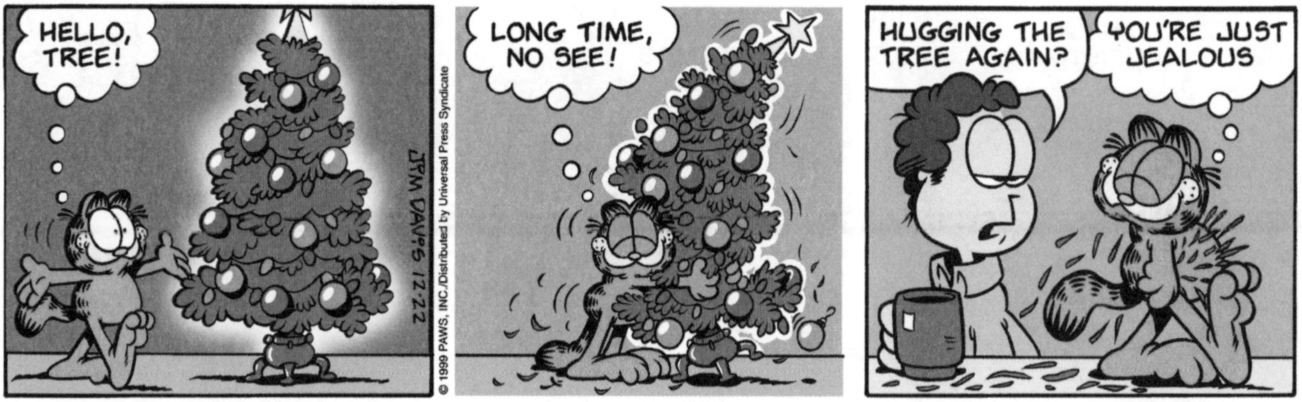
HELLO, TREE!
JIM DAVIS 12-22
© 1999 PAWS, INC./Distributed by Universal Press Syndicate
LONG TIME, NO SEE!
HUGGING THE TREE AGAIN?
YOU'RE JUST JEALOUS

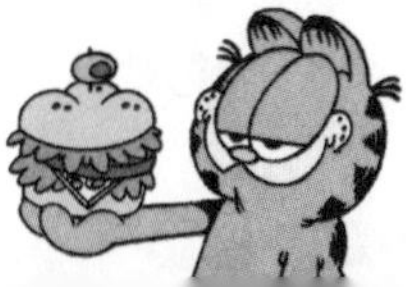

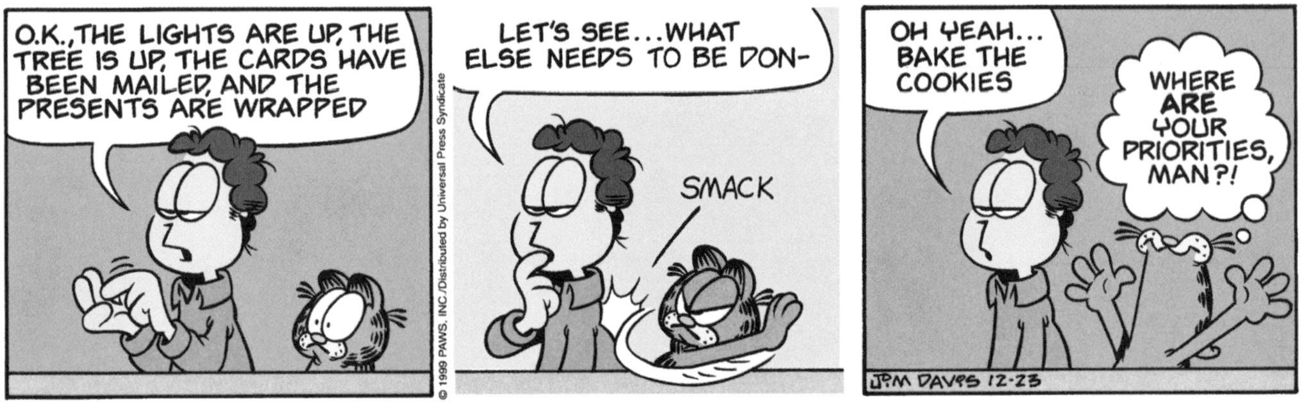
O.K., THE LIGHTS ARE UP, THE TREE IS UP, THE CARDS HAVE BEEN MAILED, AND THE PRESENTS ARE WRAPPED
© 1999 PAWS, INC./Distributed by Universal Press Syndicate
LET'S SEE...WHAT ELSE NEEDS TO BE DON-
SMACK
OH YEAH... BAKE THE COOKIES
WHERE ARE YOUR PRIORITIES, MAN?!
JIM DAVIS 12-23

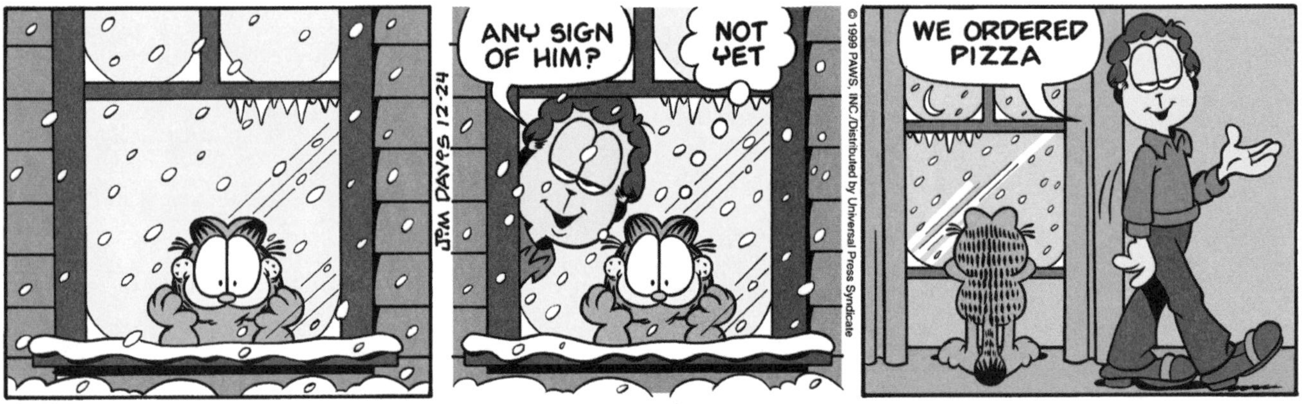
JIM DAVIS 12-24
ANY SIGN OF HIM?
NOT YET
© 1999 PAWS, INC./Distributed by Universal Press Syndicate
WE ORDERED PIZZA

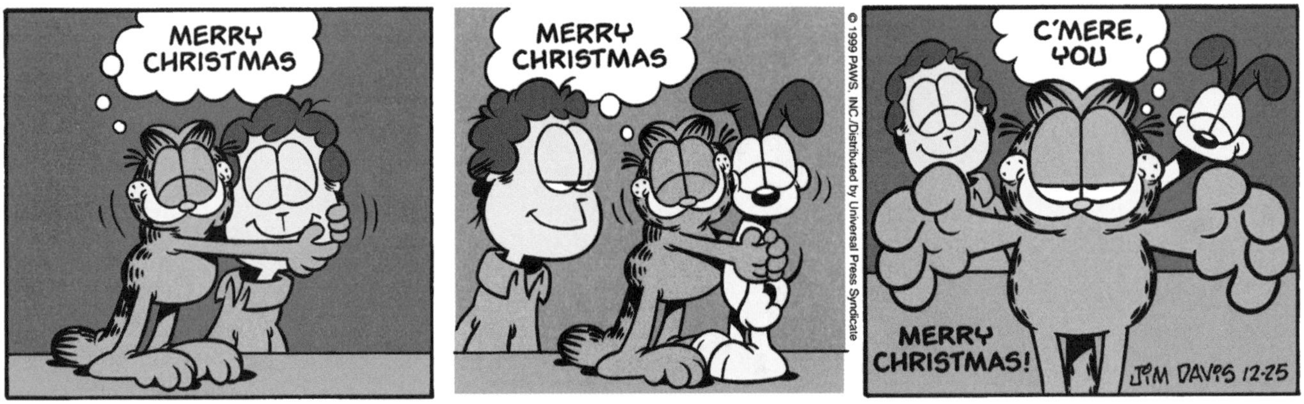
MERRY CHRISTMAS
MERRY CHRISTMAS
© 1999 PAWS, INC./Distributed by Universal Press Syndicate
C'MERE, YOU
MERRY CHRISTMAS!
JIM DAVIS 12-25

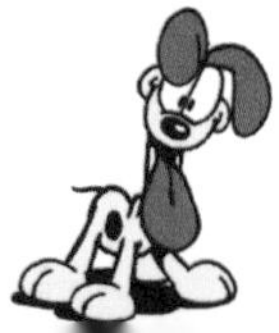

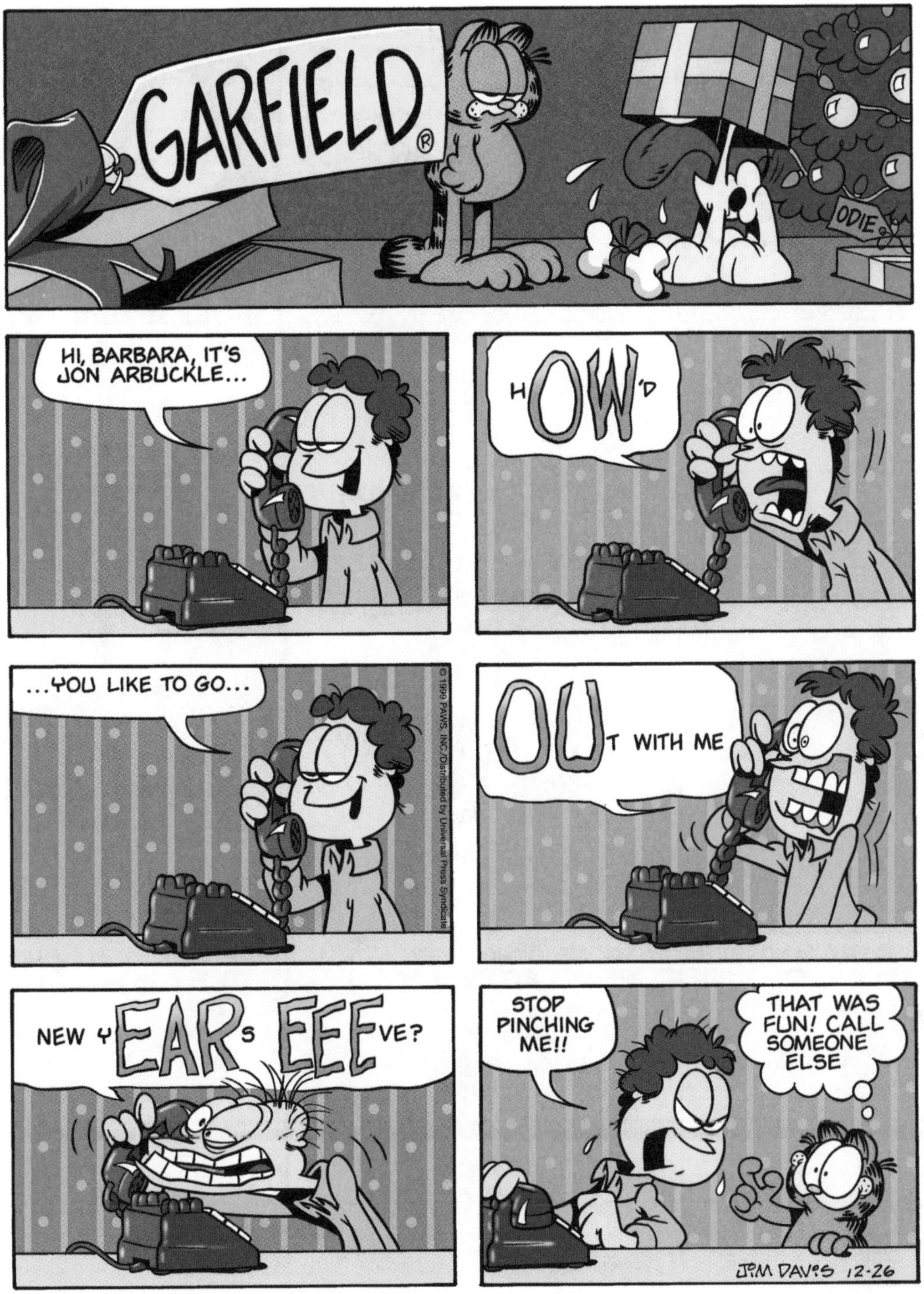
GARFIELD®
ODIE
HI, BARBARA, IT'S JON ARBUCKLE...
HOW'D
...YOU LIKE TO GO...
© 1999 PAWS, INC./Distributed by Universal Press Syndicate
OUT WITH ME
NEW YEARS EEEVE?
STOP PINCHING ME!!
THAT WAS FUN! CALL SOMEONE ELSE
JIM DAVIS 12-26

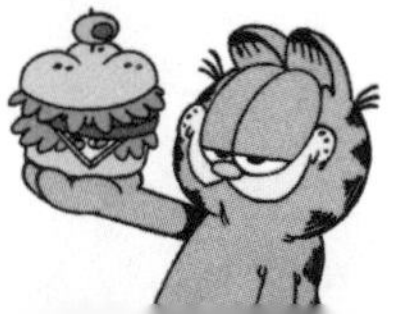

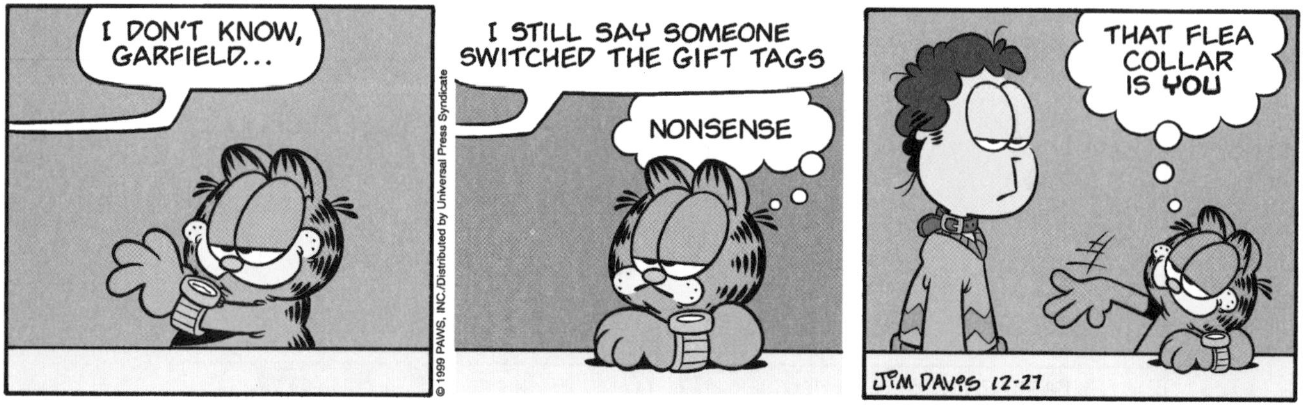
I DON'T KNOW, GARFIELD...
I STILL SAY SOMEONE SWITCHED THE GIFT TAGS
NONSENSE
THAT FLEA COLLAR IS **YOU**
JIM DAVIS 12-27
© 1999 PAWS, INC./Distributed by Universal Press Syndicate

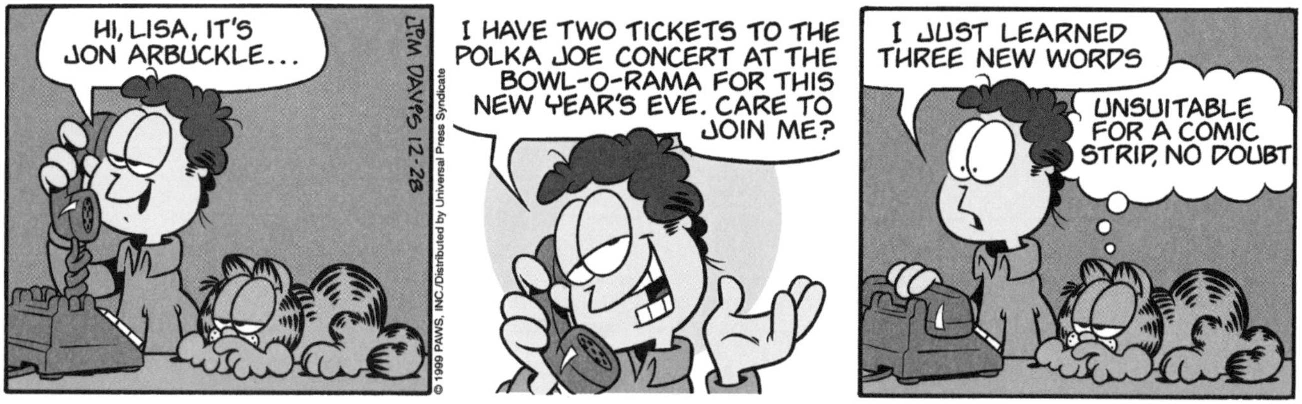
HI, LISA, IT'S JON ARBUCKLE...
JIM DAVIS 12-28
I HAVE TWO TICKETS TO THE POLKA JOE CONCERT AT THE BOWL-O-RAMA FOR THIS NEW YEAR'S EVE. CARE TO JOIN ME?
I JUST LEARNED THREE NEW WORDS
UNSUITABLE FOR A COMIC STRIP, NO DOUBT
© 1999 PAWS, INC./Distributed by Universal Press Syndicate

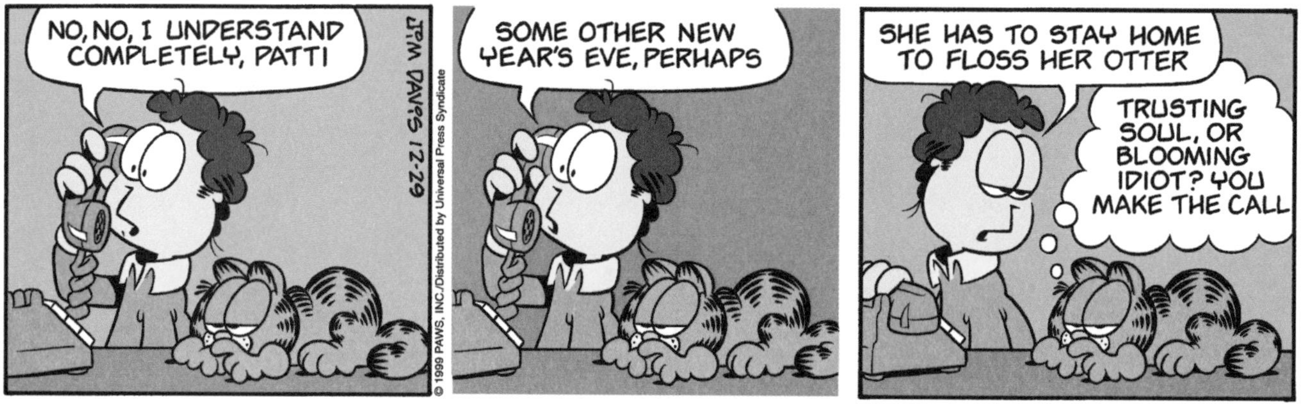
NO, NO, I UNDERSTAND COMPLETELY, PATTI
JIM DAVIS 12-29
SOME OTHER NEW YEAR'S EVE, PERHAPS
SHE HAS TO STAY HOME TO FLOSS HER OTTER
TRUSTING SOUL, OR BLOOMING IDIOT? YOU MAKE THE CALL
© 1999 PAWS, INC./Distributed by Universal Press Syndicate

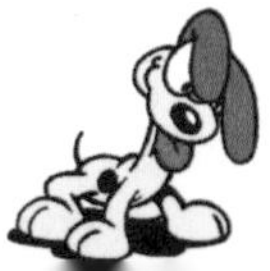

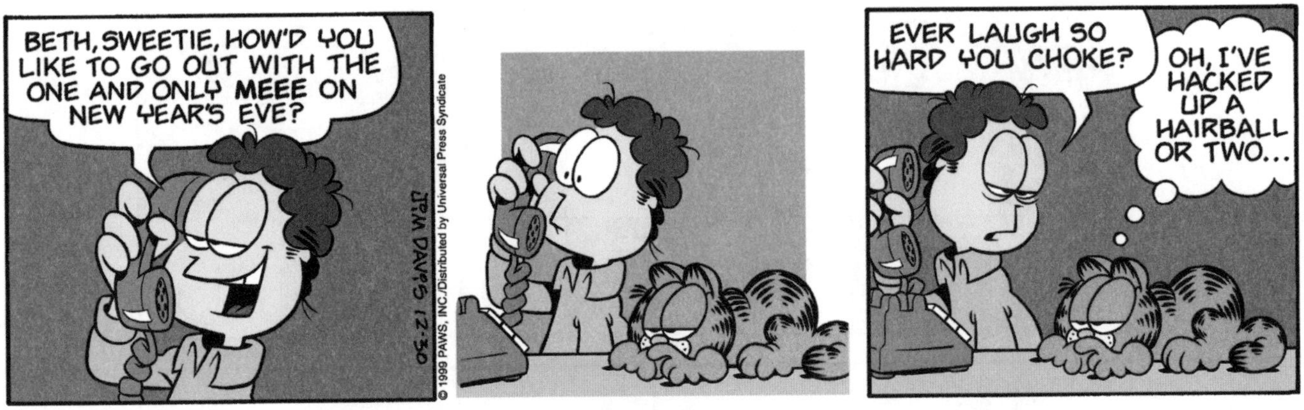
BETH, SWEETIE, HOW'D YOU LIKE TO GO OUT WITH THE ONE AND ONLY MEEE ON NEW YEAR'S EVE?
JIM DAVIS 12-30
© 1999 PAWS, INC./Distributed by Universal Press Syndicate
EVER LAUGH SO HARD YOU CHOKE?
OH, I'VE HACKED UP A HAIRBALL OR TWO...

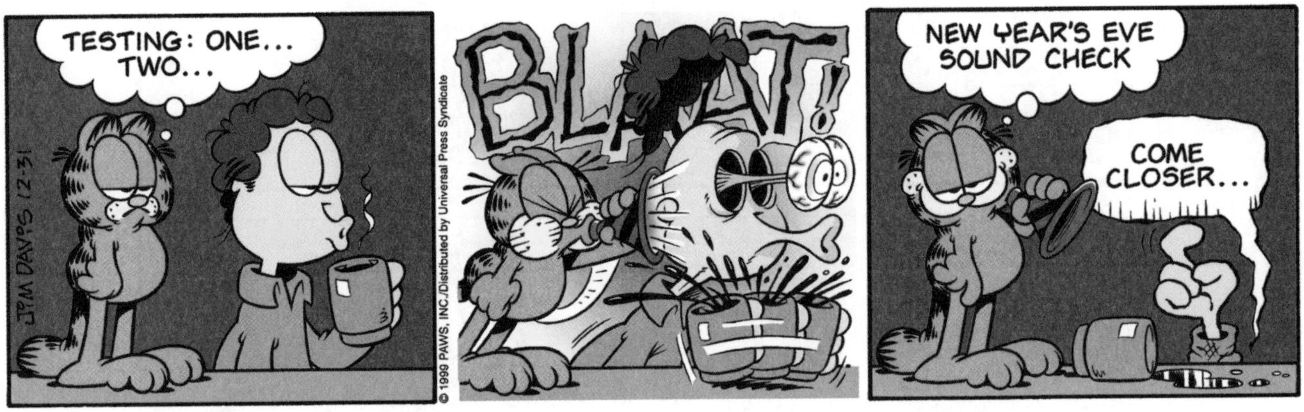
TESTING: ONE... TWO...
JIM DAVIS 12-31
© 1999 PAWS, INC./Distributed by Universal Press Syndicate
BLAAT!
NEW YEAR'S EVE SOUND CHECK
COME CLOSER...

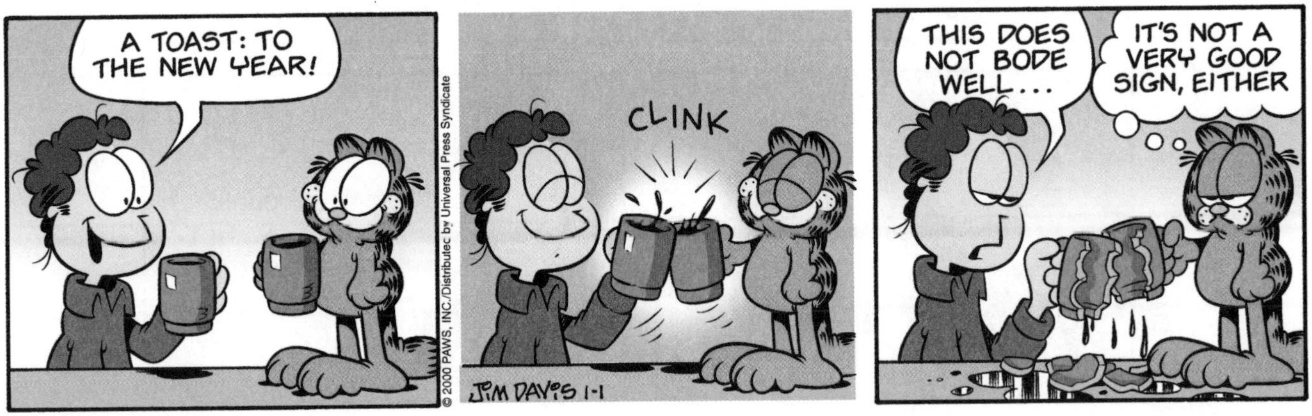
A TOAST: TO THE NEW YEAR!
© 2000 PAWS, INC./Distributec by Universal Press Syndicate
CLINK
JIM DAVIS 1-1
THIS DOES NOT BODE WELL...
IT'S NOT A VERY GOOD SIGN, EITHER

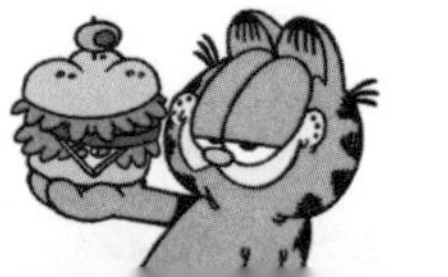

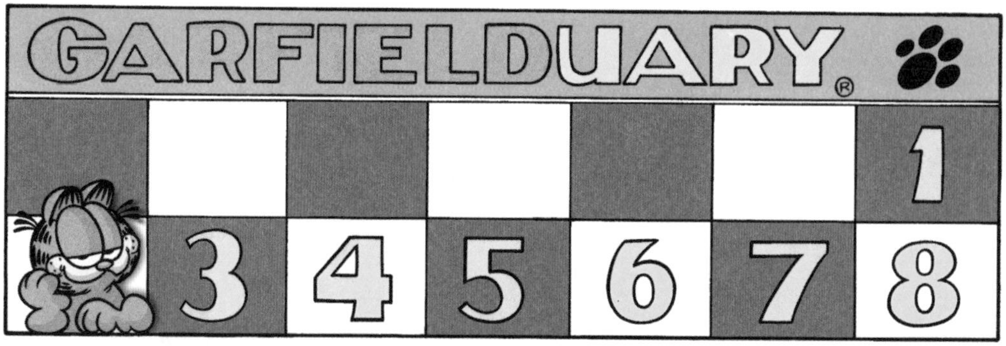
GARFIELDUARY®
1
3 4 5 6 7 8

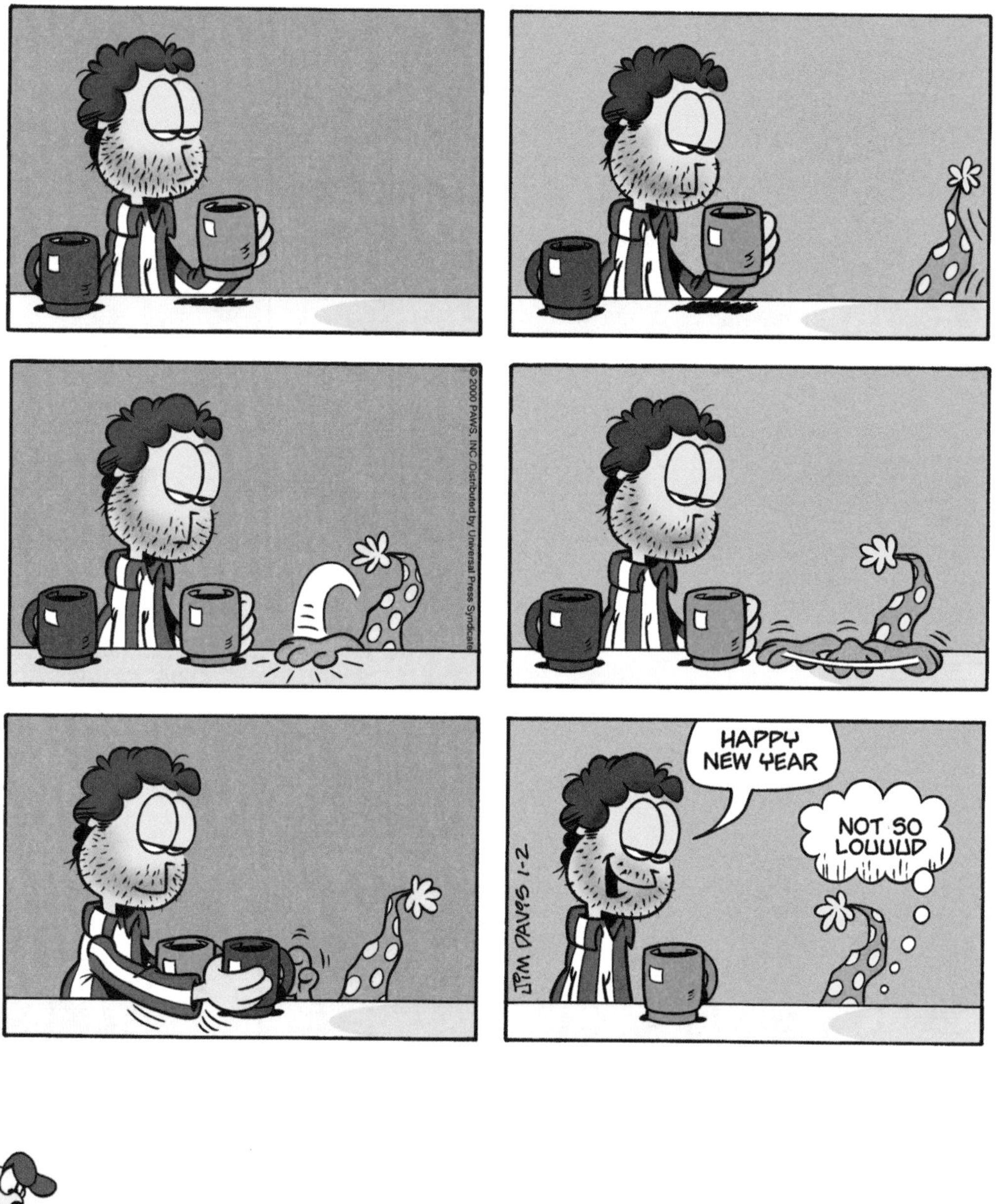
© 2000 PAWS, INC./Distributed by Universal Press Syndicate
JIM DAVIS 1-2
HAPPY NEW YEAR
NOT SO LOUUUD

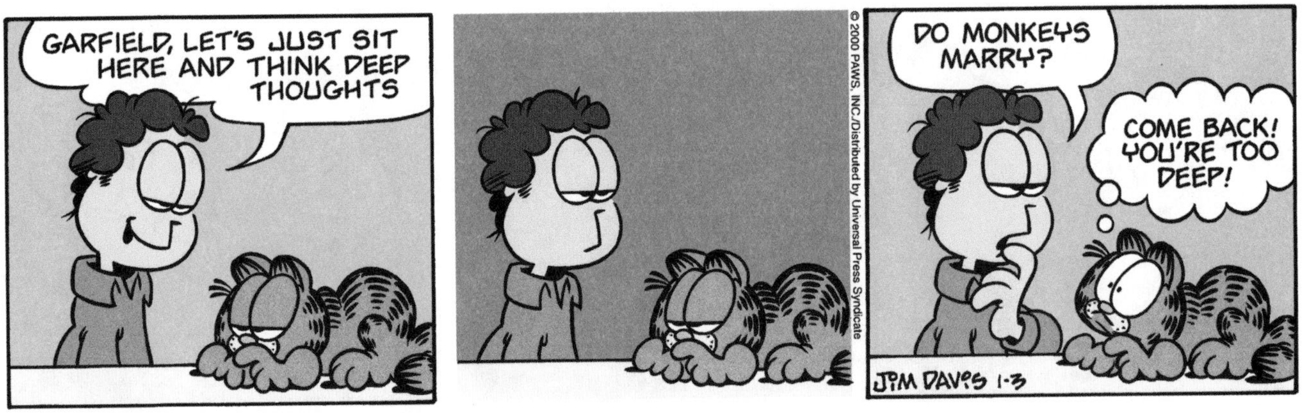
GARFIELD, LET'S JUST SIT HERE AND THINK DEEP THOUGHTS
DO MONKEYS MARRY?
COME BACK! YOU'RE TOO DEEP!
JIM DAVIS 1-3


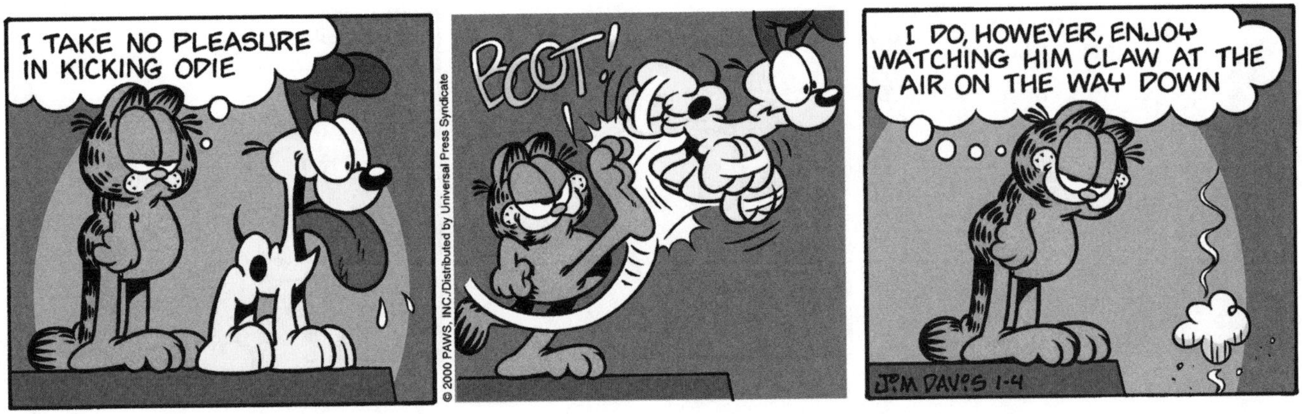
I TAKE NO PLEASURE IN KICKING ODIE
BOOT!
I DO, HOWEVER, ENJOY WATCHING HIM CLAW AT THE AIR ON THE WAY DOWN
JIM DAVIS 1-4


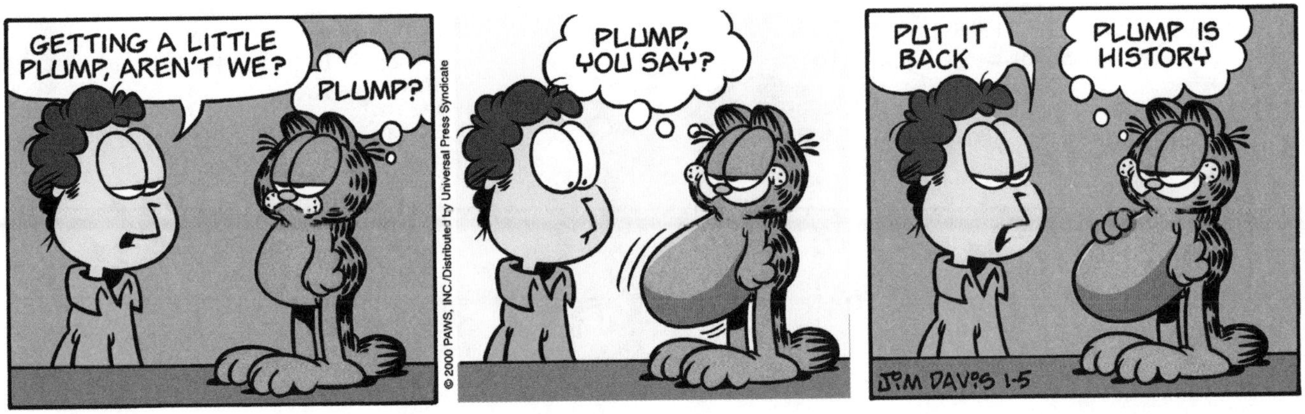
GETTING A LITTLE PLUMP, AREN'T WE?
PLUMP?
PLUMP, YOU SAY?
PUT IT BACK
PLUMP IS HISTORY
JIM DAVIS 1-5


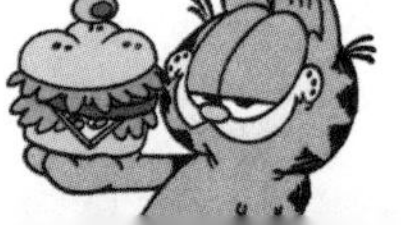

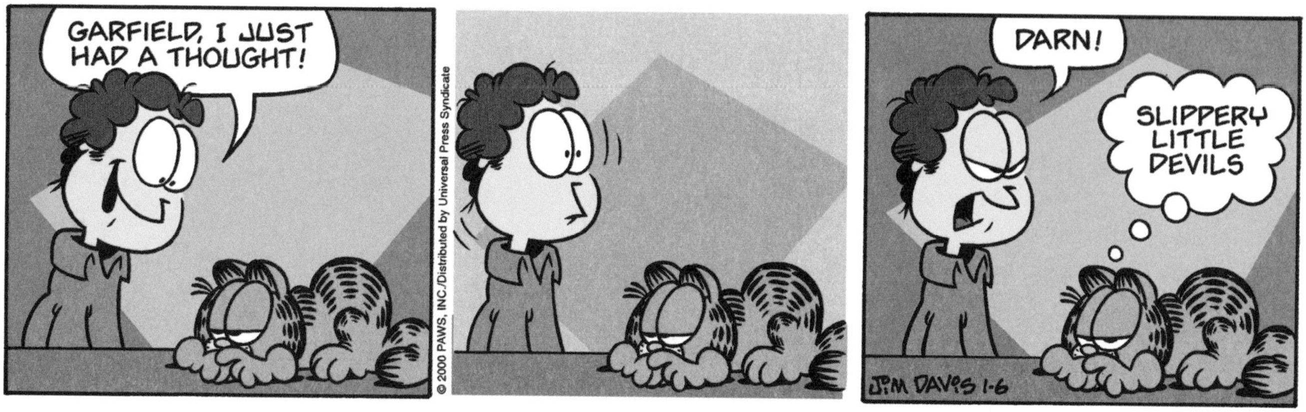
GARFIELD, I JUST HAD A THOUGHT!
© 2000 PAWS, INC./Distributed by Universal Press Syndicate
DARN!
SLIPPERY LITTLE DEVILS
JIM DAVIS 1-6

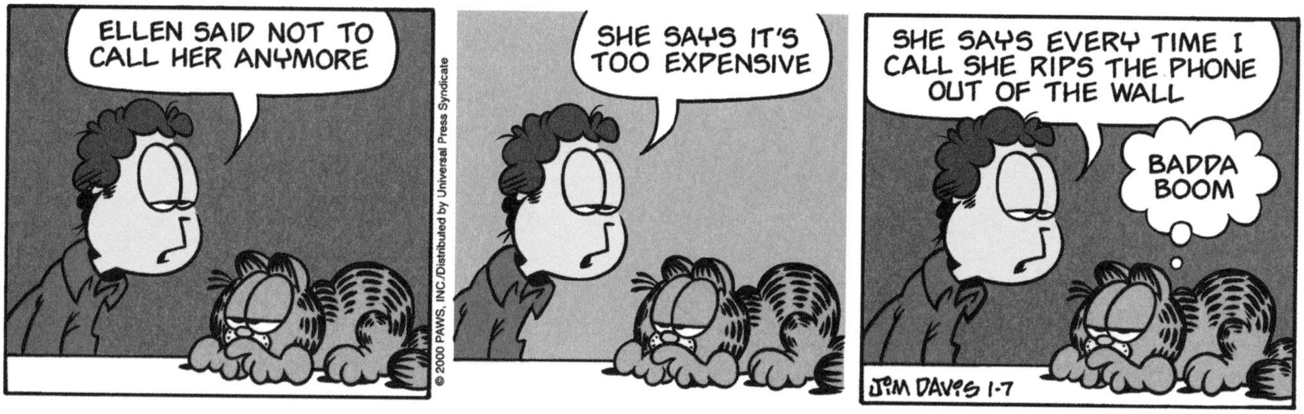
ELLEN SAID NOT TO CALL HER ANYMORE
© 2000 PAWS, INC./Distributed by Universal Press Syndicate
SHE SAYS IT'S TOO EXPENSIVE
SHE SAYS EVERY TIME I CALL SHE RIPS THE PHONE OUT OF THE WALL
BADDA BOOM
JIM DAVIS 1-7

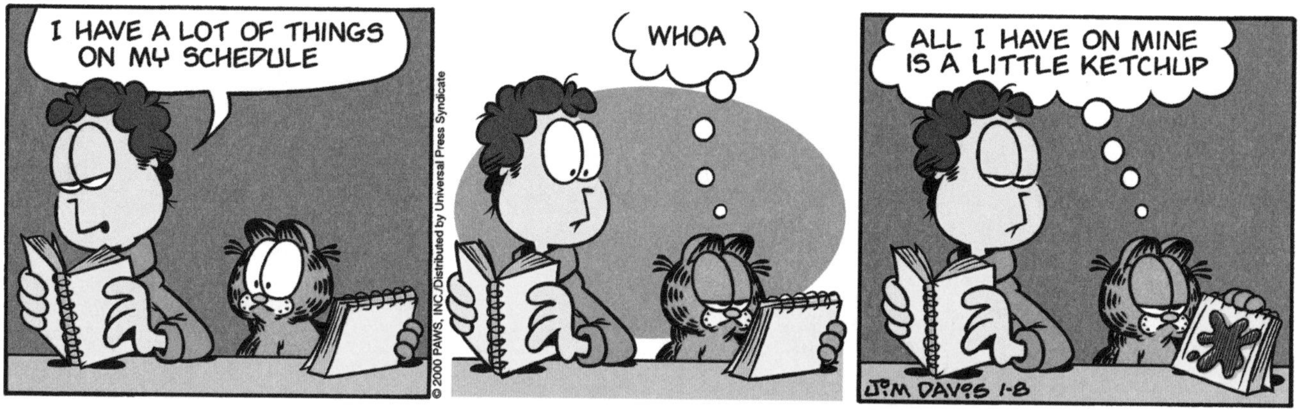
I HAVE A LOT OF THINGS ON MY SCHEDULE
© 2000 PAWS, INC./Distributed by Universal Press Syndicate
WHOA
ALL I HAVE ON MINE IS A LITTLE KETCHUP
JIM DAVIS 1-8

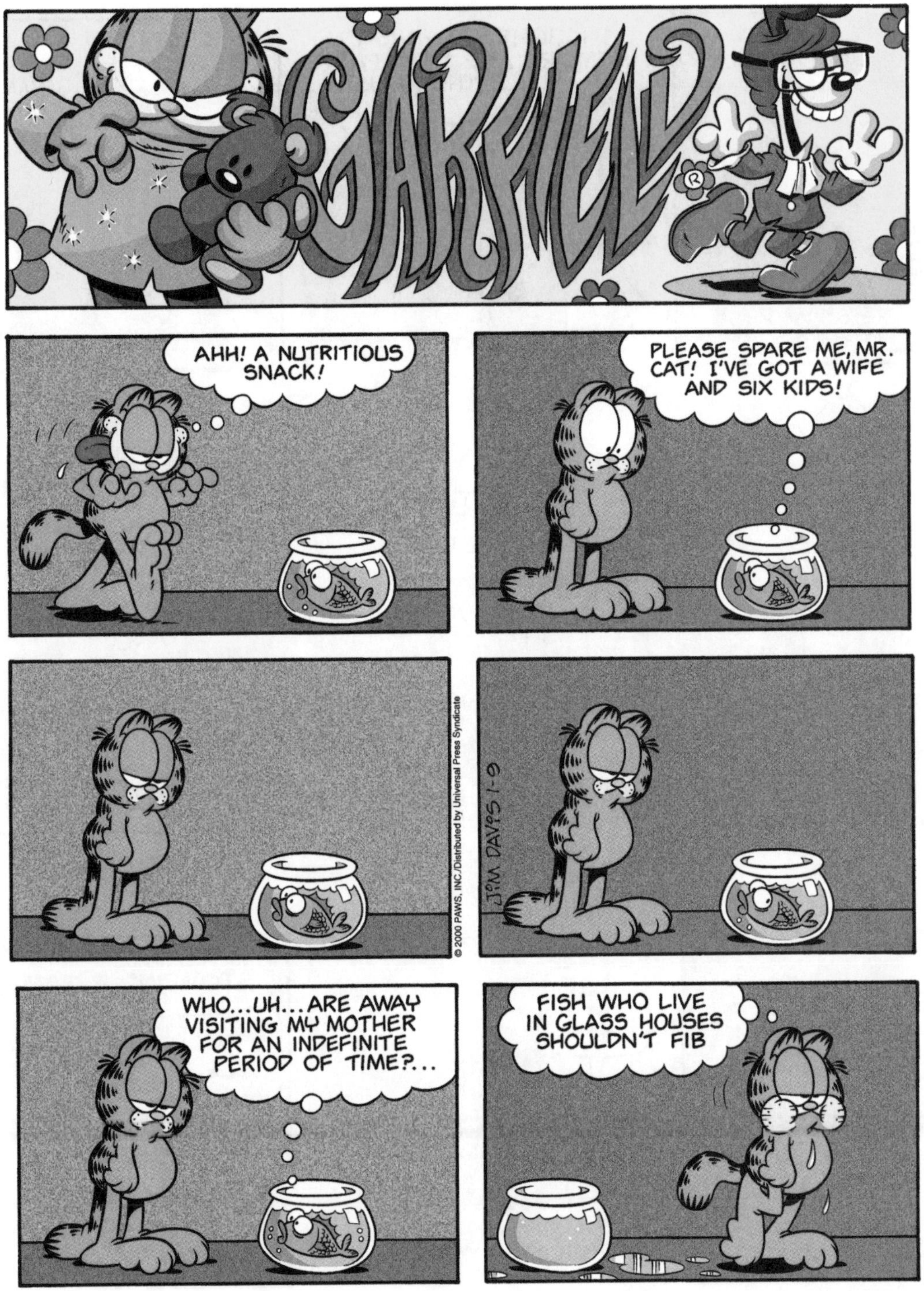
GARFIELD
AHH! A NUTRITIOUS SNACK!
PLEASE SPARE ME, MR. CAT! I'VE GOT A WIFE AND SIX KIDS!
© 2000 PAWS, INC./Distributed by Universal Press Syndicate
JIM DAVIS 1-9
WHO...UH...ARE AWAY VISITING MY MOTHER FOR AN INDEFINITE PERIOD OF TIME?...
FISH WHO LIVE IN GLASS HOUSES SHOULDN'T FIB

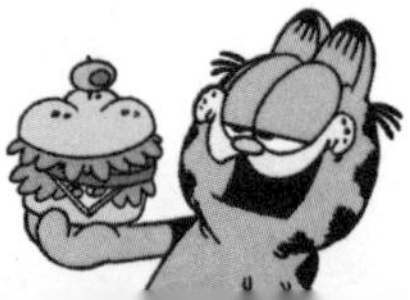

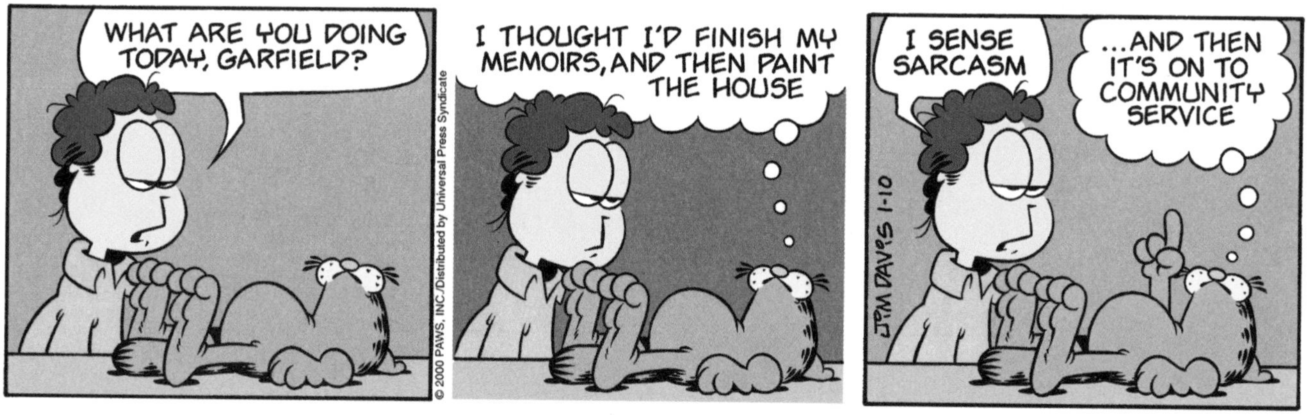
WHAT ARE YOU DOING TODAY, GARFIELD?
I THOUGHT I'D FINISH MY MEMOIRS, AND THEN PAINT THE HOUSE
I SENSE SARCASM
...AND THEN IT'S ON TO COMMUNITY SERVICE
JIM DAVIS 1-10
© 2000 PAWS, INC./Distributed by Universal Press Syndicate

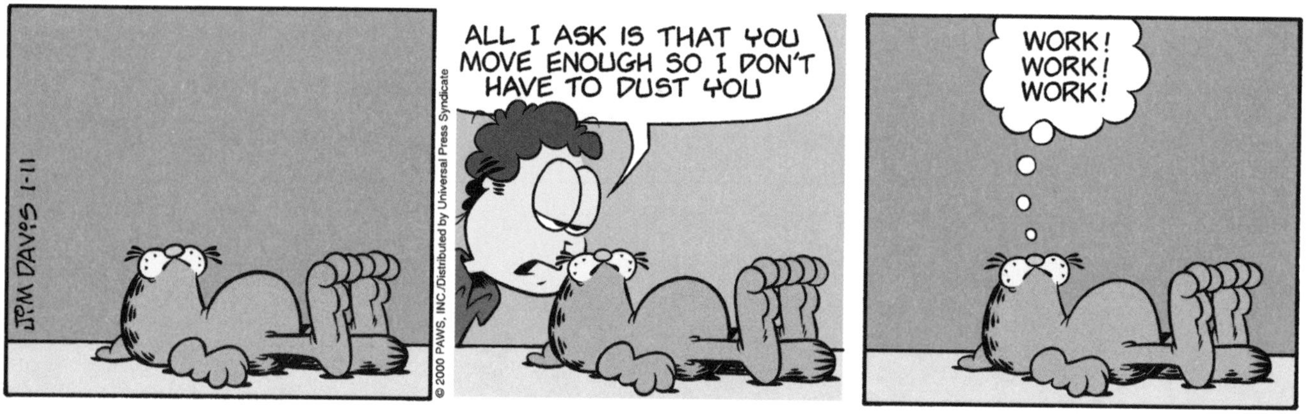
JIM DAVIS 1-11
ALL I ASK IS THAT YOU MOVE ENOUGH SO I DON'T HAVE TO DUST YOU
WORK! WORK! WORK!
© 2000 PAWS, INC./Distributed by Universal Press Syndicate

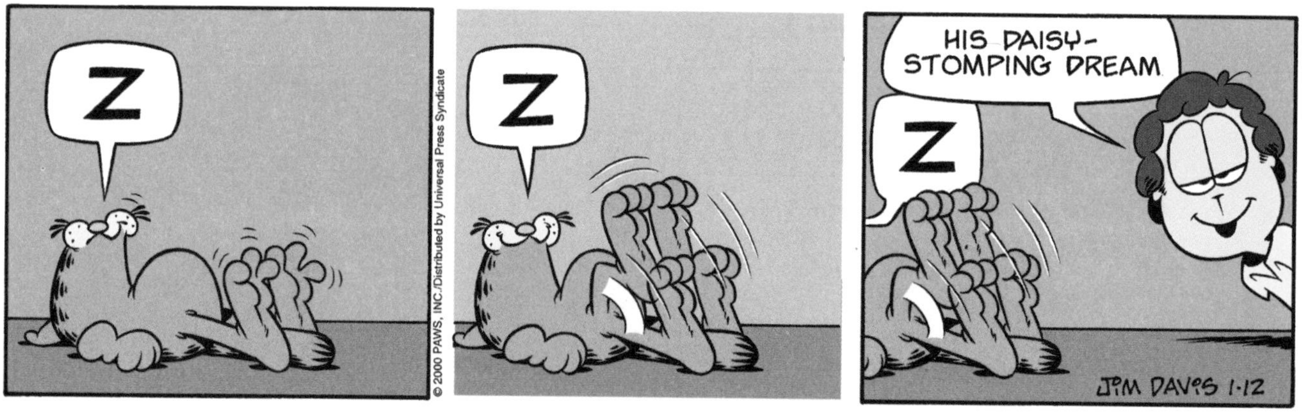
Z
Z
HIS DAISY-STOMPING DREAM
Z
JIM DAVIS 1-12
© 2000 PAWS, INC./Distributed by Universal Press Syndicate



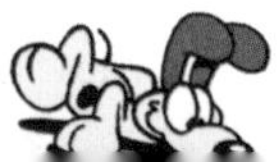

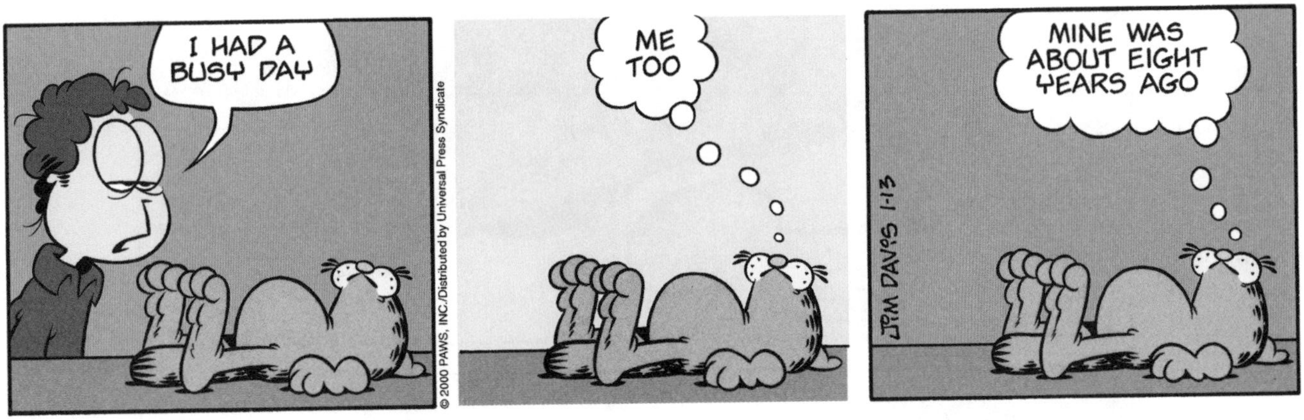
I HAD A BUSY DAY
ME TOO
MINE WAS ABOUT EIGHT YEARS AGO
© 2000 PAWS, INC./Distributed by Universal Press Syndicate
JIM DAVIS 1-13

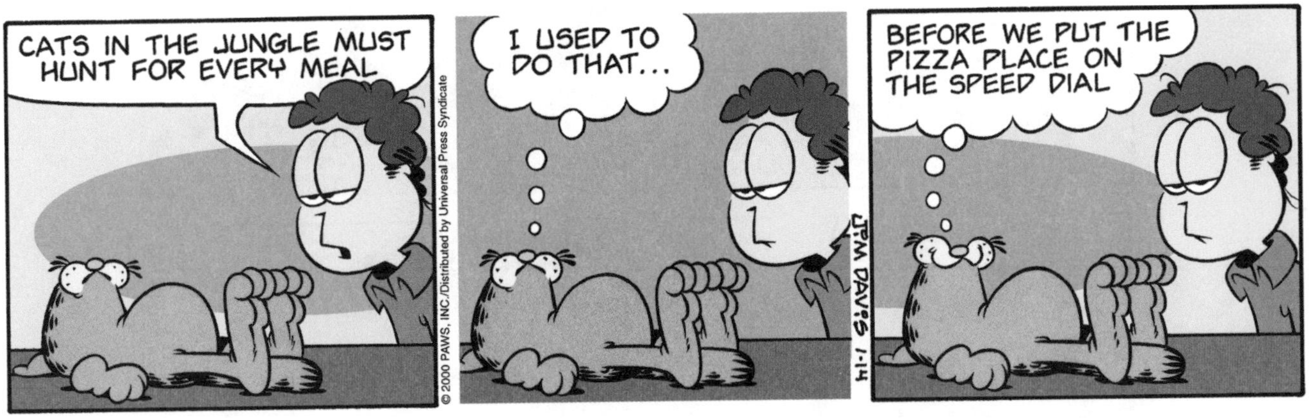
CATS IN THE JUNGLE MUST HUNT FOR EVERY MEAL
I USED TO DO THAT...
BEFORE WE PUT THE PIZZA PLACE ON THE SPEED DIAL
© 2000 PAWS, INC./Distributed by Universal Press Syndicate
JIM DAVIS 1-14

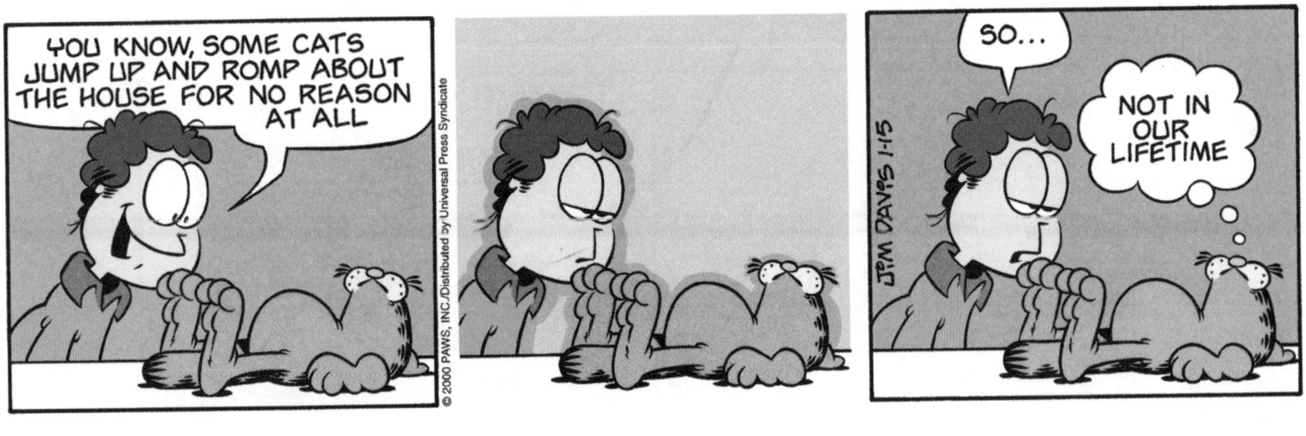
YOU KNOW, SOME CATS JUMP UP AND ROMP ABOUT THE HOUSE FOR NO REASON AT ALL
SO...
NOT IN OUR LIFETIME
© 2000 PAWS, INC./Distributed by Universal Press Syndicate
JIM DAVIS 1-15

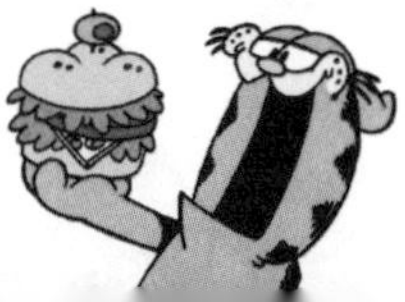

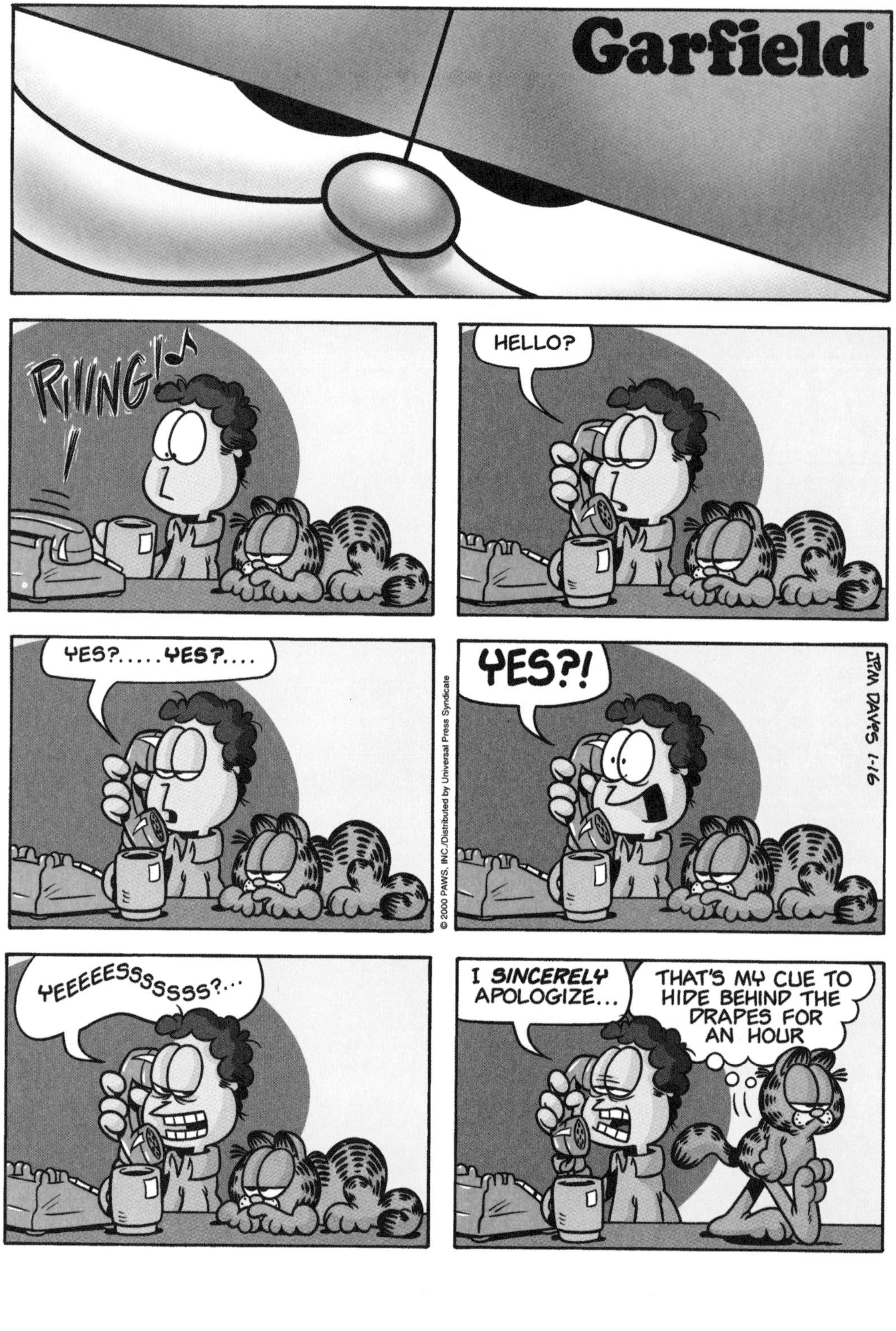
Garfield
RIIING!
HELLO?
YES?.....YES?....
YES?!
YEEEEESSSSSSS?...
I SINCERELY APOLOGIZE...
THAT'S MY CUE TO HIDE BEHIND THE DRAPES FOR AN HOUR
JPM DAVIS 1-16
© 2000 PAWS, INC./Distributed by Universal Press Syndicate

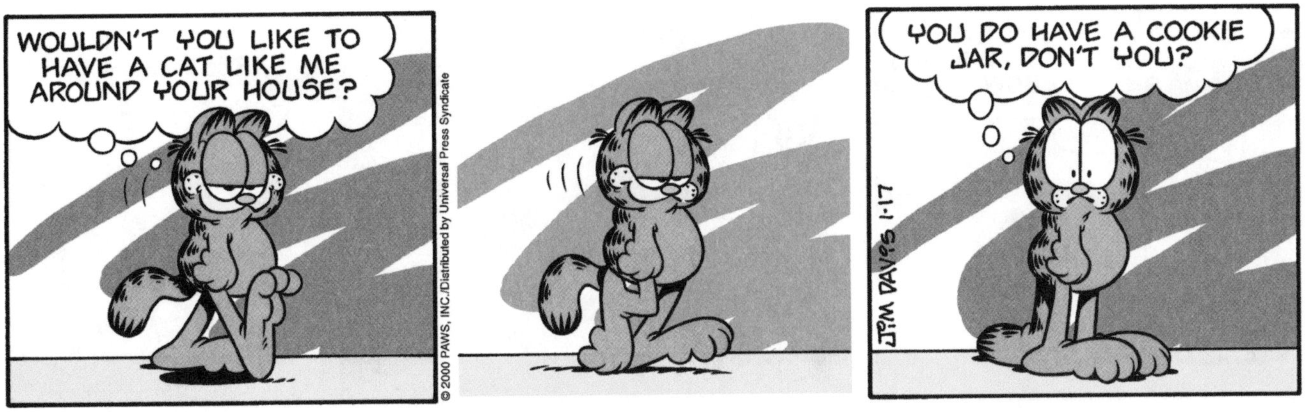
WOULDN'T YOU LIKE TO HAVE A CAT LIKE ME AROUND YOUR HOUSE?
© 2000 PAWS, INC./Distributed by Universal Press Syndicate
YOU DO HAVE A COOKIE JAR, DON'T YOU?
JIM DAVIS 1-17

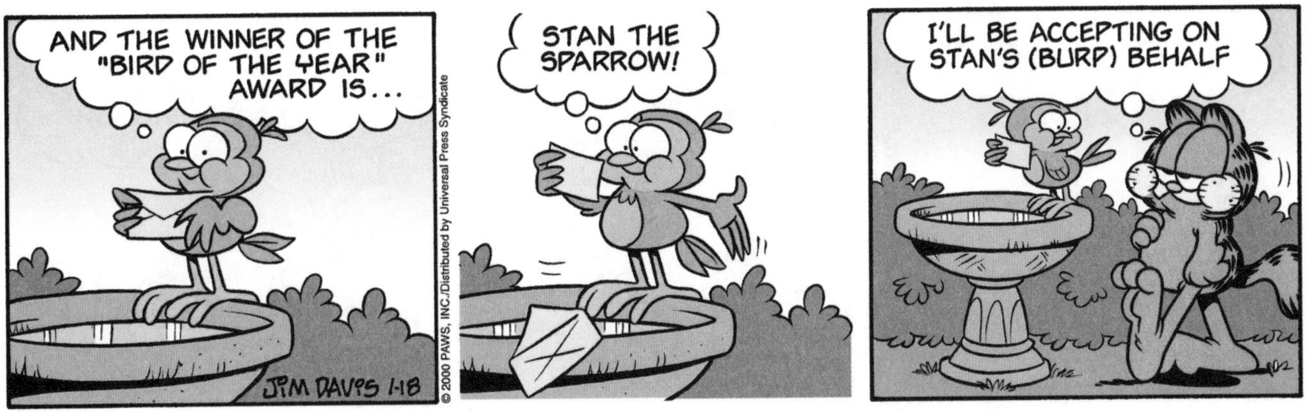
AND THE WINNER OF THE "BIRD OF THE YEAR" AWARD IS...
JIM DAVIS 1-18
© 2000 PAWS, INC./Distributed by Universal Press Syndicate
STAN THE SPARROW!
I'LL BE ACCEPTING ON STAN'S (BURP) BEHALF

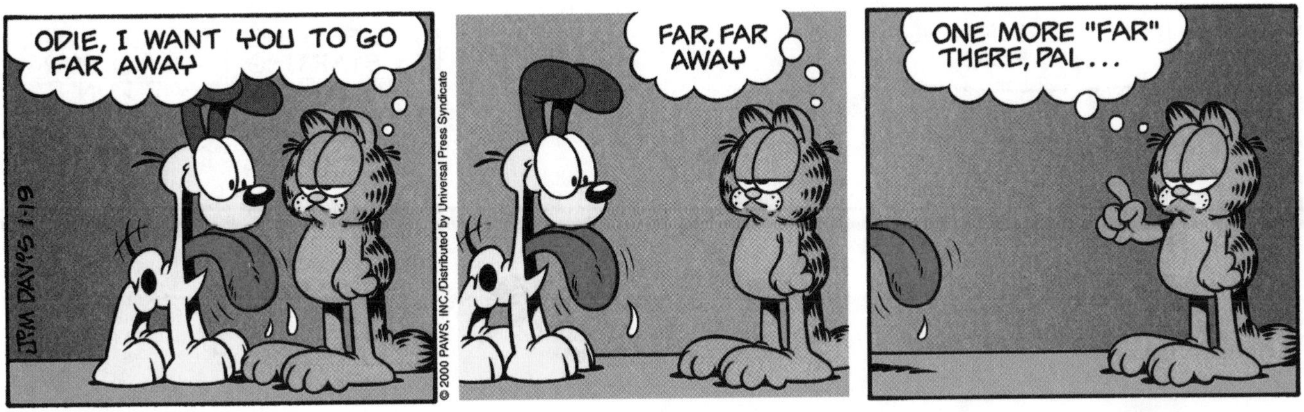
ODIE, I WANT YOU TO GO FAR AWAY
JIM DAVIS 1-19
© 2000 PAWS, INC./Distributed by Universal Press Syndicate
FAR, FAR AWAY
ONE MORE "FAR" THERE, PAL...

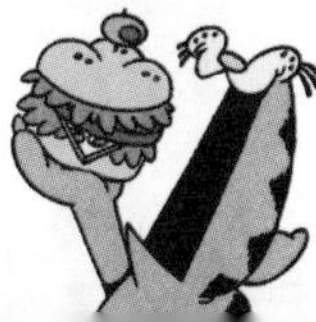

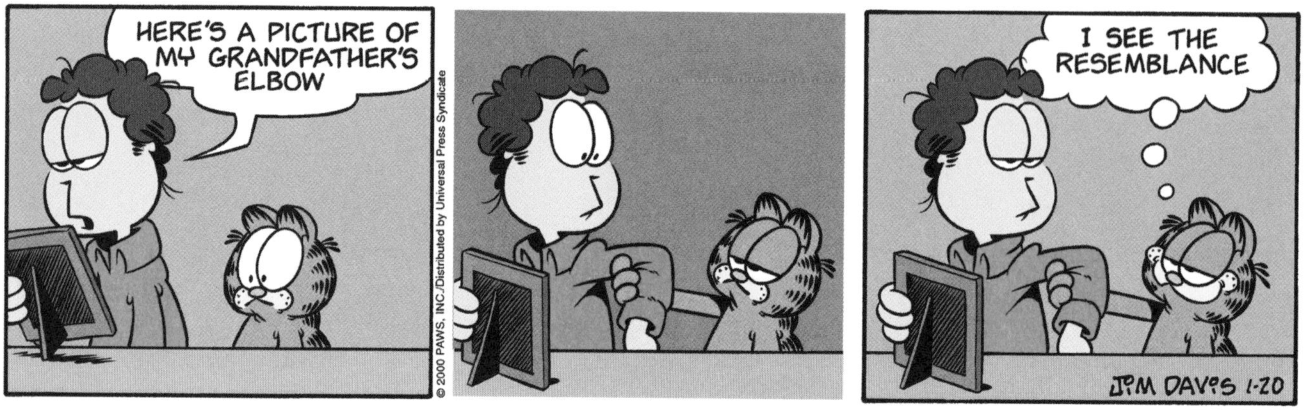
HERE'S A PICTURE OF MY GRANDFATHER'S ELBOW
© 2000 PAWS, INC./Distributed by Universal Press Syndicate
I SEE THE RESEMBLANCE
JIM DAVIS 1-20

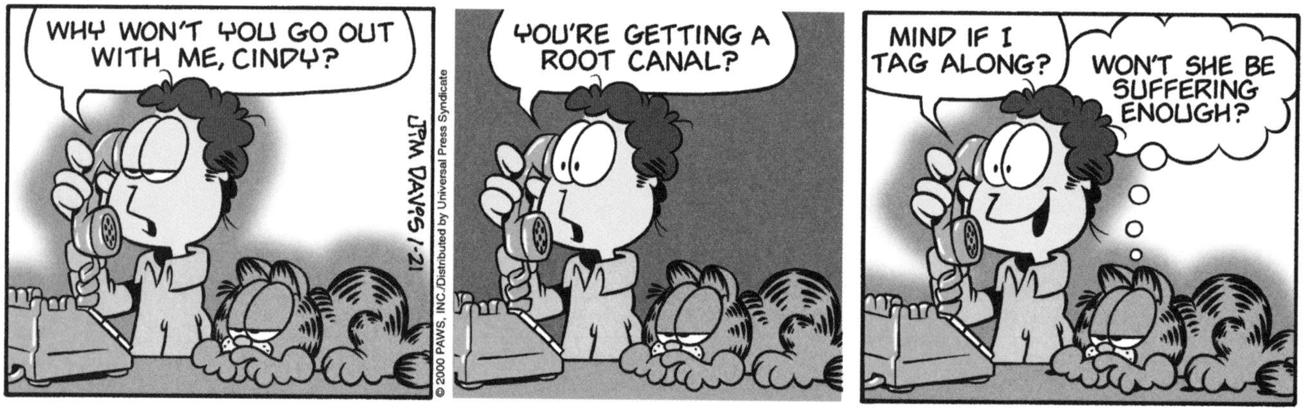
WHY WON'T YOU GO OUT WITH ME, CINDY?
JIM DAVIS 1-21
© 2000 PAWS, INC./Distributed by Universal Press Syndicate
YOU'RE GETTING A ROOT CANAL?
MIND IF I TAG ALONG?
WON'T SHE BE SUFFERING ENOUGH?

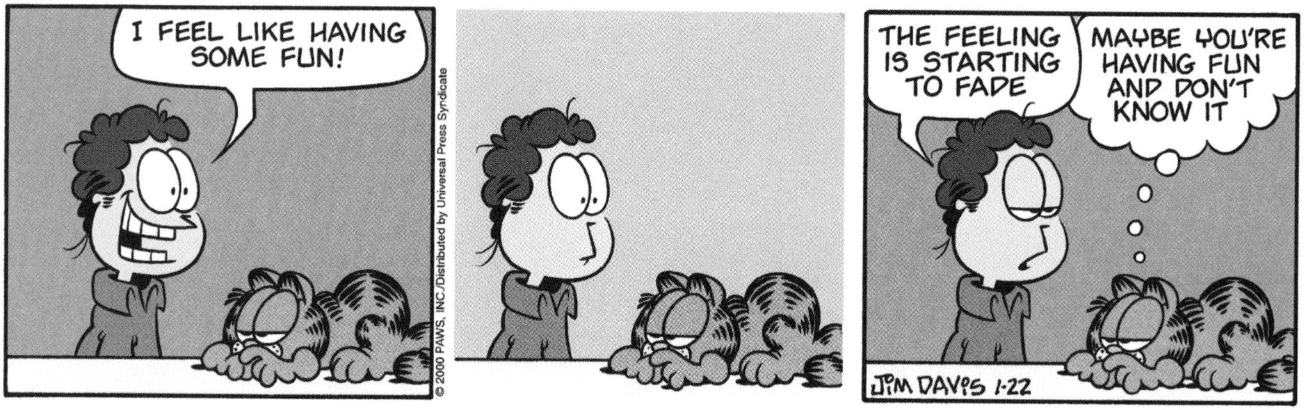
I FEEL LIKE HAVING SOME FUN!
© 2000 PAWS, INC./Distributed by Universal Press Syndicate
THE FEELING IS STARTING TO FADE
MAYBE YOU'RE HAVING FUN AND DON'T KNOW IT
JIM DAVIS 1-22



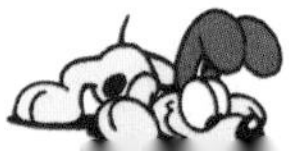

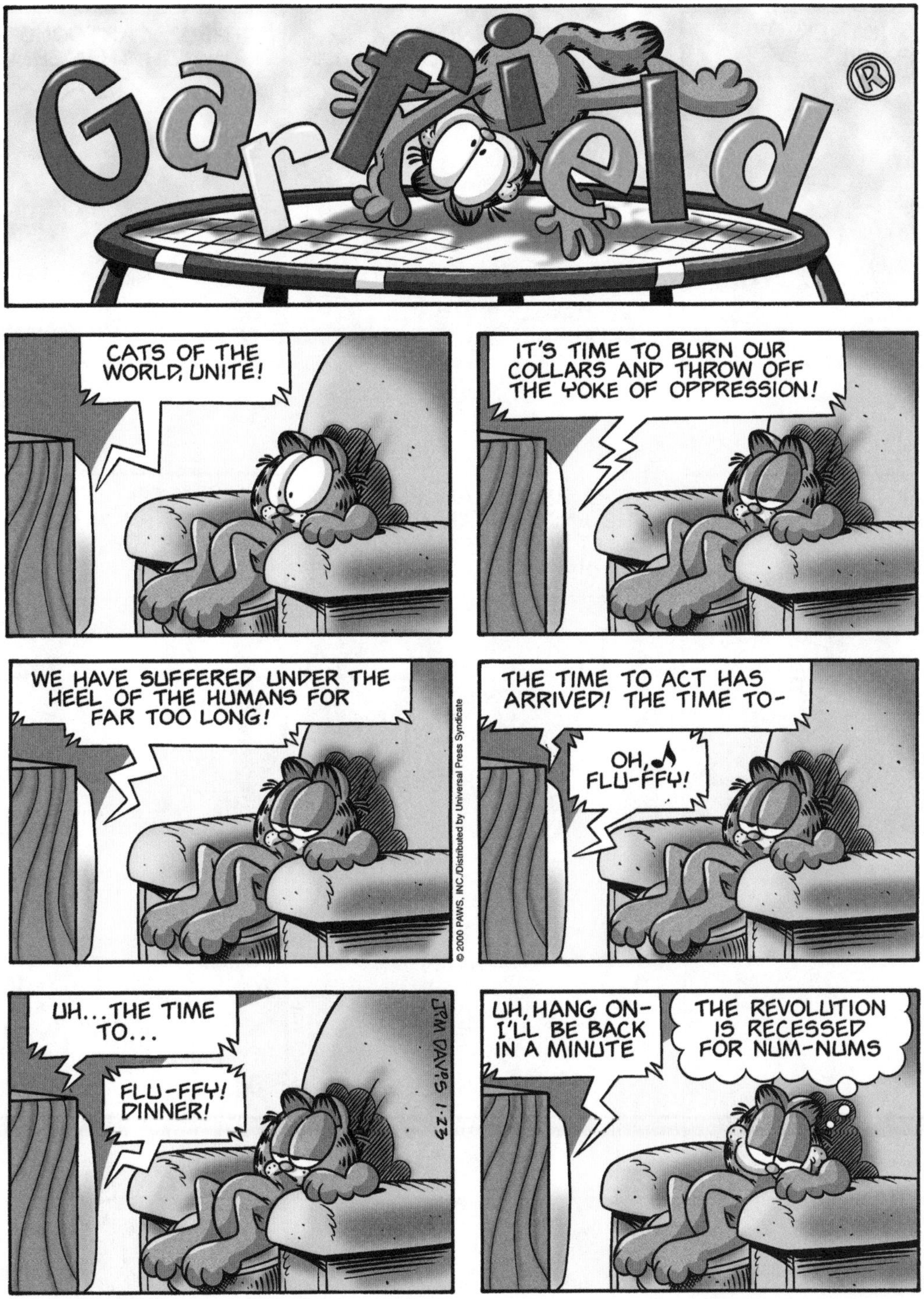
Garfield®
CATS OF THE WORLD, UNITE!
IT'S TIME TO BURN OUR COLLARS AND THROW OFF THE YOKE OF OPPRESSION!
WE HAVE SUFFERED UNDER THE HEEL OF THE HUMANS FOR FAR TOO LONG!
THE TIME TO ACT HAS ARRIVED! THE TIME TO-
OH, ♪ FLU-FFY!
UH... THE TIME TO...
FLU-FFY! DINNER!
UH, HANG ON- I'LL BE BACK IN A MINUTE
THE REVOLUTION IS RECESSED FOR NUM-NUMS
JPM DAVIS 1-23
© 2000 PAWS, INC./Distributed by Universal Press Syndicate

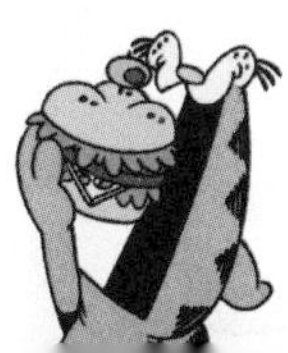

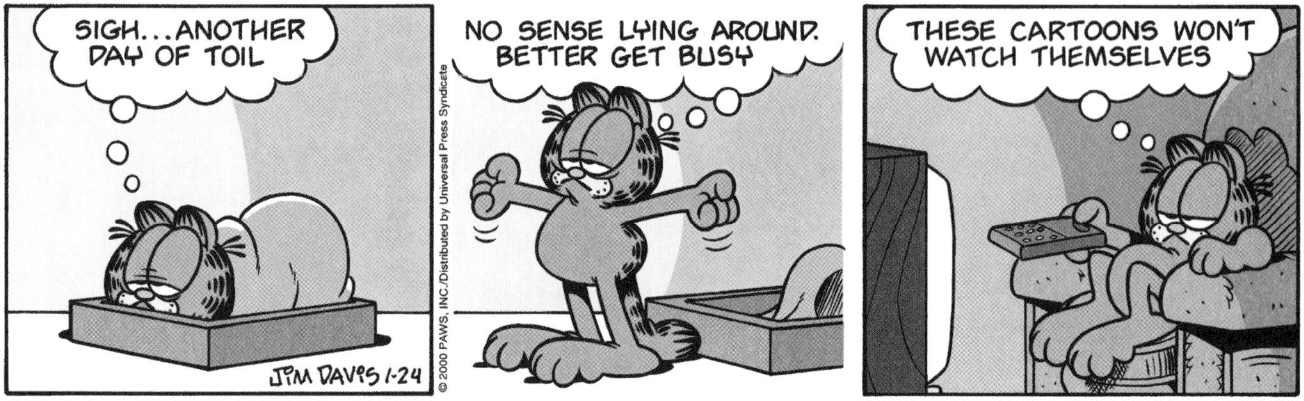
SIGH...ANOTHER DAY OF TOIL
JIM DAVIS 1-24
© 2000 PAWS, INC./Distributed by Universal Press Syndicate
NO SENSE LYING AROUND. BETTER GET BUSY
THESE CARTOONS WON'T WATCH THEMSELVES

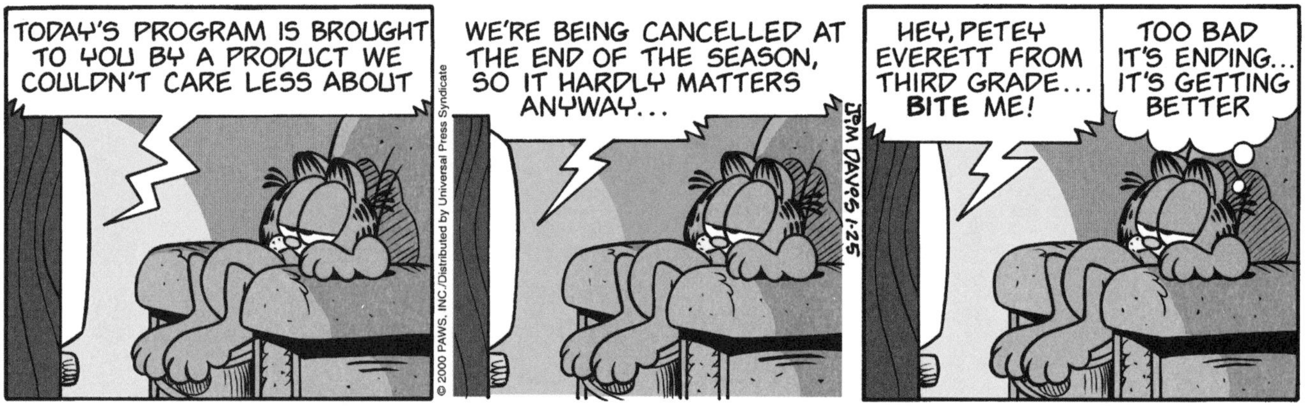
TODAY'S PROGRAM IS BROUGHT TO YOU BY A PRODUCT WE COULDN'T CARE LESS ABOUT
© 2000 PAWS, INC./Distributed by Universal Press Syndicate
WE'RE BEING CANCELLED AT THE END OF THE SEASON, SO IT HARDLY MATTERS ANYWAY...
JIM DAVIS 1-25
HEY, PETEY EVERETT FROM THIRD GRADE... BITE ME!
TOO BAD IT'S ENDING... IT'S GETTING BETTER

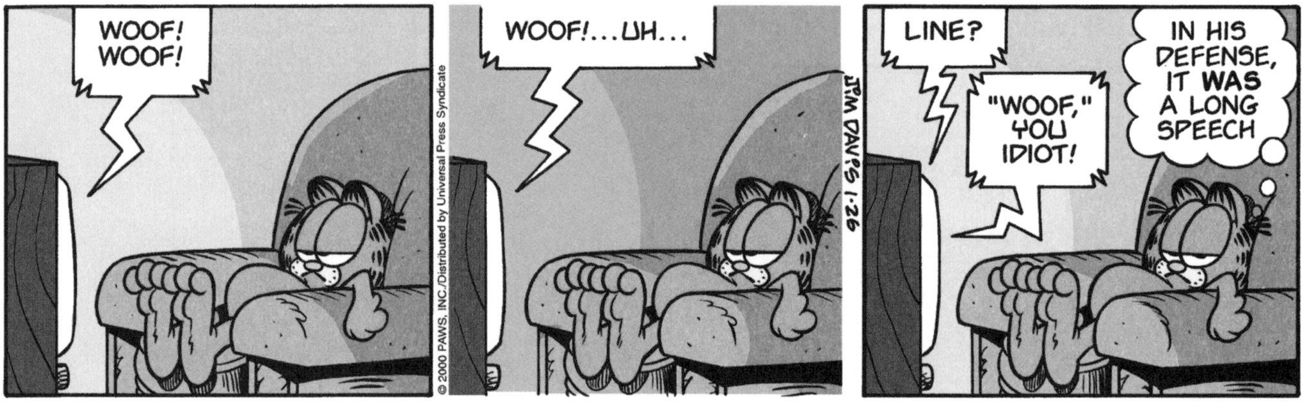
WOOF! WOOF!
© 2000 PAWS, INC./Distributed by Universal Press Syndicate
WOOF!...UH...
JIM DAVIS 1-26
LINE?
"WOOF," YOU IDIOT!
IN HIS DEFENSE, IT WAS A LONG SPEECH

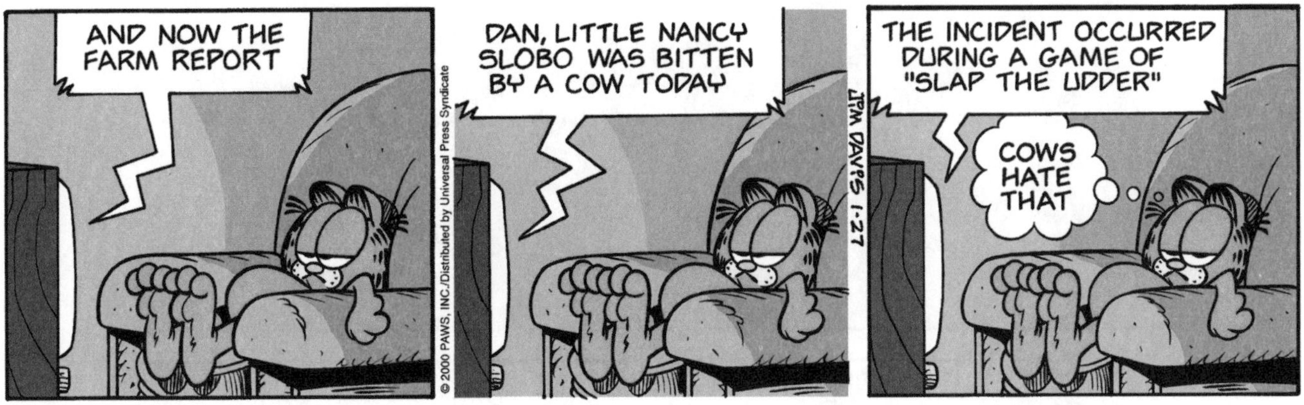
AND NOW THE FARM REPORT
© 2000 PAWS, INC./Distributed by Universal Press Syndicate
DAN, LITTLE NANCY SLOBO WAS BITTEN BY A COW TODAY
JPM DAVPS 1-27
THE INCIDENT OCCURRED DURING A GAME OF "SLAP THE UDDER"
COWS HATE THAT

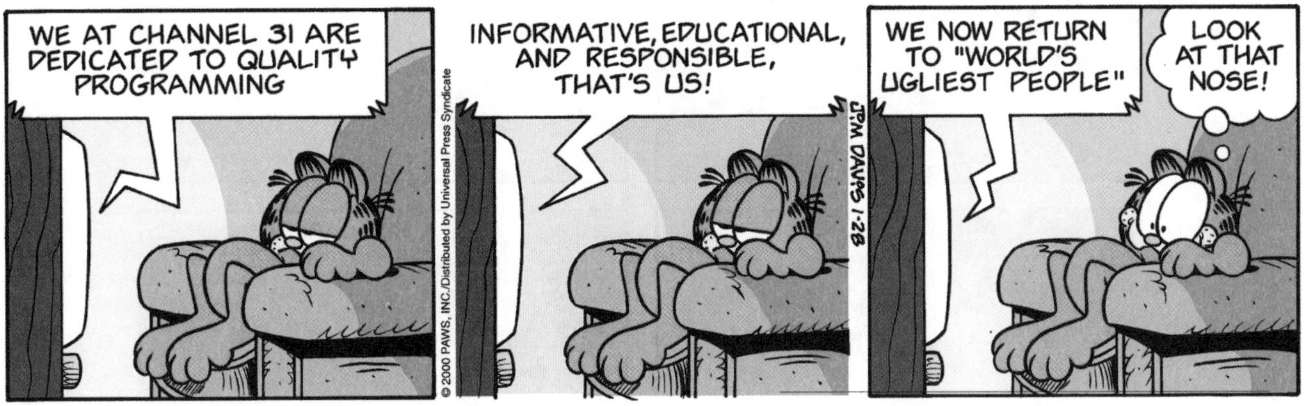
WE AT CHANNEL 31 ARE DEDICATED TO QUALITY PROGRAMMING
© 2000 PAWS, INC./Distributed by Universal Press Syndicate
INFORMATIVE, EDUCATIONAL, AND RESPONSIBLE, THAT'S US!
JPM DAVPS 1-28
WE NOW RETURN TO "WORLD'S UGLIEST PEOPLE"
LOOK AT THAT NOSE!

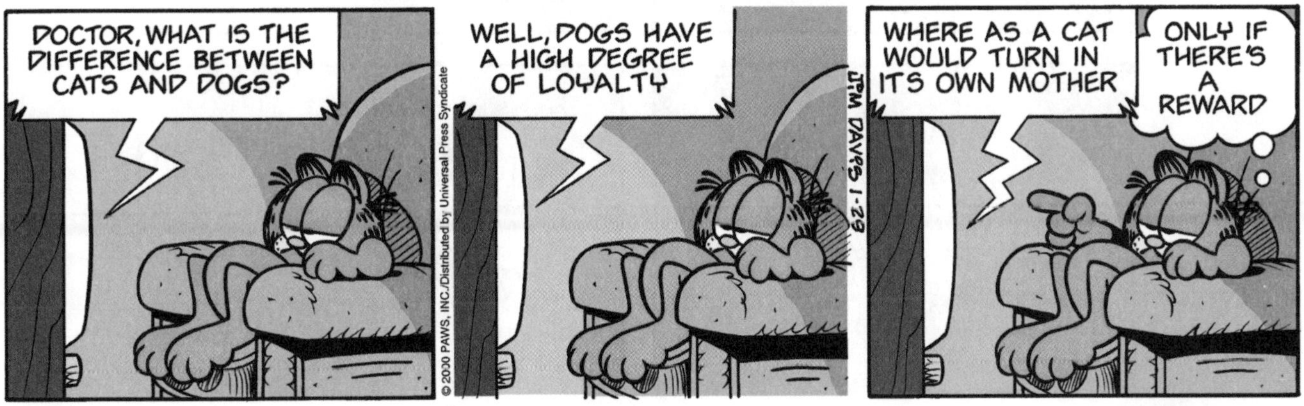
DOCTOR, WHAT IS THE DIFFERENCE BETWEEN CATS AND DOGS?
© 2000 PAWS, INC./Distributed by Universal Press Syndicate
WELL, DOGS HAVE A HIGH DEGREE OF LOYALTY
JPM DAVPS 1-29
WHERE AS A CAT WOULD TURN IN ITS OWN MOTHER
ONLY IF THERE'S A REWARD

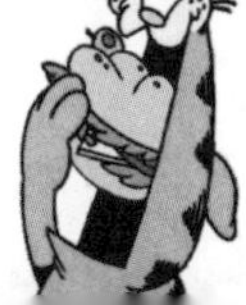

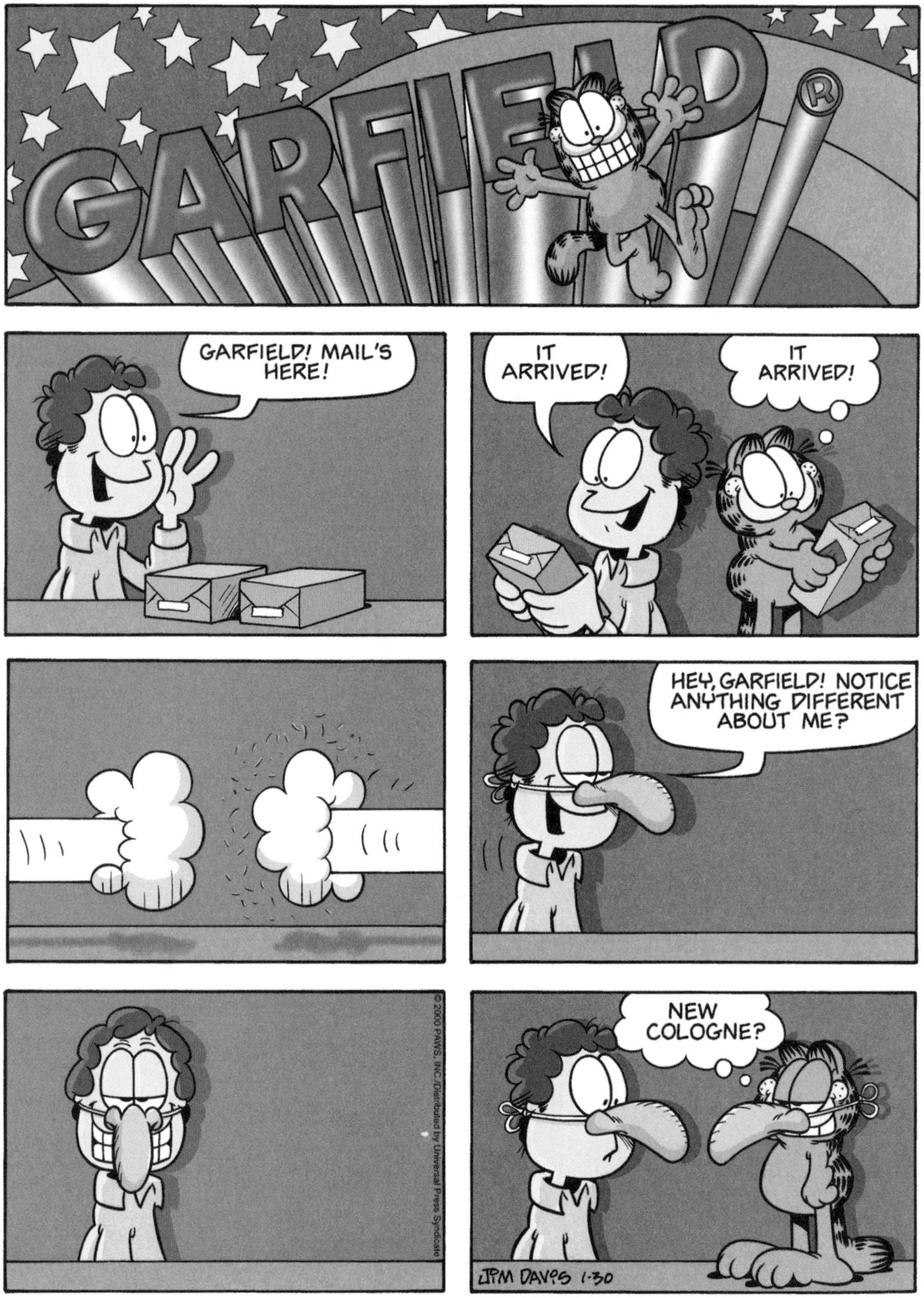
GARFIELD®
GARFIELD! MAIL'S HERE!
IT ARRIVED!
IT ARRIVED!
HEY, GARFIELD! NOTICE ANYTHING DIFFERENT ABOUT ME?
© 2000 PAWS, INC./Distributed by Universal Press Syndicate
NEW COLOGNE?
JIM DAVIS 1-30

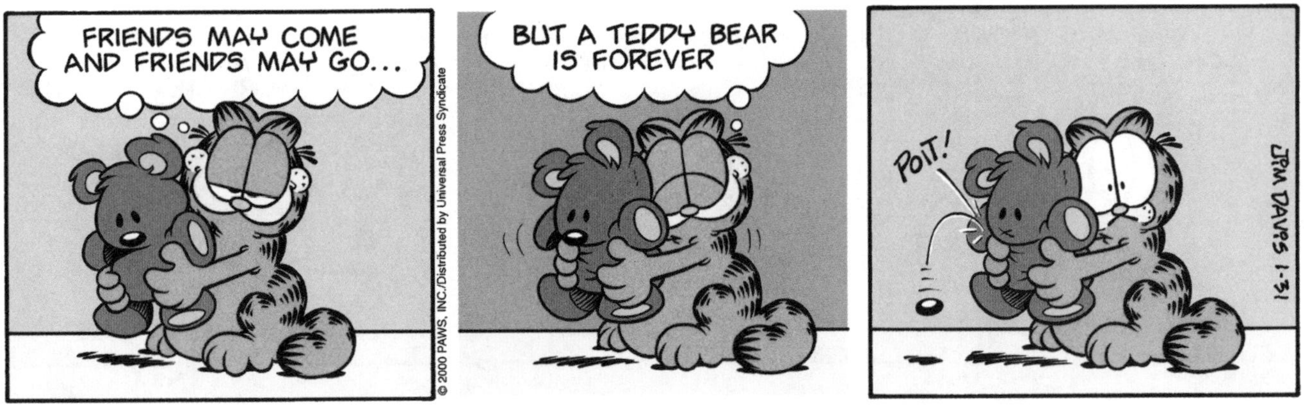
FRIENDS MAY COME AND FRIENDS MAY GO...
BUT A TEDDY BEAR IS FOREVER
POIT!
JIM DAVIS 1-31



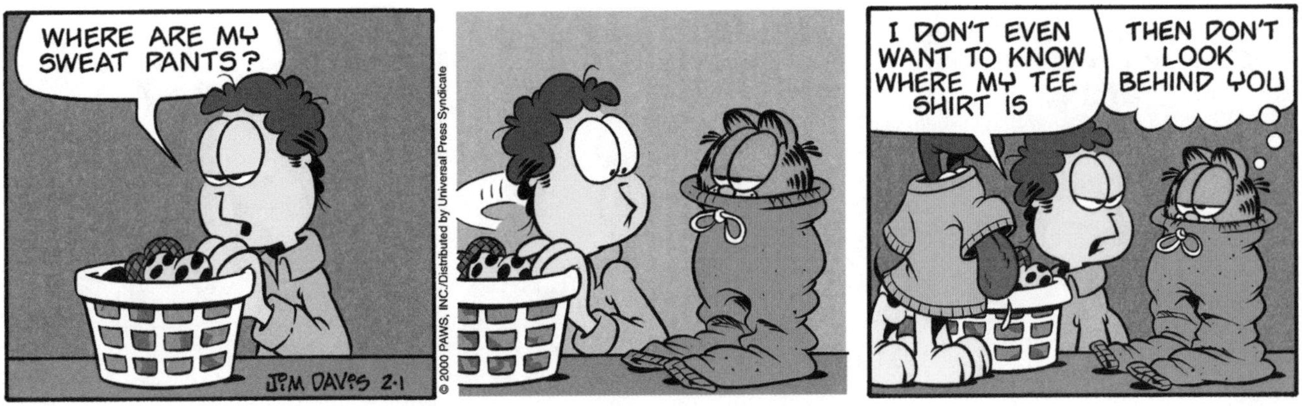
WHERE ARE MY SWEAT PANTS?
JIM DAVIS 2-1
I DON'T EVEN WANT TO KNOW WHERE MY TEE SHIRT IS
THEN DON'T LOOK BEHIND YOU



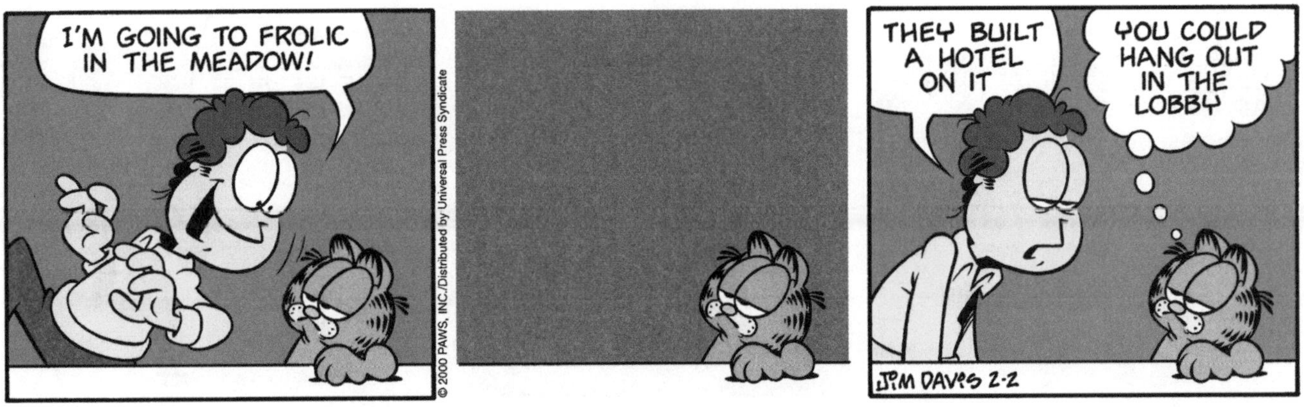
I'M GOING TO FROLIC IN THE MEADOW!
THEY BUILT A HOTEL ON IT
YOU COULD HANG OUT IN THE LOBBY
JIM DAVIS 2-2



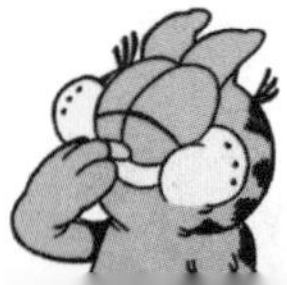

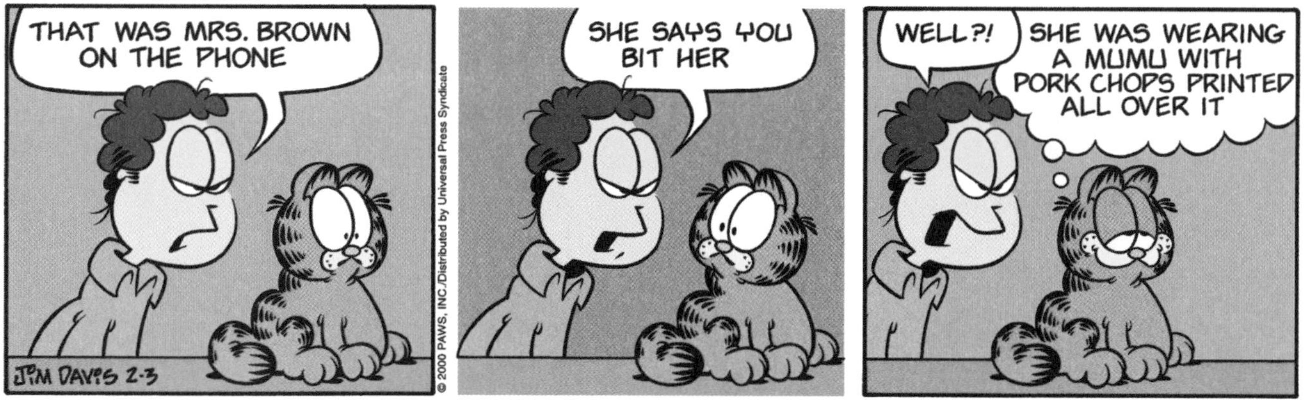
THAT WAS MRS. BROWN ON THE PHONE
JIM DAVIS 2-3
© 2000 PAWS, INC./Distributed by Universal Press Syndicate
SHE SAYS YOU BIT HER
WELL?!
SHE WAS WEARING A MUMU WITH PORK CHOPS PRINTED ALL OVER IT

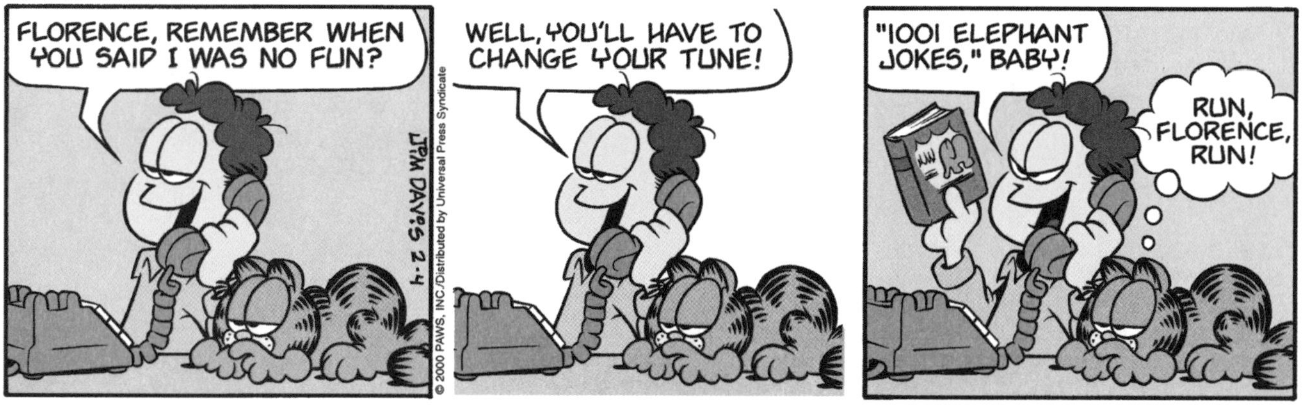
FLORENCE, REMEMBER WHEN YOU SAID I WAS NO FUN?
JIM DAVIS 2-4
© 2000 PAWS, INC./Distributed by Universal Press Syndicate
WELL, YOU'LL HAVE TO CHANGE YOUR TUNE!
"1001 ELEPHANT JOKES," BABY!
RUN, FLORENCE, RUN!

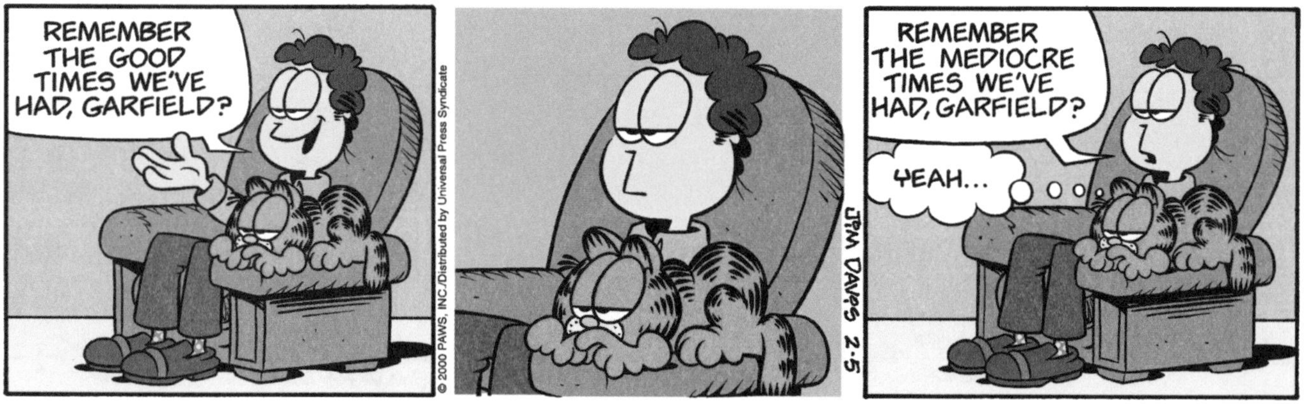
REMEMBER THE GOOD TIMES WE'VE HAD, GARFIELD?
© 2000 PAWS, INC./Distributed by Universal Press Syndicate
JIM DAVIS 2-5
REMEMBER THE MEDIOCRE TIMES WE'VE HAD, GARFIELD?
YEAH...



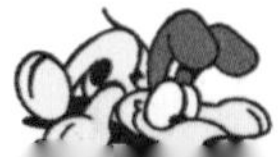

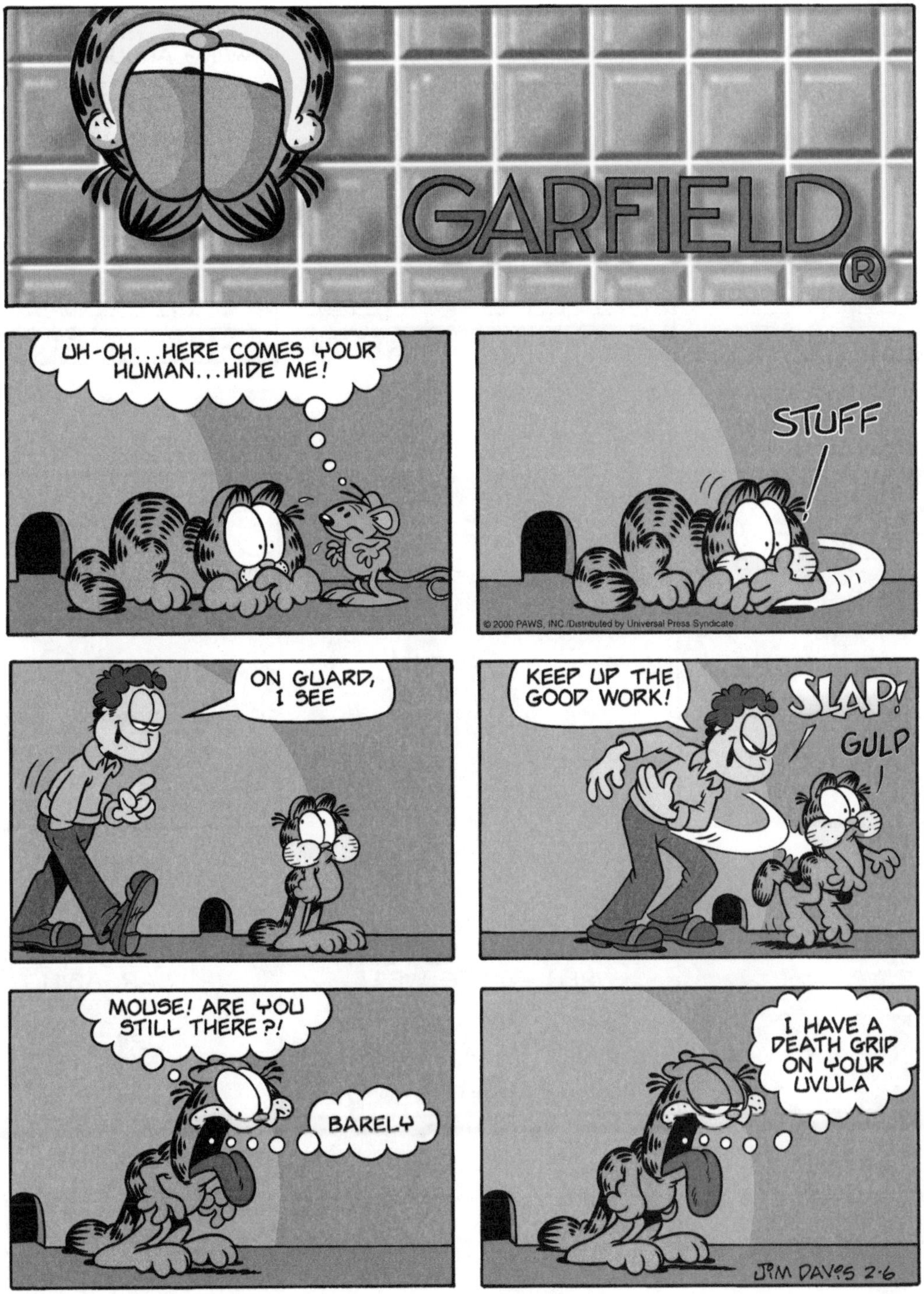
GARFIELD®
UH-OH...HERE COMES YOUR HUMAN...HIDE ME!
STUFF
© 2000 PAWS, INC./Distributed by Universal Press Syndicate
ON GUARD, I SEE
KEEP UP THE GOOD WORK!
SLAP!
GULP
MOUSE! ARE YOU STILL THERE?!
BARELY
I HAVE A DEATH GRIP ON YOUR UVULA
JIM DAVIS 2-6

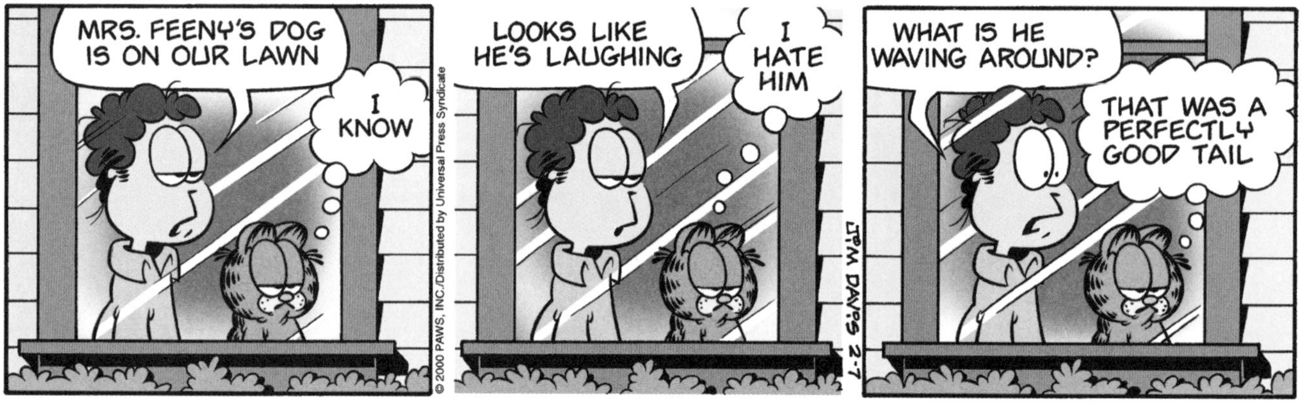
MRS. FEENY'S DOG IS ON OUR LAWN
I KNOW
LOOKS LIKE HE'S LAUGHING
I HATE HIM
WHAT IS HE WAVING AROUND?
THAT WAS A PERFECTLY GOOD TAIL
© 2000 PAWS, INC./Distributed by Universal Press Syndicate
JIM DAVIS 2-7

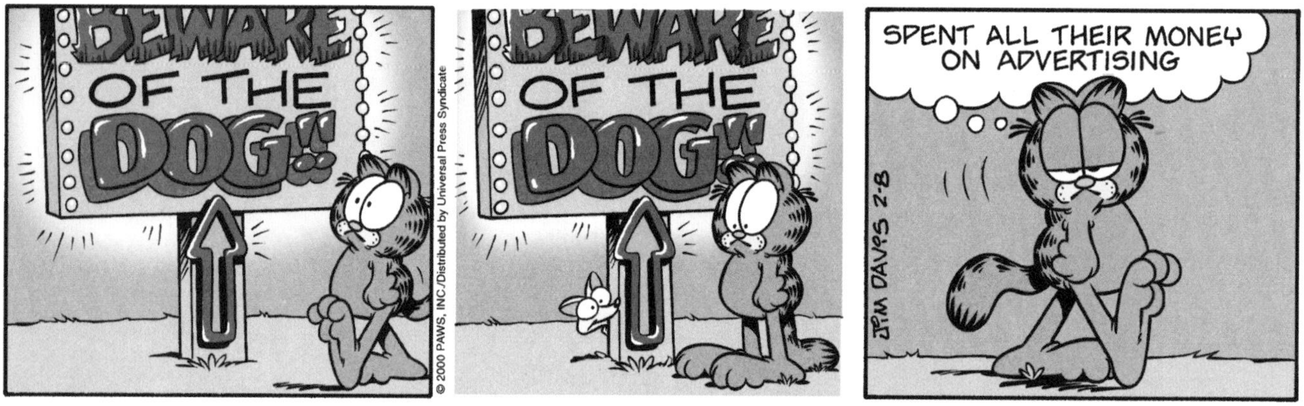
BEWARE OF THE DOG!!
SPENT ALL THEIR MONEY ON ADVERTISING
© 2000 PAWS, INC./Distributed by Universal Press Syndicate
JIM DAVIS 2-8

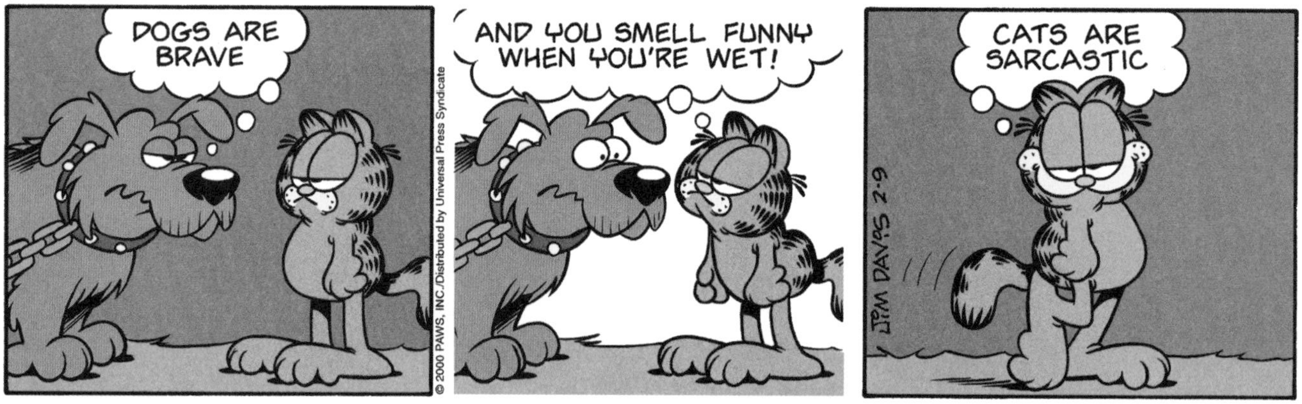
DOGS ARE BRAVE
AND YOU SMELL FUNNY WHEN YOU'RE WET!
CATS ARE SARCASTIC
© 2000 PAWS, INC./Distributed by Universal Press Syndicate
JIM DAVIS 2-9

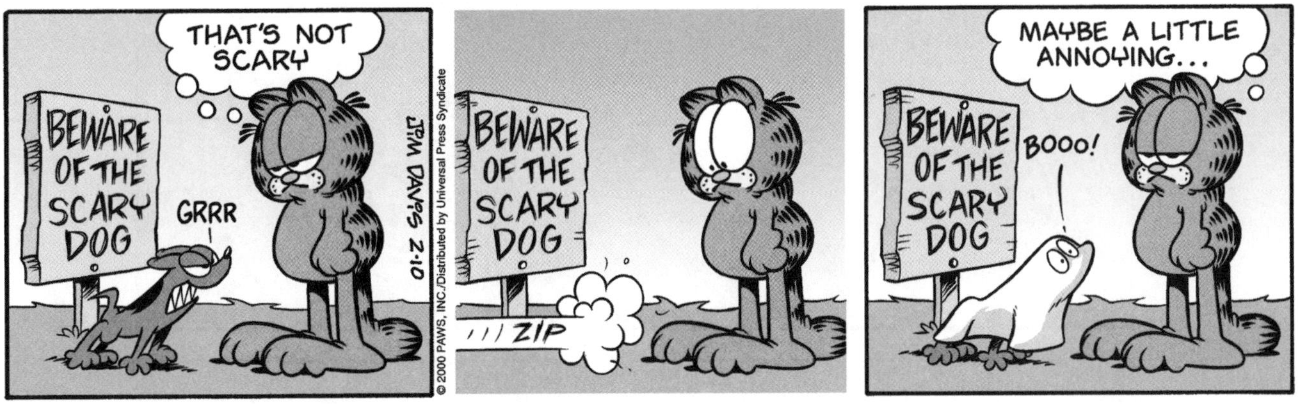
THAT'S NOT SCARY
BEWARE OF THE SCARY DOG
GRRR
JIM DAVIS 2-10
© 2000 PAWS, INC./Distributed by Universal Press Syndicate
BEWARE OF THE SCARY DOG
ZIP
MAYBE A LITTLE ANNOYING...
BEWARE OF THE SCARY DOG
BOOO!

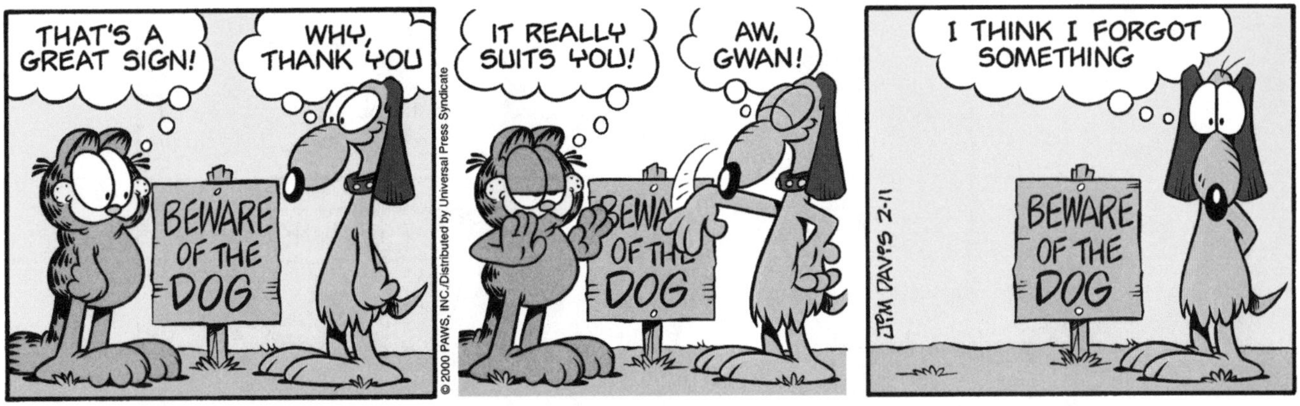
THAT'S A GREAT SIGN!
WHY, THANK YOU
BEWARE OF THE DOG
© 2000 PAWS, INC./Distributed by Universal Press Syndicate
IT REALLY SUITS YOU!
AW, GWAN!
I THINK I FORGOT SOMETHING
JIM DAVIS 2-11
BEWARE OF THE DOG

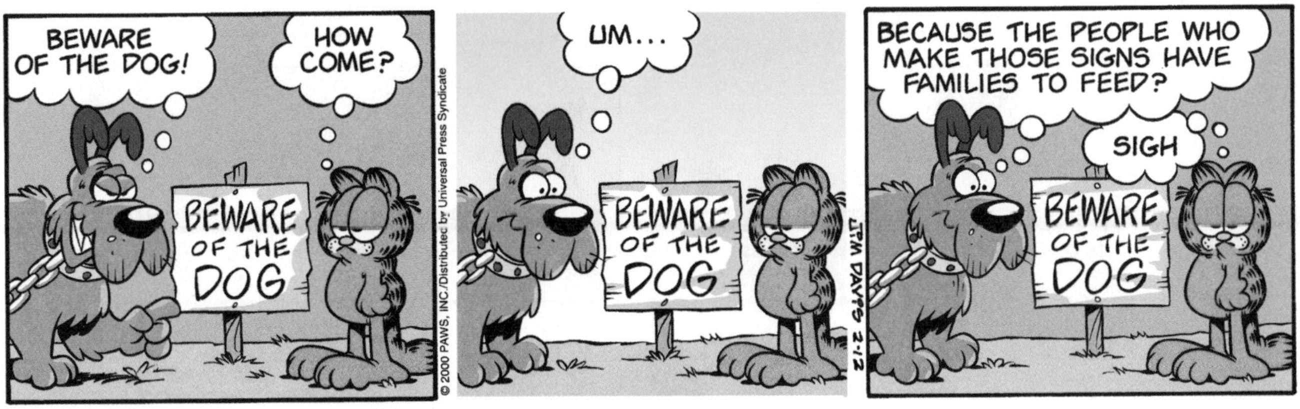
BEWARE OF THE DOG!
HOW COME?
BEWARE OF THE DOG
© 2000 PAWS, INC./Distributed by Universal Press Syndicate
UM...
BEWARE OF THE DOG
JIM DAVIS 2-12
BECAUSE THE PEOPLE WHO MAKE THOSE SIGNS HAVE FAMILIES TO FEED?
SIGH
BEWARE OF THE DOG

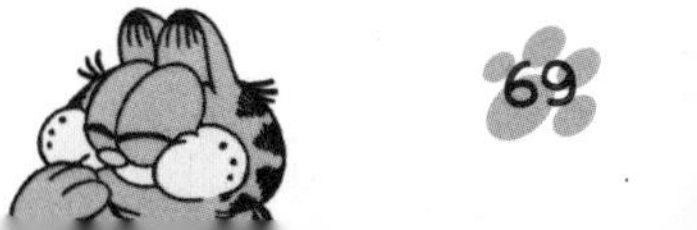

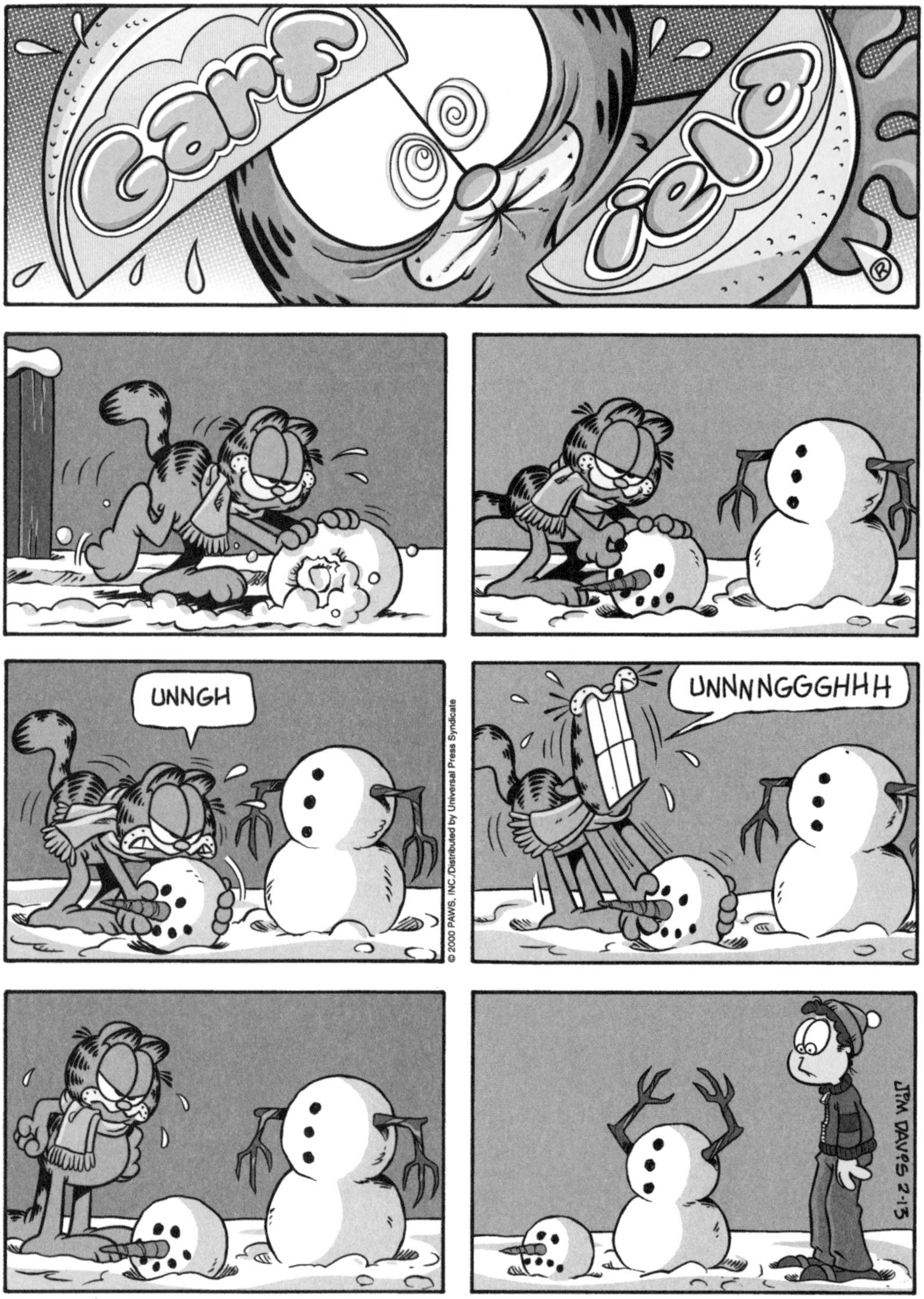
Garfield
UNNGH
UNNNNGGGHHH
© 2000 PAWS, INC./Distributed by Universal Press Syndicate
JIM DAVIS 2-13

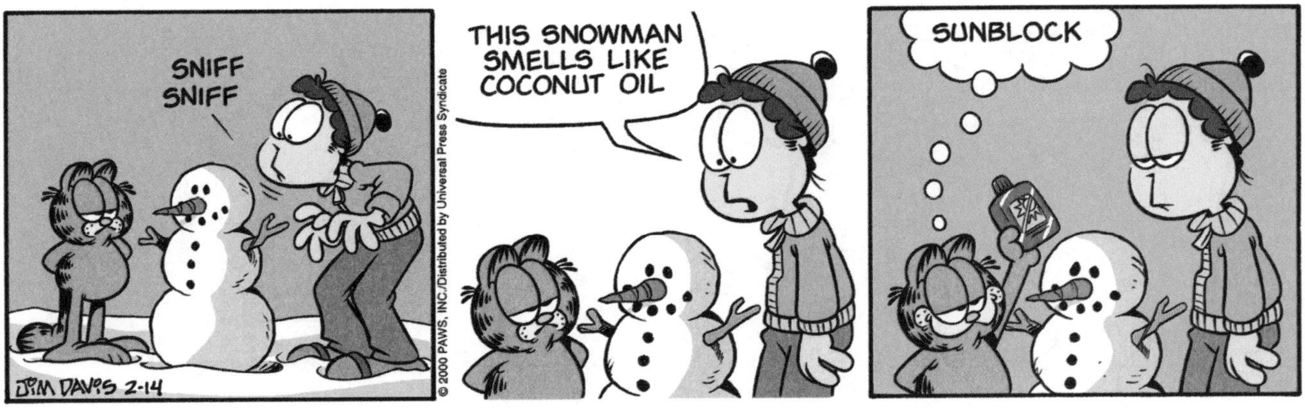
SNIFF SNIFF
JIM DAVIS 2-14
© 2000 PAWS, INC./Distributed by Universal Press Syndicate
THIS SNOWMAN SMELLS LIKE COCONUT OIL
SUNBLOCK

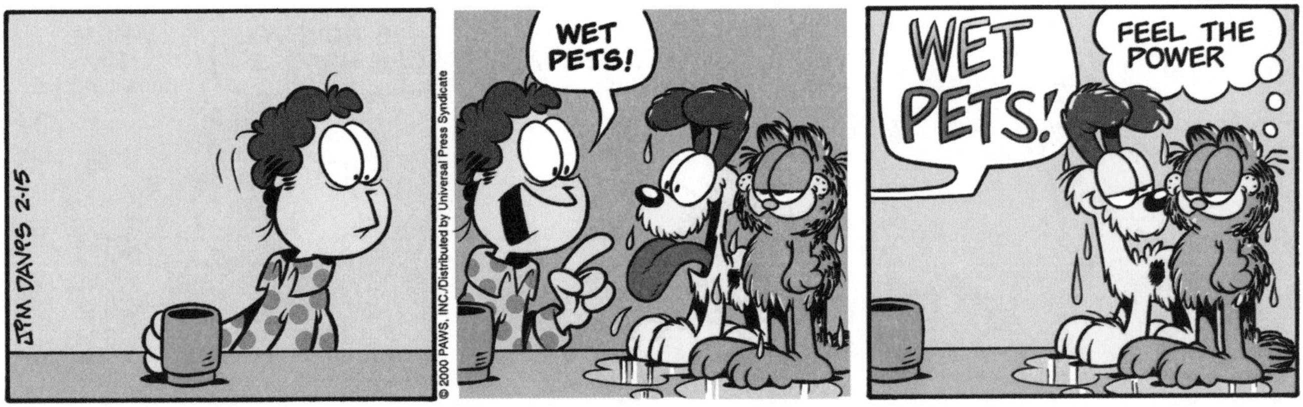
JIM DAVIS 2-15
© 2000 PAWS, INC./Distributed by Universal Press Syndicate
WET PETS!
WET PETS!
FEEL THE POWER

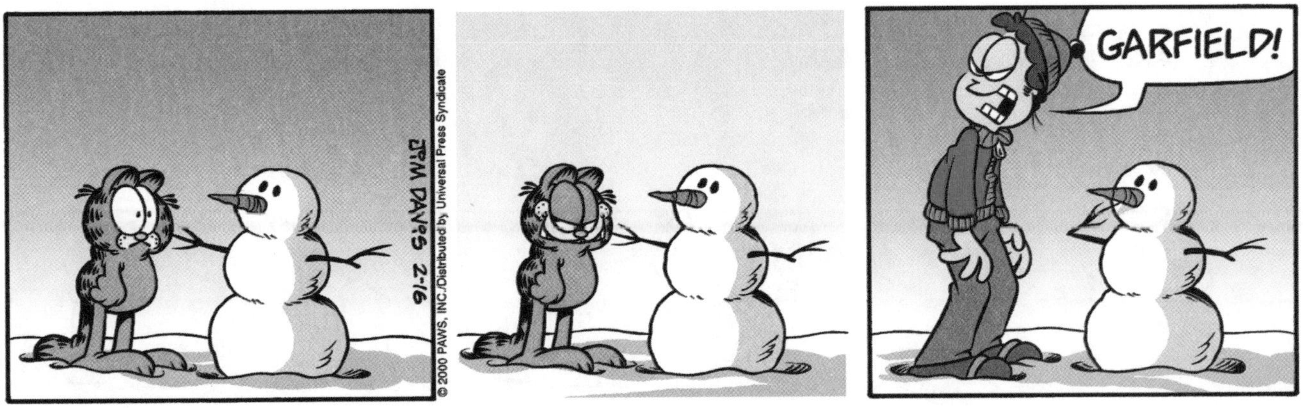
JIM DAVIS 2-16
© 2000 PAWS, INC./Distributed by Universal Press Syndicate
GARFIELD!

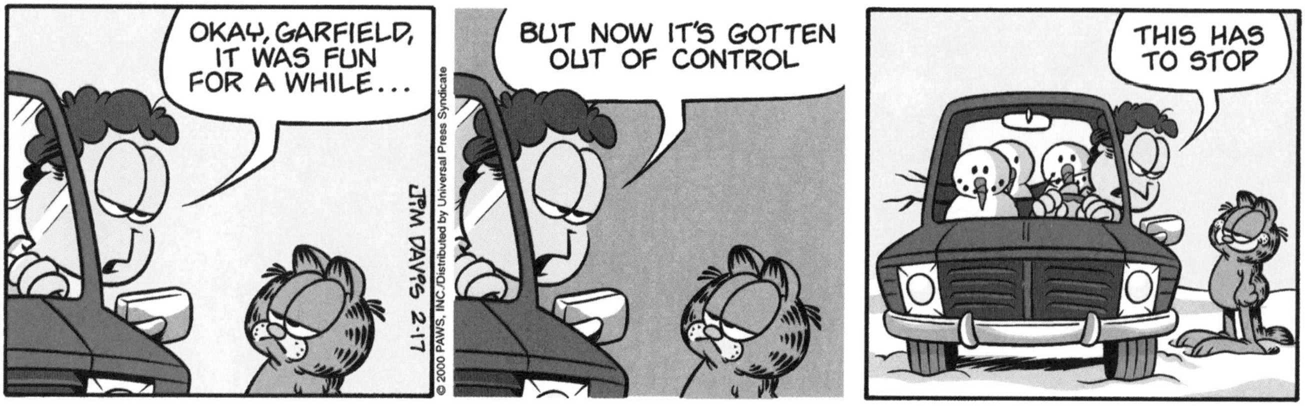
OKAY, GARFIELD, IT WAS FUN FOR A WHILE...
JIM DAVIS 2-17
© 2000 PAWS, INC./Distributed by Universal Press Syndicate
BUT NOW IT'S GOTTEN OUT OF CONTROL
THIS HAS TO STOP

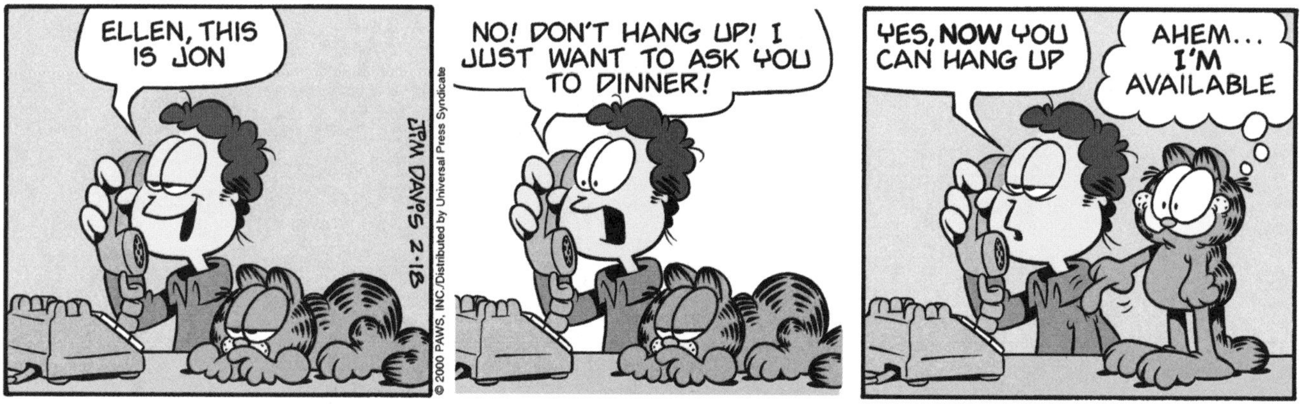
ELLEN, THIS IS JON
JIM DAVIS 2-18
© 2000 PAWS, INC./Distributed by Universal Press Syndicate
NO! DON'T HANG UP! I JUST WANT TO ASK YOU TO DINNER!
YES, **NOW** YOU CAN HANG UP
AHEM... **I'M** AVAILABLE

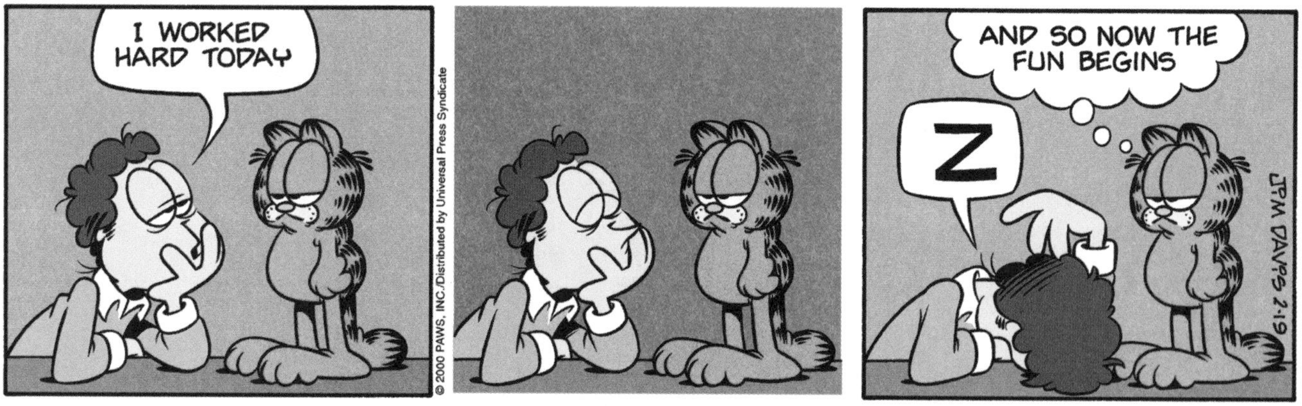
I WORKED HARD TODAY
© 2000 PAWS, INC./Distributed by Universal Press Syndicate
Z
AND SO NOW THE FUN BEGINS
JIM DAVIS 2-19

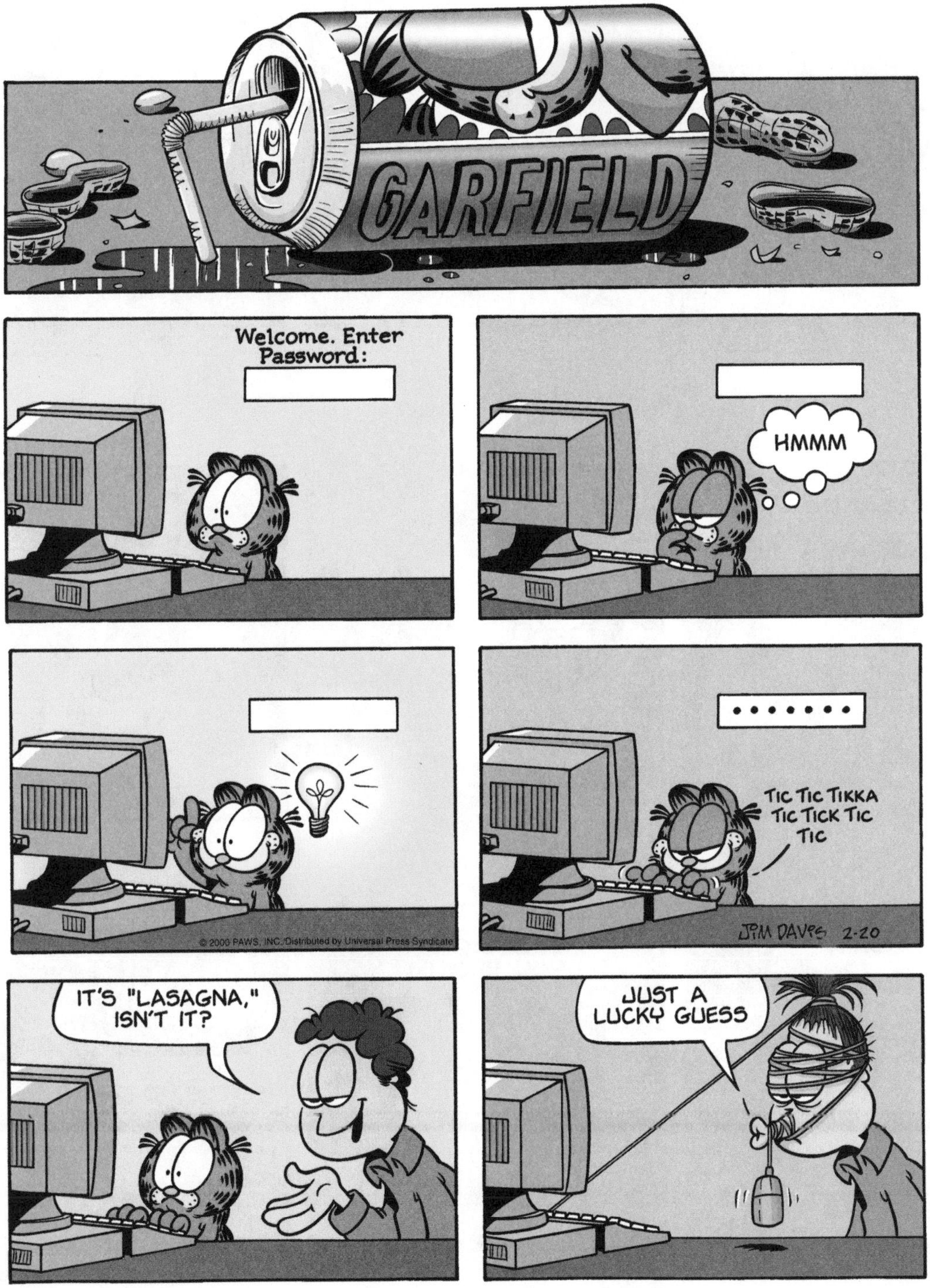
GARFIELD
Welcome. Enter Password:
HMMM
TIC TIC TIKKA TIC TICK TIC TIC
© 2000 PAWS, INC. Distributed by Universal Press Syndicate
JIM DAVIS 2-20
IT'S "LASAGNA," ISN'T IT?
JUST A LUCKY GUESS

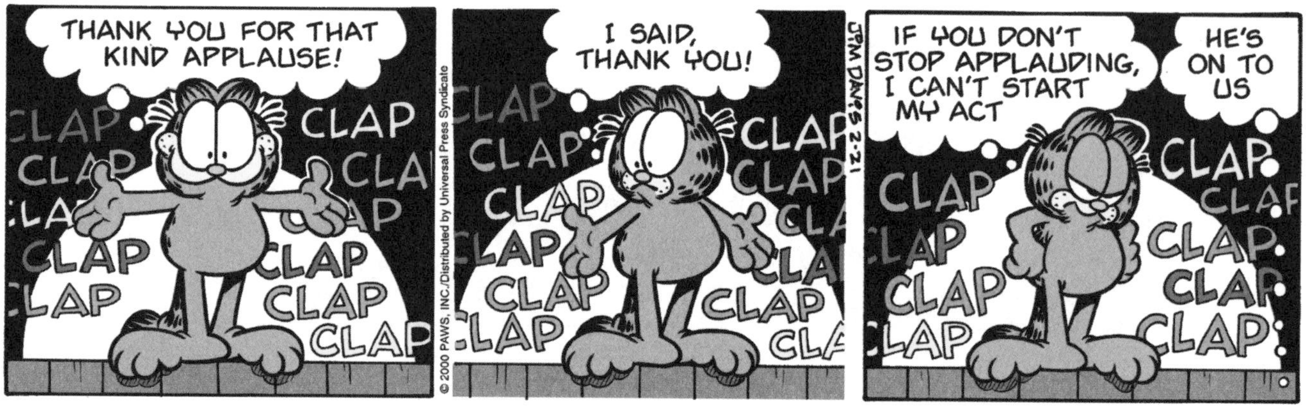
THANK YOU FOR THAT KIND APPLAUSE!
CLAP CLAP CLAP CLAP CLAP CLAP CLAP CLAP CLAP
© 2000 PAWS, INC./Distributed by Universal Press Syndicate
I SAID, THANK YOU!
CLAP CLAP CLAP CLAP CLAP CLAP
JIM DAVIS 2-21
IF YOU DON'T STOP APPLAUDING, I CAN'T START MY ACT
HE'S ON TO US
CLAP CLAP CLAP CLAP CLAP CLAP CLAP

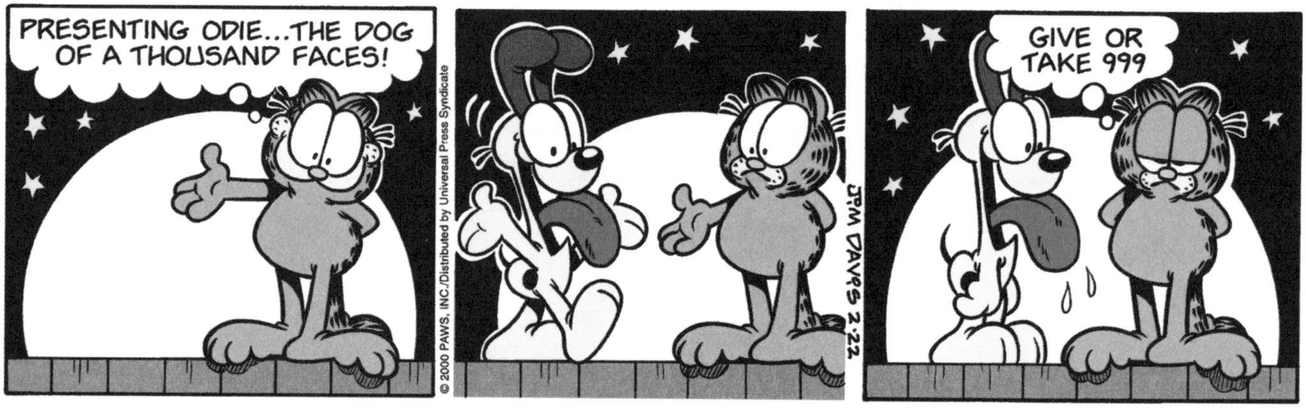
PRESENTING ODIE...THE DOG OF A THOUSAND FACES!
© 2000 PAWS, INC./Distributed by Universal Press Syndicate
JIM DAVIS 2-22
GIVE OR TAKE 999

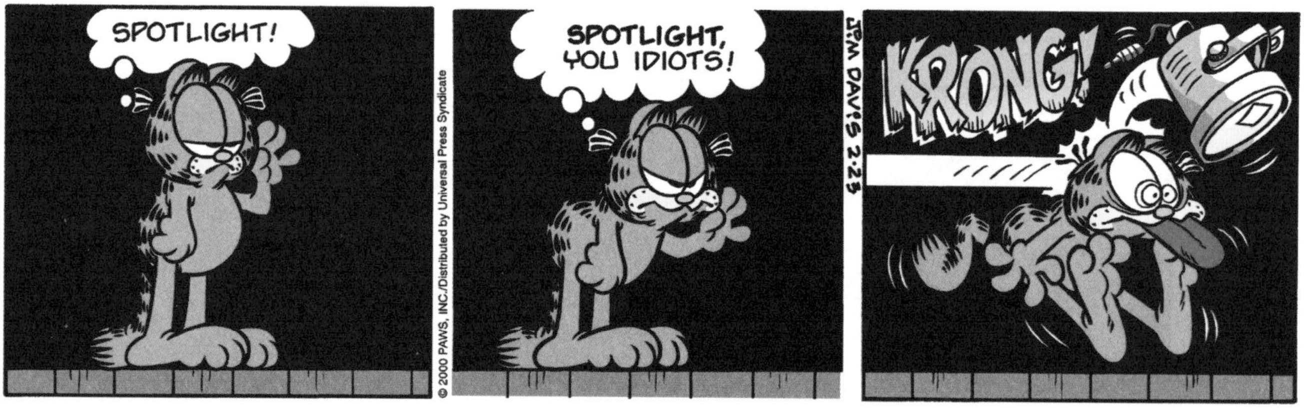
SPOTLIGHT!
© 2000 PAWS, INC./Distributed by Universal Press Syndicate
SPOTLIGHT, YOU IDIOTS!
JIM DAVIS 2-23
KRONG!



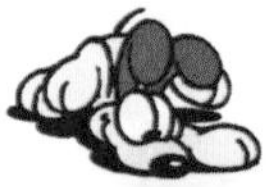

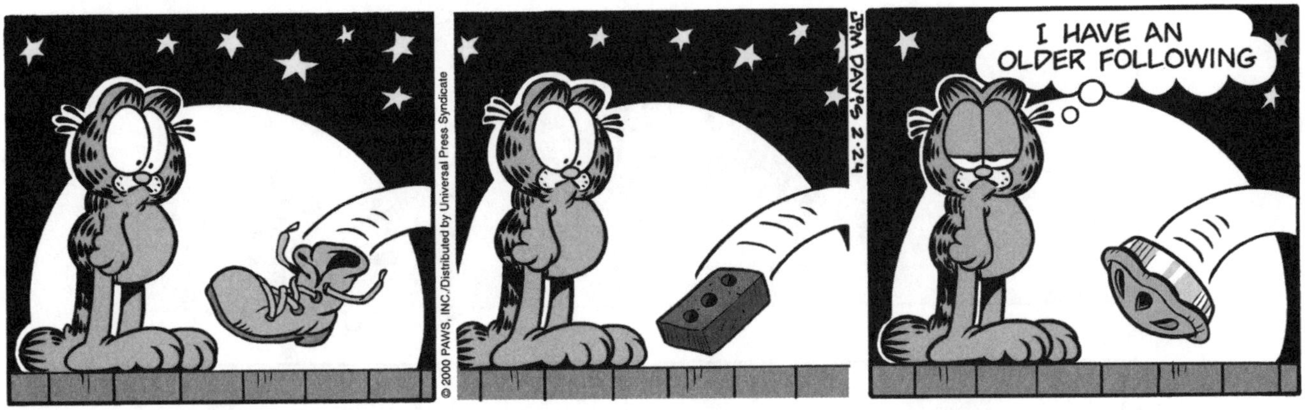
© 2000 PAWS, INC./Distributed by Universal Press Syndicate
I HAVE AN OLDER FOLLOWING

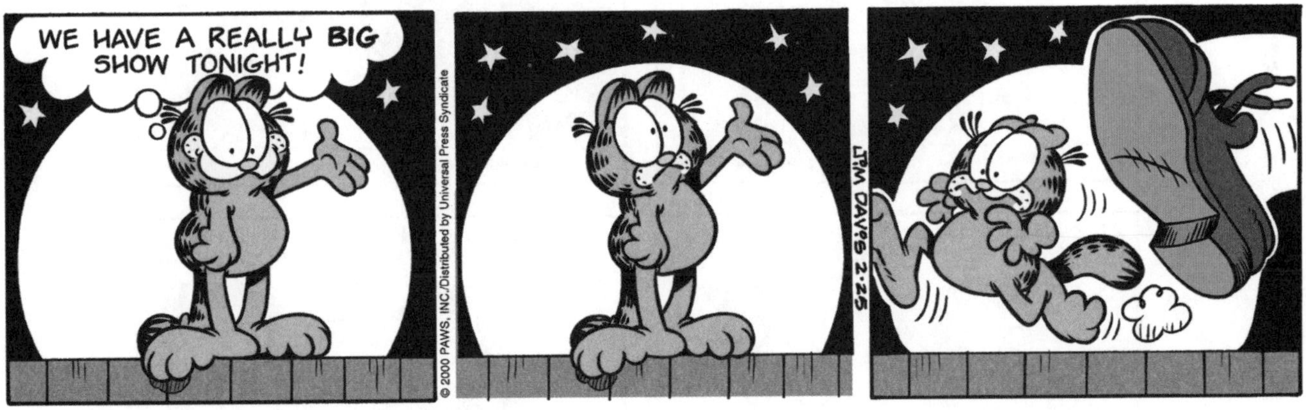
WE HAVE A REALLY BIG SHOW TONIGHT!
© 2000 PAWS, INC./Distributed by Universal Press Syndicate

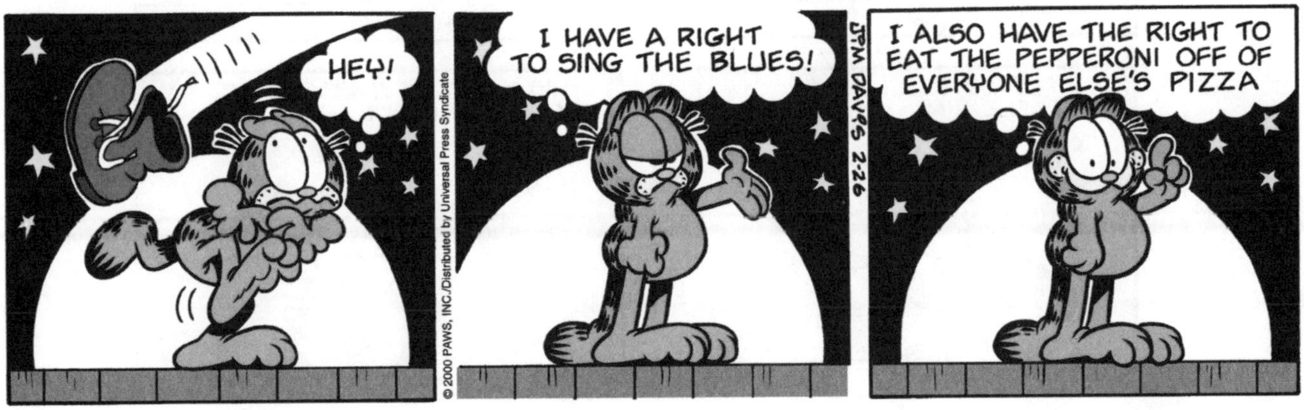
HEY!
© 2000 PAWS, INC./Distributed by Universal Press Syndicate
I HAVE A RIGHT TO SING THE BLUES!
I ALSO HAVE THE RIGHT TO EAT THE PEPPERONI OFF OF EVERYONE ELSE'S PIZZA

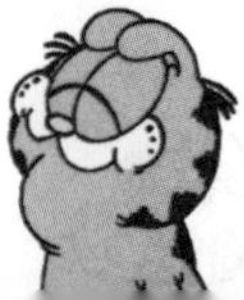

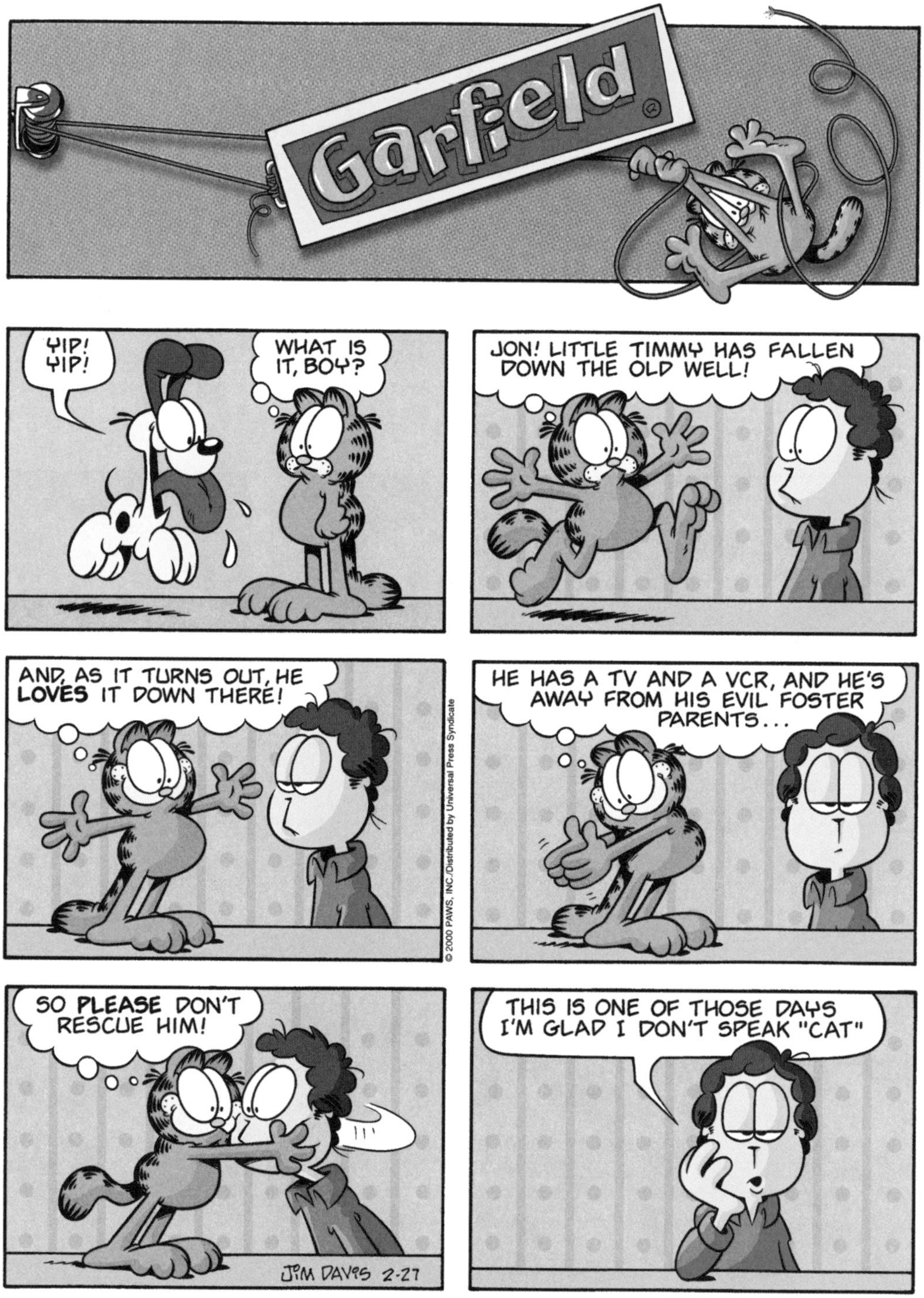
Garfield
YIP! YIP!
WHAT IS IT, BOY?
JON! LITTLE TIMMY HAS FALLEN DOWN THE OLD WELL!
AND, AS IT TURNS OUT, HE **LOVES** IT DOWN THERE!
HE HAS A TV AND A VCR, AND HE'S AWAY FROM HIS EVIL FOSTER PARENTS...
SO **PLEASE** DON'T RESCUE HIM!
THIS IS ONE OF THOSE DAYS I'M GLAD I DON'T SPEAK "CAT"
JIM DAVIS 2-27

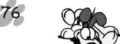

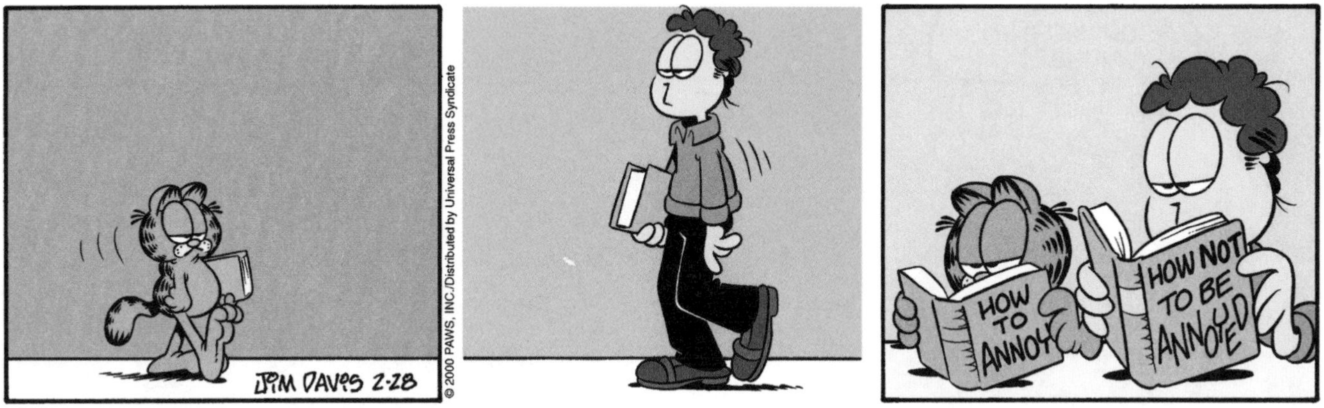
HOW TO ANNOY
HOW NOT TO BE ANNOYED
JIM DAVIS 2-28
© 2000 PAWS, INC./Distributed by Universal Press Syndicate

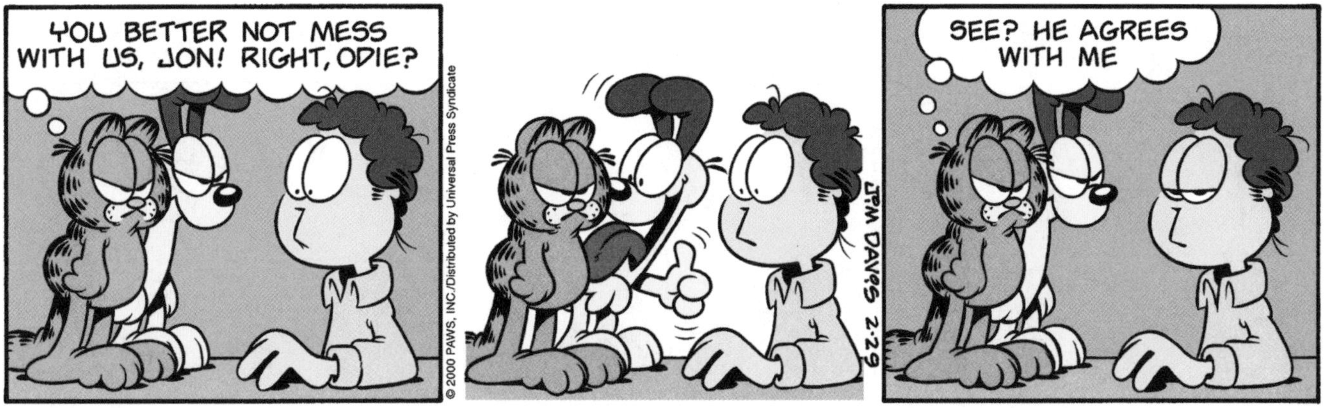
YOU BETTER NOT MESS WITH US, JON! RIGHT, ODIE?
SEE? HE AGREES WITH ME
JIM DAVIS 2-29
© 2000 PAWS, INC./Distributed by Universal Press Syndicate

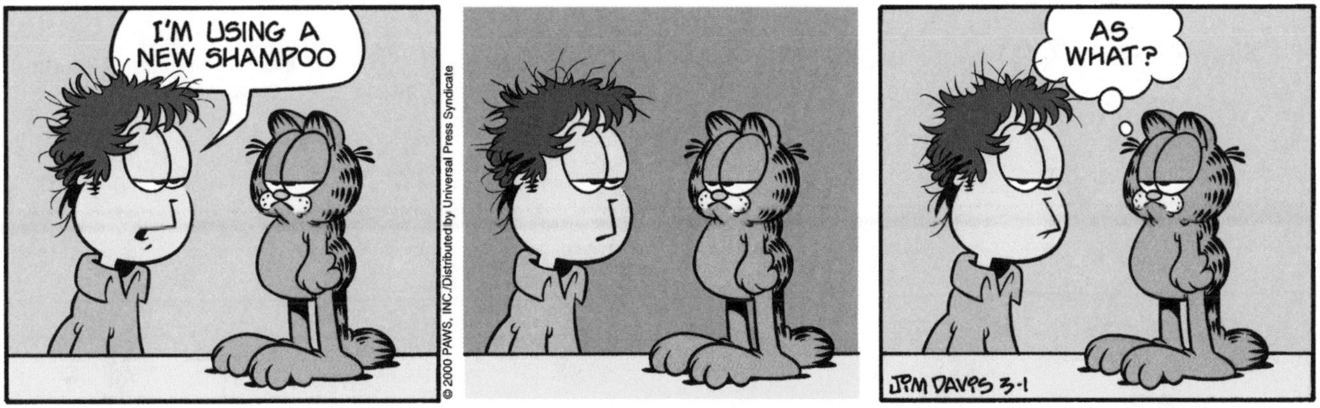
I'M USING A NEW SHAMPOO
AS WHAT?
JIM DAVIS 3-1
© 2000 PAWS, INC./Distributed by Universal Press Syndicate

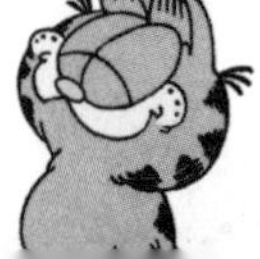

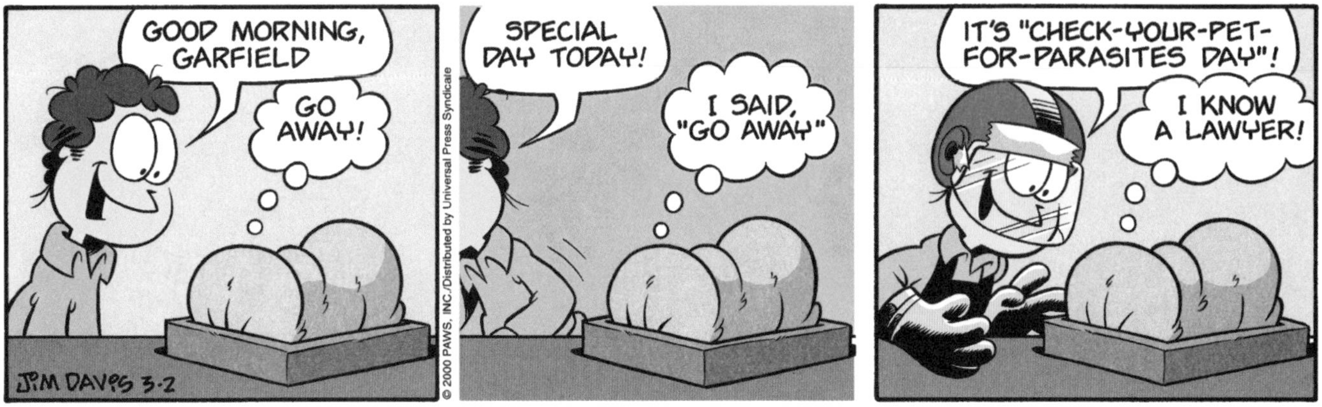
GOOD MORNING, GARFIELD
GO AWAY!
SPECIAL DAY TODAY!
I SAID, "GO AWAY"
IT'S "CHECK-YOUR-PET-FOR-PARASITES DAY"!
I KNOW A LAWYER!
JIM DAVIS 3-2
© 2000 PAWS, INC./Distributed by Universal Press Syndicate

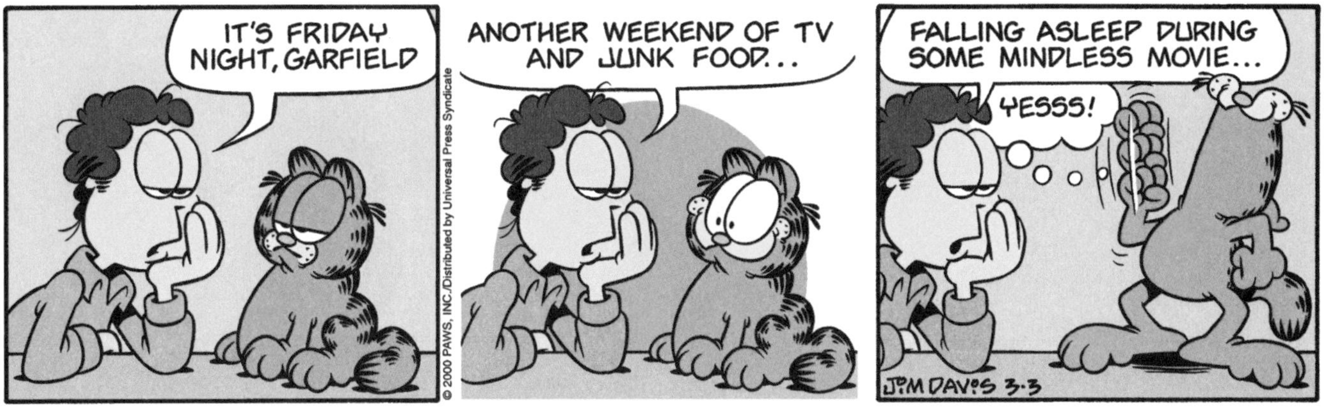
IT'S FRIDAY NIGHT, GARFIELD
ANOTHER WEEKEND OF TV AND JUNK FOOD...
FALLING ASLEEP DURING SOME MINDLESS MOVIE...
YESSS!
JIM DAVIS 3-3
© 2000 PAWS, INC./Distributed by Universal Press Syndicate

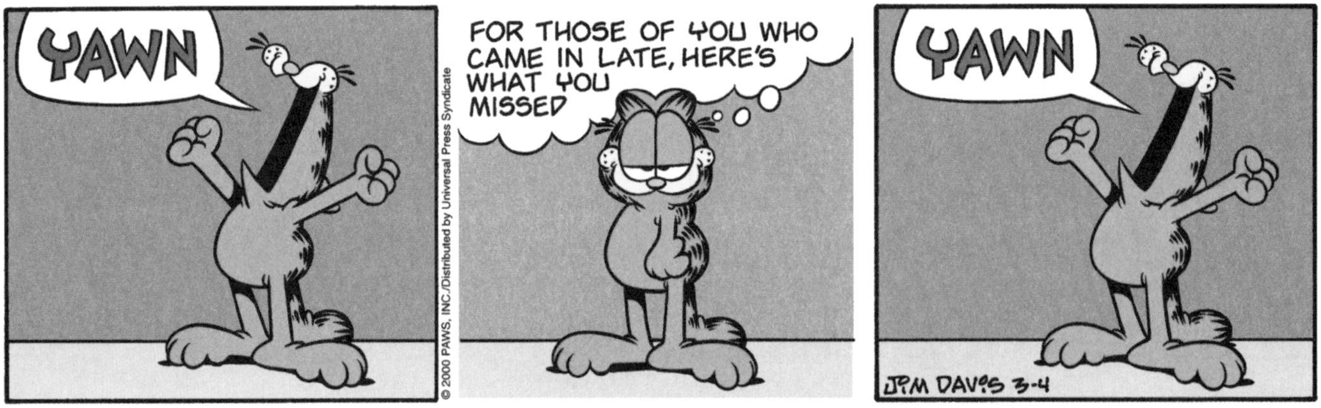
YAWN
FOR THOSE OF YOU WHO CAME IN LATE, HERE'S WHAT YOU MISSED
YAWN
JIM DAVIS 3-4
© 2000 PAWS, INC./Distributed by Universal Press Syndicate

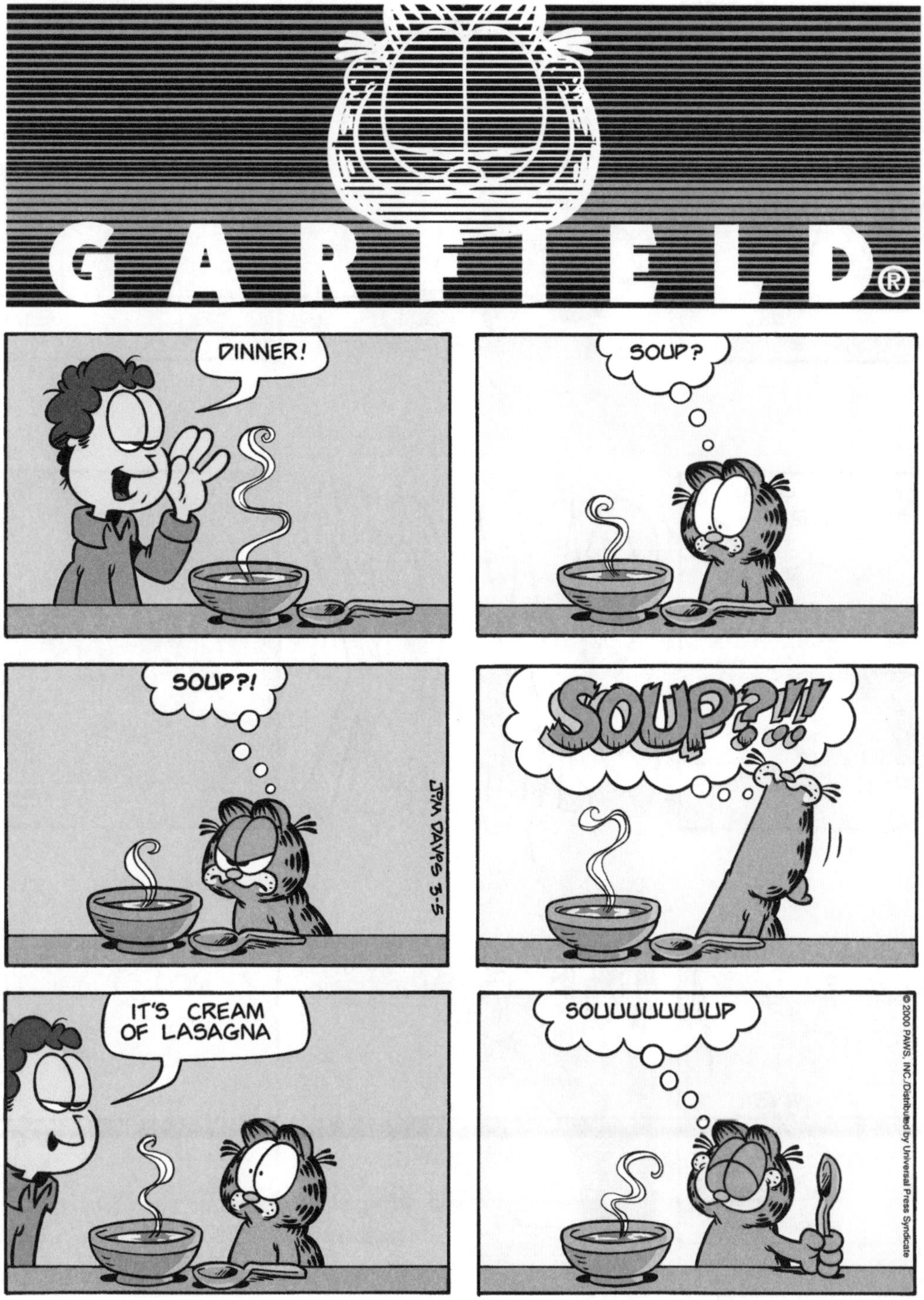
GARFIELD®
DINNER!
SOUP?
SOUP?!
JPM DAVIS 3-5
SOUP?!!
IT'S CREAM OF LASAGNA
SOUUUUUUUUP
© 2000 PAWS, INC./Distributed by Universal Press Syndicate

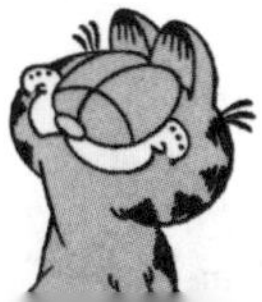

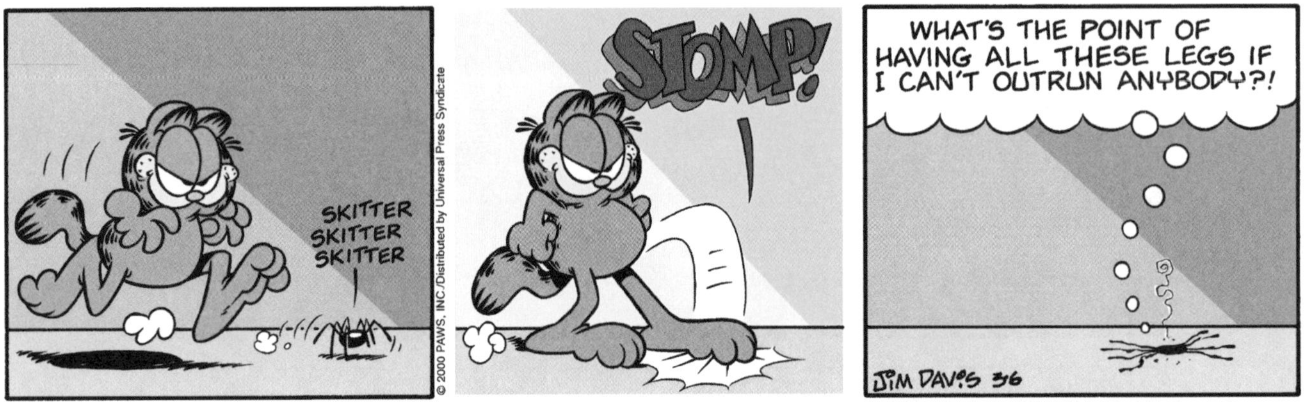
SKITTER
SKITTER
SKITTER
© 2000 PAWS, INC./Distributed by Universal Press Syndicate
STOMP!
WHAT'S THE POINT OF HAVING ALL THESE LEGS IF I CAN'T OUTRUN ANYBODY?!
JIM DAVIS 3-6

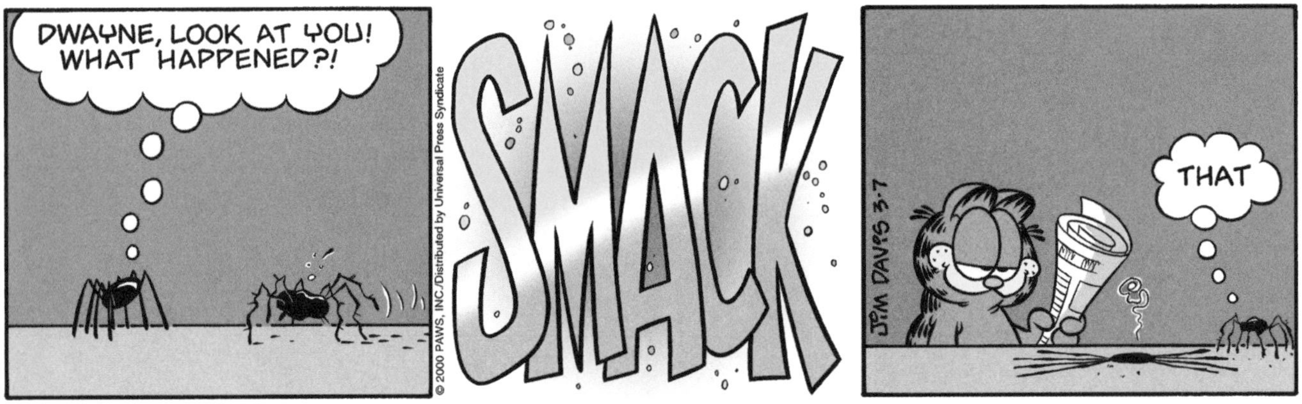
DWAYNE, LOOK AT YOU! WHAT HAPPENED?!
© 2000 PAWS, INC./Distributed by Universal Press Syndicate
SMACK
JIM DAVIS 3-7
THAT

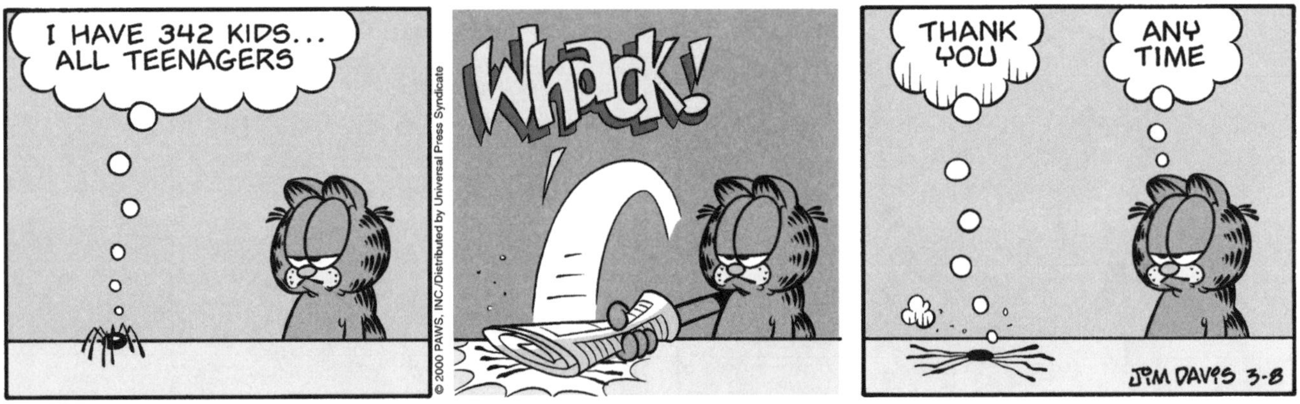
I HAVE 342 KIDS... ALL TEENAGERS
© 2000 PAWS, INC./Distributed by Universal Press Syndicate
Whack!
THANK YOU
ANY TIME
JIM DAVIS 3-8



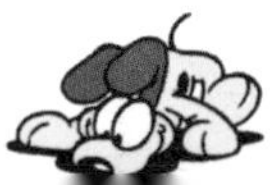

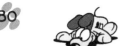

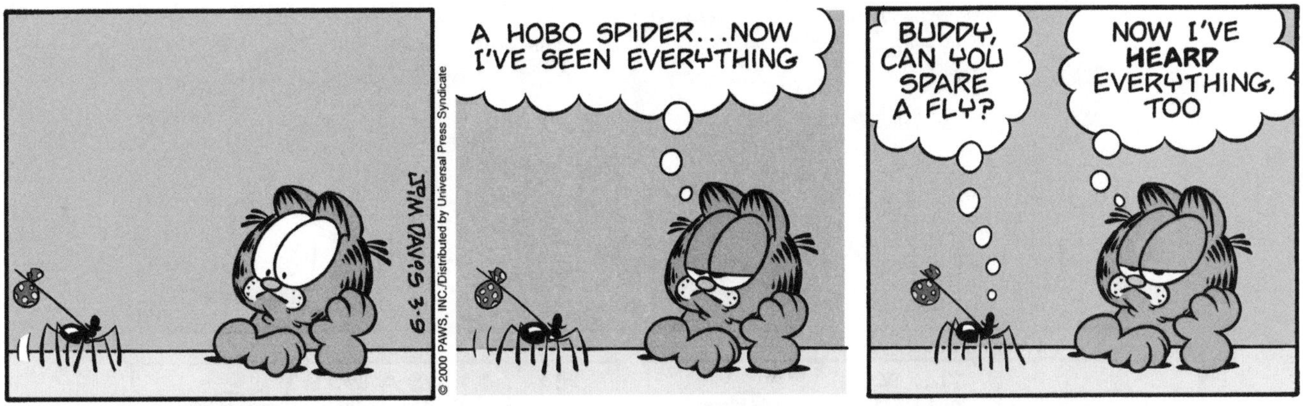
JIM DAVIS 3-9
© 2000 PAWS, INC./Distributed by Universal Press Syndicate
A HOBO SPIDER...NOW I'VE SEEN EVERYTHING
BUDDY, CAN YOU SPARE A FLY?
NOW I'VE **HEARD** EVERYTHING, TOO

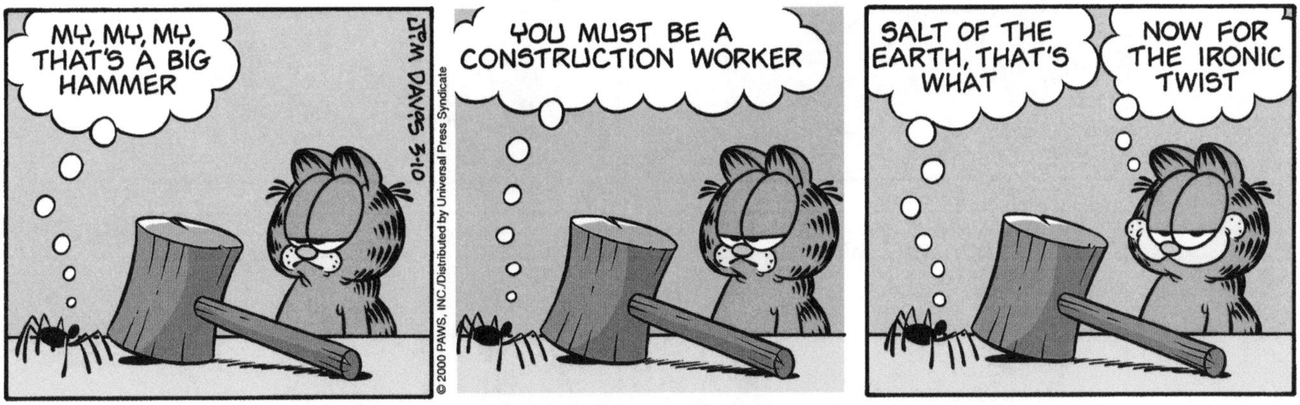
MY, MY, MY, THAT'S A BIG HAMMER
JIM DAVIS 3-10
© 2000 PAWS, INC./Distributed by Universal Press Syndicate
YOU MUST BE A CONSTRUCTION WORKER
SALT OF THE EARTH, THAT'S WHAT
NOW FOR THE IRONIC TWIST

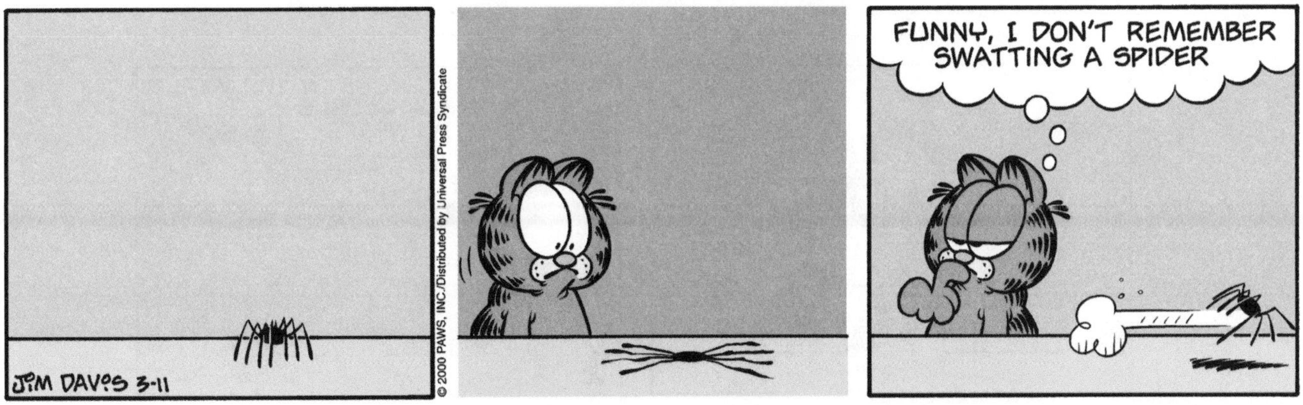
JIM DAVIS 3-11
© 2000 PAWS, INC./Distributed by Universal Press Syndicate
FUNNY, I DON'T REMEMBER SWATTING A SPIDER

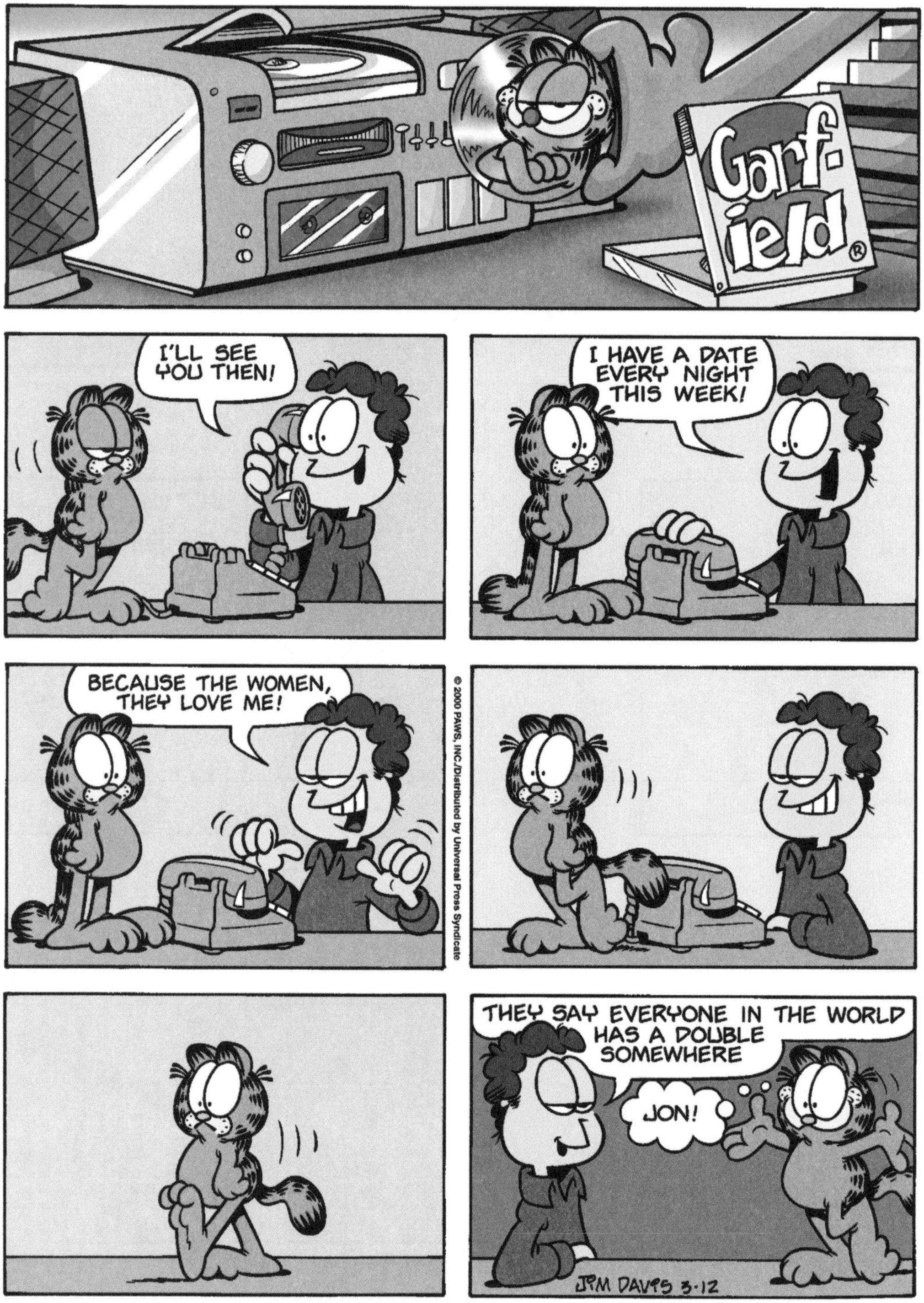
Garfield®
I'LL SEE YOU THEN!
I HAVE A DATE EVERY NIGHT THIS WEEK!
BECAUSE THE WOMEN, THEY LOVE ME!
THEY SAY EVERYONE IN THE WORLD HAS A DOUBLE SOMEWHERE
JON!
JIM DAVIS 3-12
© 2000 PAWS, INC./Distributed by Universal Press Syndicate

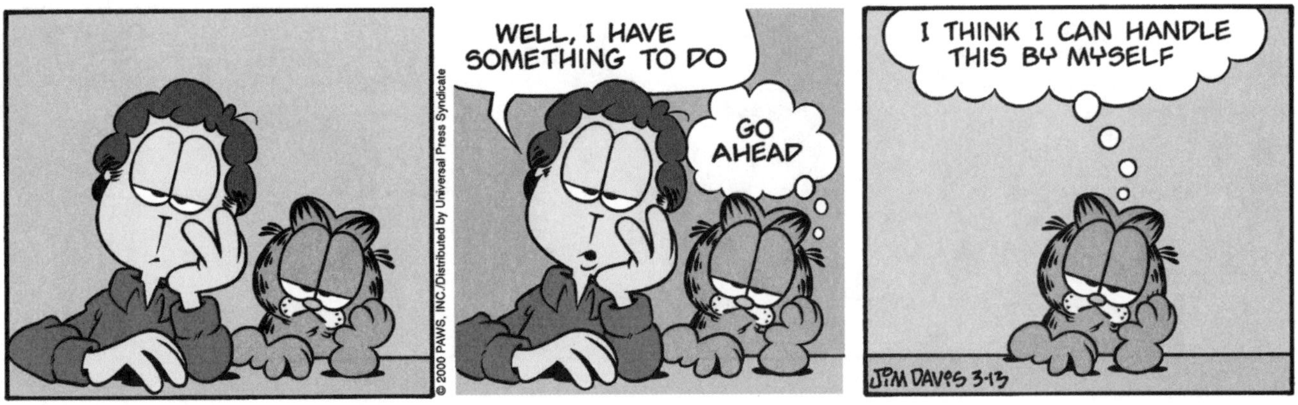
WELL, I HAVE SOMETHING TO DO
GO AHEAD
I THINK I CAN HANDLE THIS BY MYSELF
© 2000 PAWS, INC./Distributed by Universal Press Syndicate
JIM DAVIS 3-13

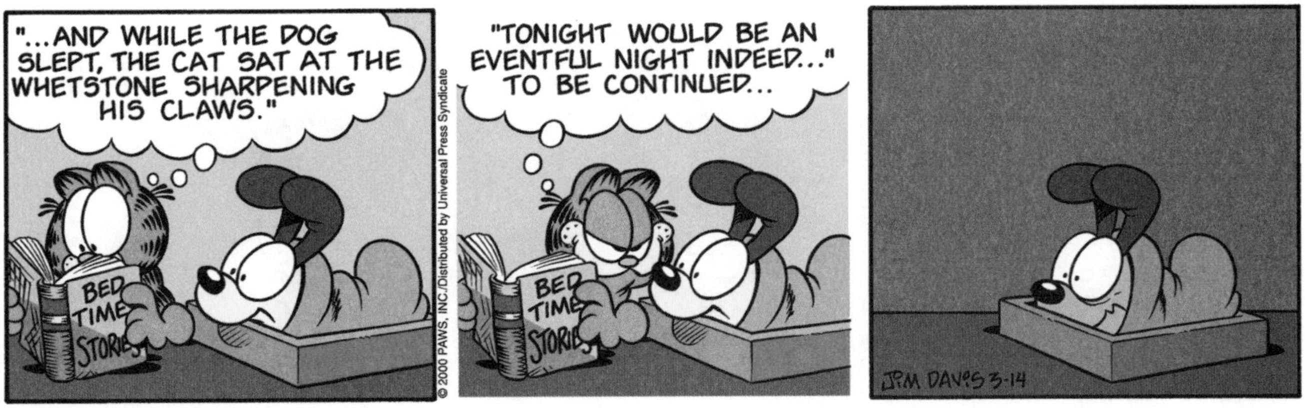
"...AND WHILE THE DOG SLEPT, THE CAT SAT AT THE WHETSTONE SHARPENING HIS CLAWS."
BED TIME STORIES
"TONIGHT WOULD BE AN EVENTFUL NIGHT INDEED..." TO BE CONTINUED...
© 2000 PAWS, INC./Distributed by Universal Press Syndicate
JIM DAVIS 3-14

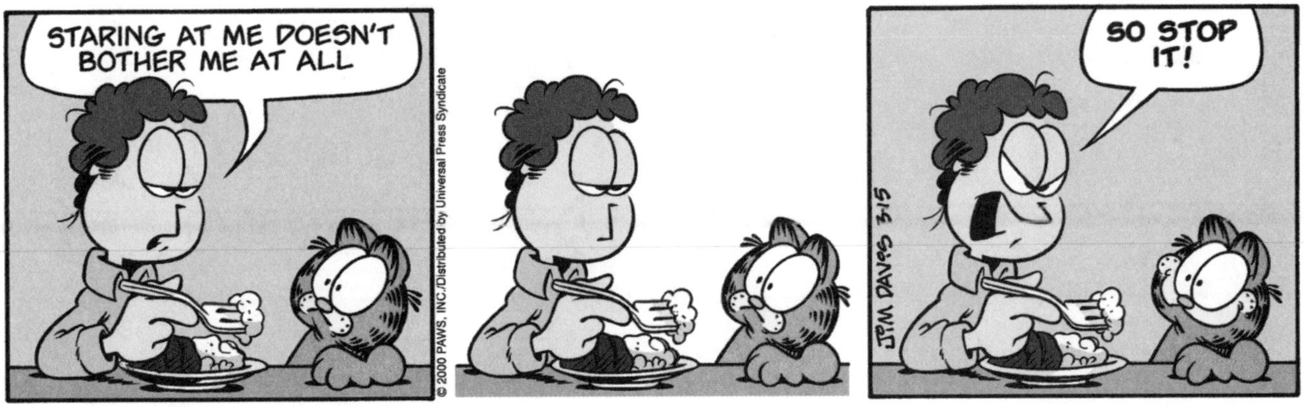
STARING AT ME DOESN'T BOTHER ME AT ALL
SO STOP IT!
© 2000 PAWS, INC./Distributed by Universal Press Syndicate
JIM DAVIS 3-15

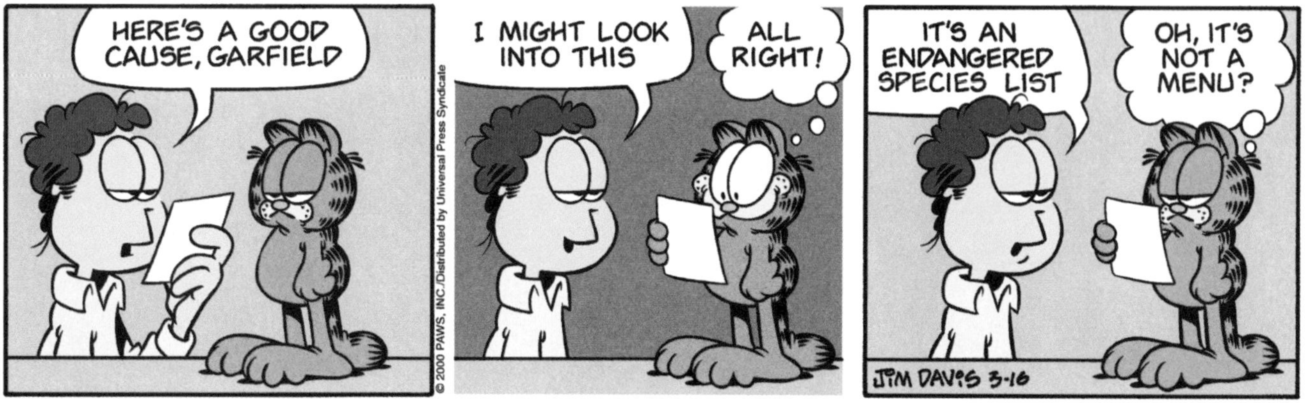
HERE'S A GOOD CAUSE, GARFIELD
© 2000 PAWS, INC./Distributed by Universal Press Syndicate
I MIGHT LOOK INTO THIS
ALL RIGHT!
IT'S AN ENDANGERED SPECIES LIST
OH, IT'S NOT A MENU?
JIM DAVIS 3-16

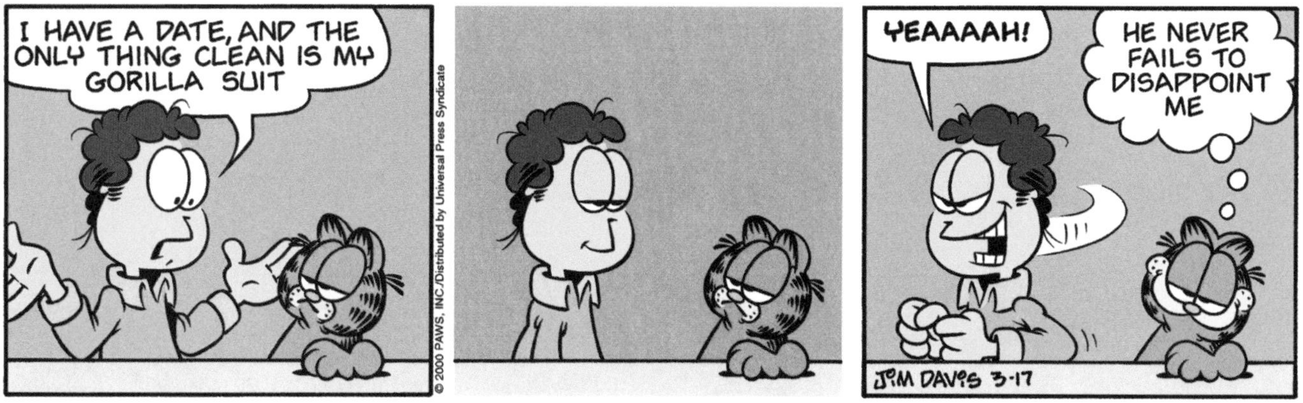
I HAVE A DATE, AND THE ONLY THING CLEAN IS MY GORILLA SUIT
© 2000 PAWS, INC./Distributed by Universal Press Syndicate
YEAAAAH!
HE NEVER FAILS TO DISAPPOINT ME
JIM DAVIS 3-17

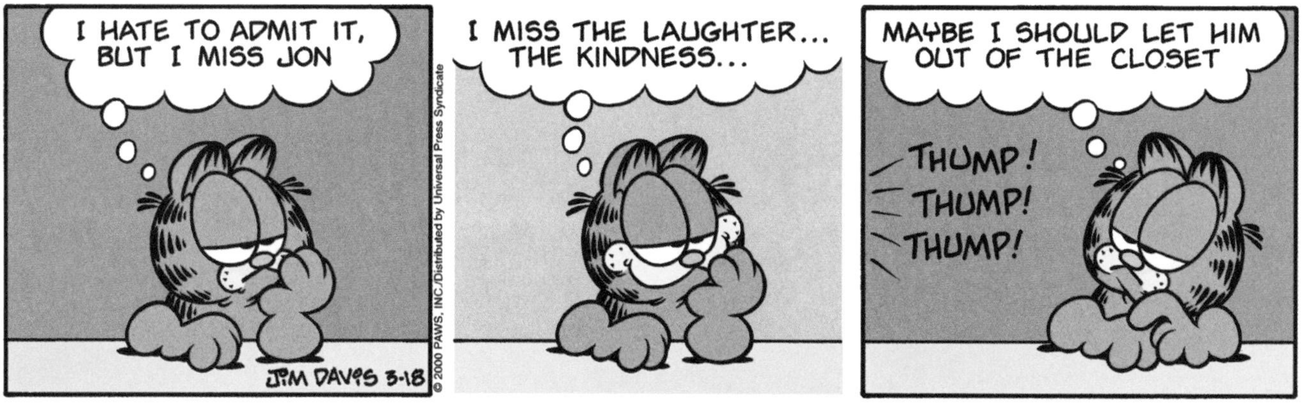
I HATE TO ADMIT IT, BUT I MISS JON
JIM DAVIS 3-18
© 2000 PAWS, INC./Distributed by Universal Press Syndicate
I MISS THE LAUGHTER... THE KINDNESS...
MAYBE I SHOULD LET HIM OUT OF THE CLOSET
THUMP!
THUMP!
THUMP!

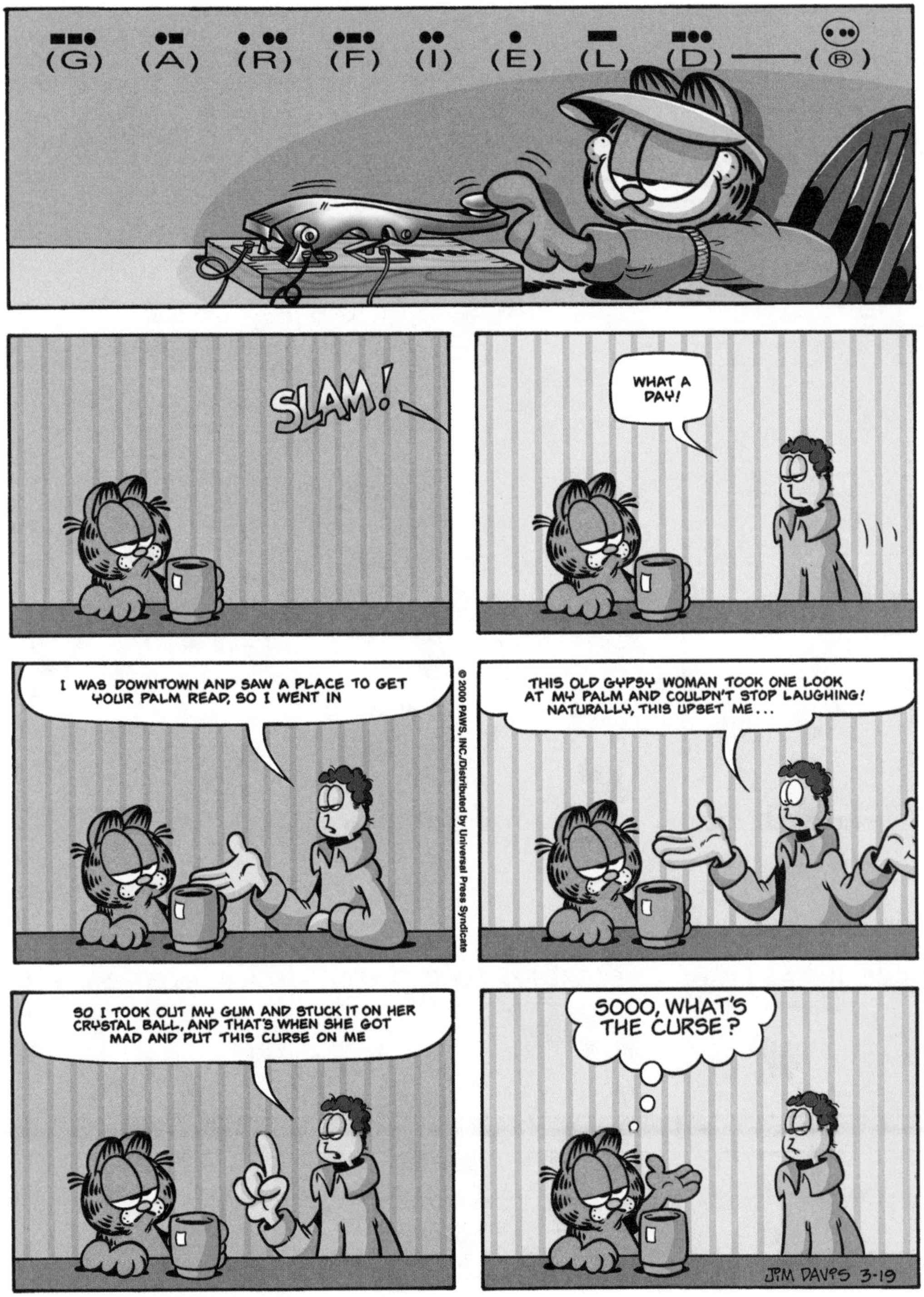
(G) (A) (R) (F) (I) (E) (L) (D) —— (®)
SLAM!
WHAT A DAY!
I WAS DOWNTOWN AND SAW A PLACE TO GET YOUR PALM READ, SO I WENT IN
© 2000 PAWS, INC./Distributed by Universal Press Syndicate
THIS OLD GYPSY WOMAN TOOK ONE LOOK AT MY PALM AND COULDN'T STOP LAUGHING! NATURALLY, THIS UPSET ME...
SO I TOOK OUT MY GUM AND STUCK IT ON HER CRYSTAL BALL, AND THAT'S WHEN SHE GOT MAD AND PUT THIS CURSE ON ME
SOOO, WHAT'S THE CURSE?
JIM DAVIS 3-19

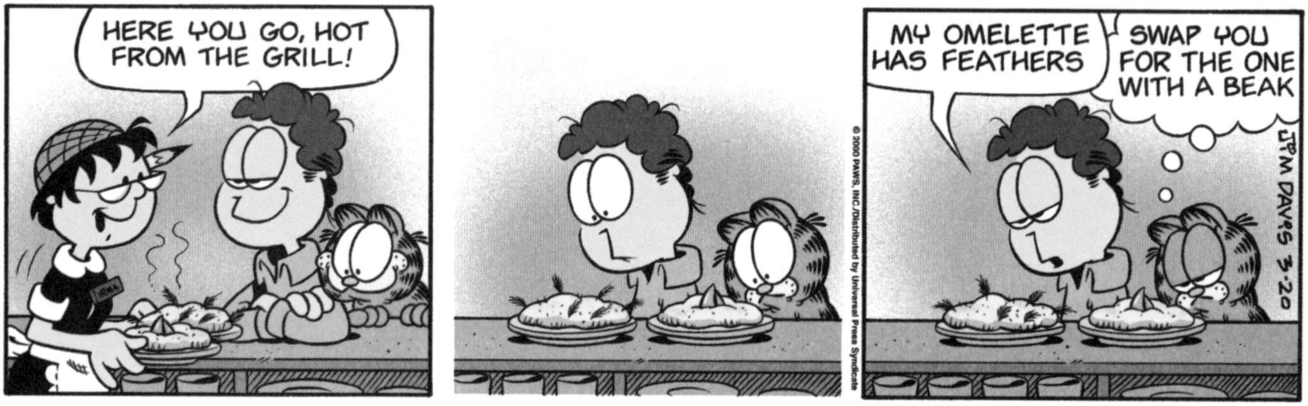
HERE YOU GO, HOT FROM THE GRILL!
© 2000 PAWS, INC./Distributed by Universal Press Syndicate
MY OMELETTE HAS FEATHERS
SWAP YOU FOR THE ONE WITH A BEAK
JIM DAVIS 3-20

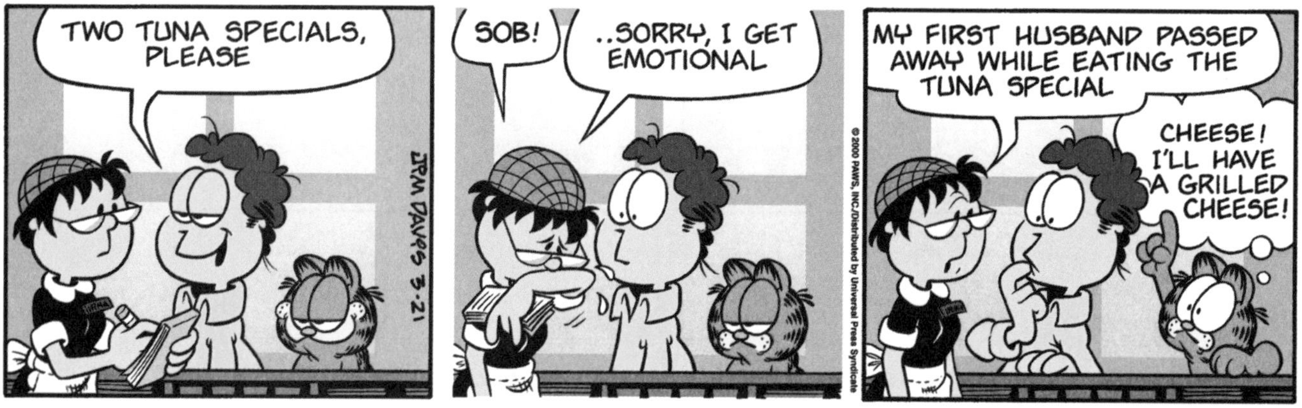
TWO TUNA SPECIALS, PLEASE
JIM DAVIS 3-21
SOB!
..SORRY, I GET EMOTIONAL
© 2000 PAWS, INC./Distributed by Universal Press Syndicate
MY FIRST HUSBAND PASSED AWAY WHILE EATING THE TUNA SPECIAL
CHEESE! I'LL HAVE A GRILLED CHEESE!

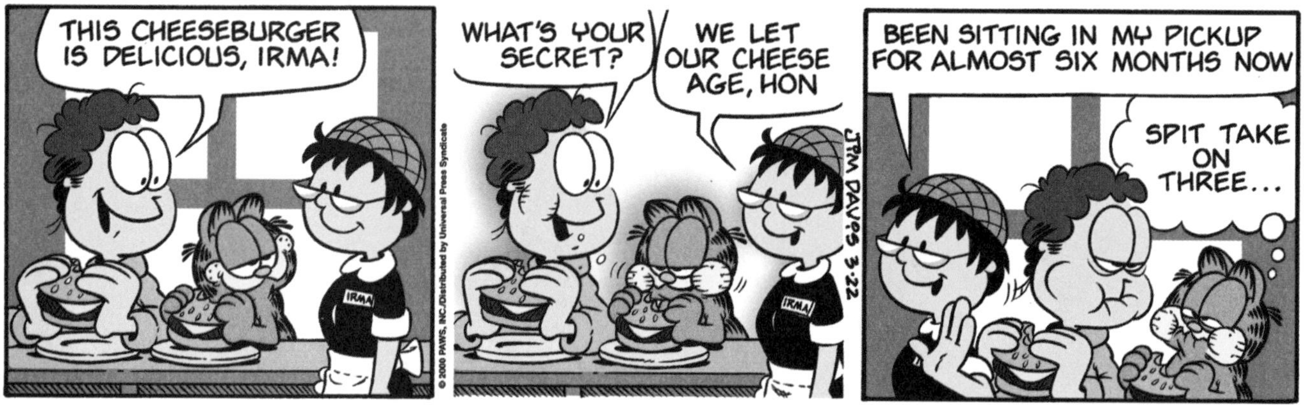
THIS CHEESEBURGER IS DELICIOUS, IRMA!
© 2000 PAWS, INC./Distributed by Universal Press Syndicate
WHAT'S YOUR SECRET?
WE LET OUR CHEESE AGE, HON
JIM DAVIS 3-22
BEEN SITTING IN MY PICKUP FOR ALMOST SIX MONTHS NOW
SPIT TAKE ON THREE...



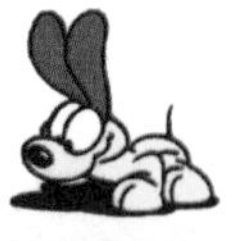

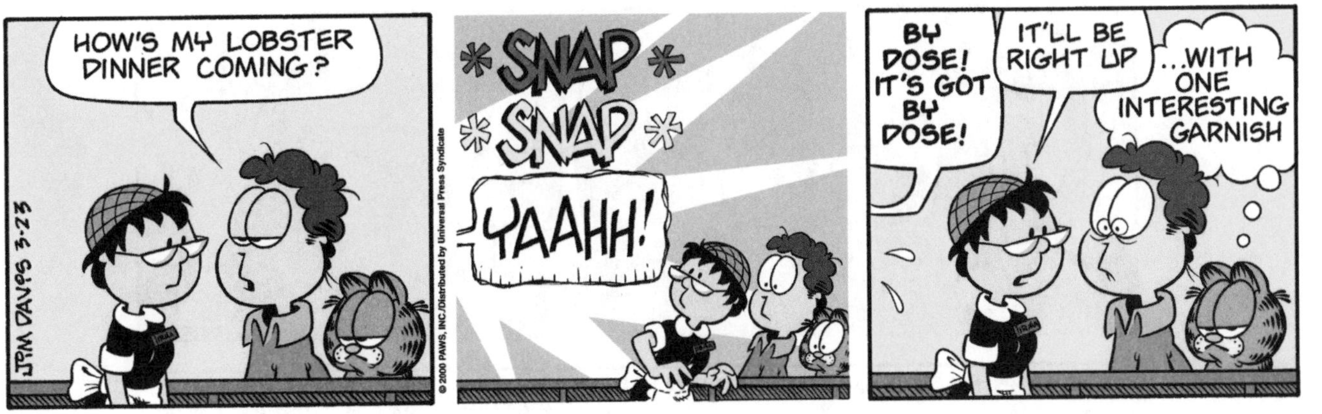
HOW'S MY LOBSTER DINNER COMING?
JIM DAVIS 3-23
© 2000 PAWS, INC./Distributed by Universal Press Syndicate
*SNAP*
*SNAP*
YAAHH!
BY DOSE! IT'S GOT BY DOSE!
IT'LL BE RIGHT UP
...WITH ONE INTERESTING GARNISH

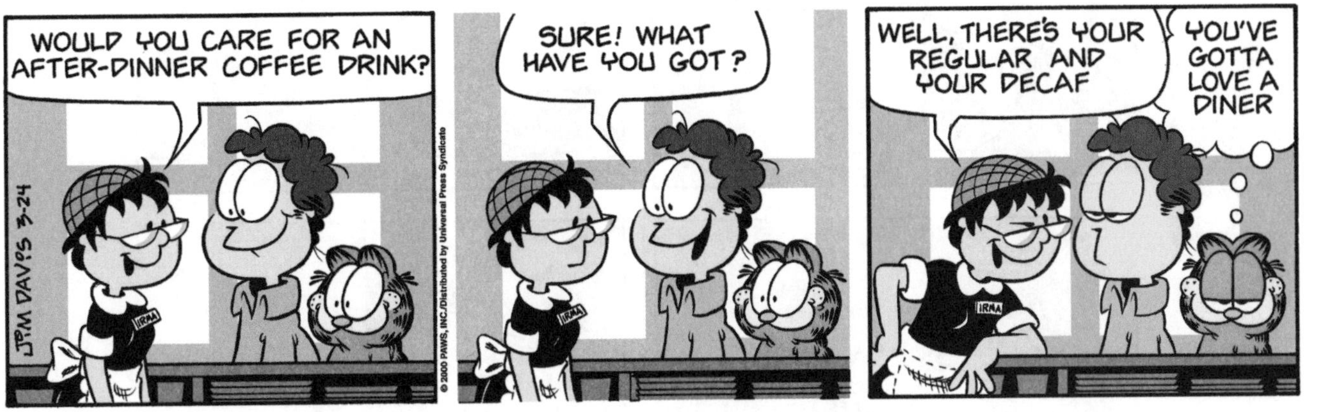
WOULD YOU CARE FOR AN AFTER-DINNER COFFEE DRINK?
JIM DAVIS 3-24
© 2000 PAWS, INC./Distributed by Universal Press Syndicate
SURE! WHAT HAVE YOU GOT?
WELL, THERE'S YOUR REGULAR AND YOUR DECAF
YOU'VE GOTTA LOVE A DINER

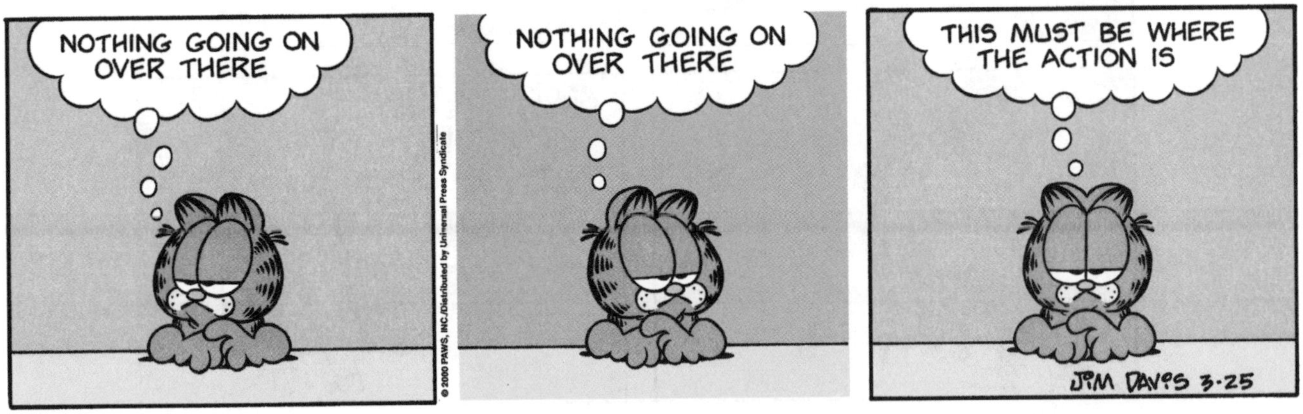
NOTHING GOING ON OVER THERE
© 2000 PAWS, INC./Distributed by Universal Press Syndicate
NOTHING GOING ON OVER THERE
THIS MUST BE WHERE THE ACTION IS
JIM DAVIS 3-25

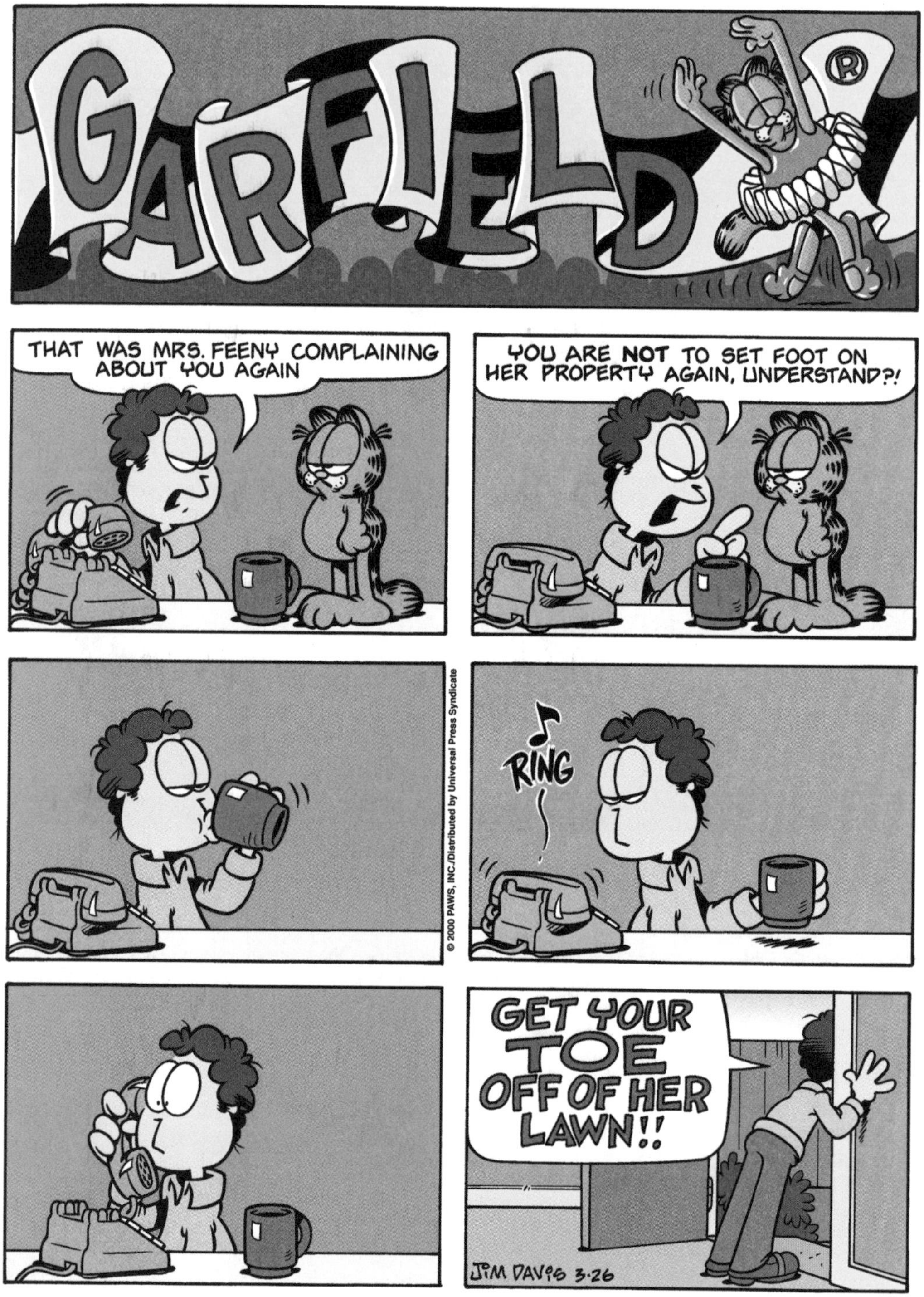
GARFIELD ®
THAT WAS MRS. FEENY COMPLAINING ABOUT YOU AGAIN
YOU ARE **NOT** TO SET FOOT ON HER PROPERTY AGAIN, UNDERSTAND?!
© 2000 PAWS, INC./Distributed by Universal Press Syndicate
RING
GET YOUR TOE OFF OF HER LAWN!!
JIM DAVIS 3-26

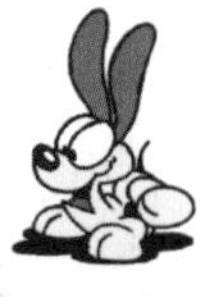

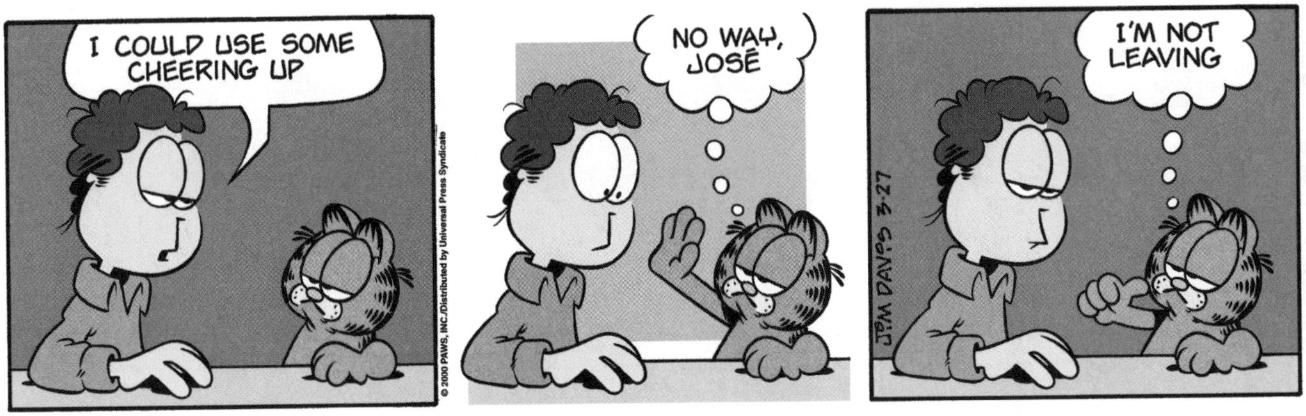
I COULD USE SOME CHEERING UP
© 2000 PAWS, INC./Distributed by Universal Press Syndicate
NO WAY, JOSÉ
I'M NOT LEAVING
JIM DAVIS 3-27

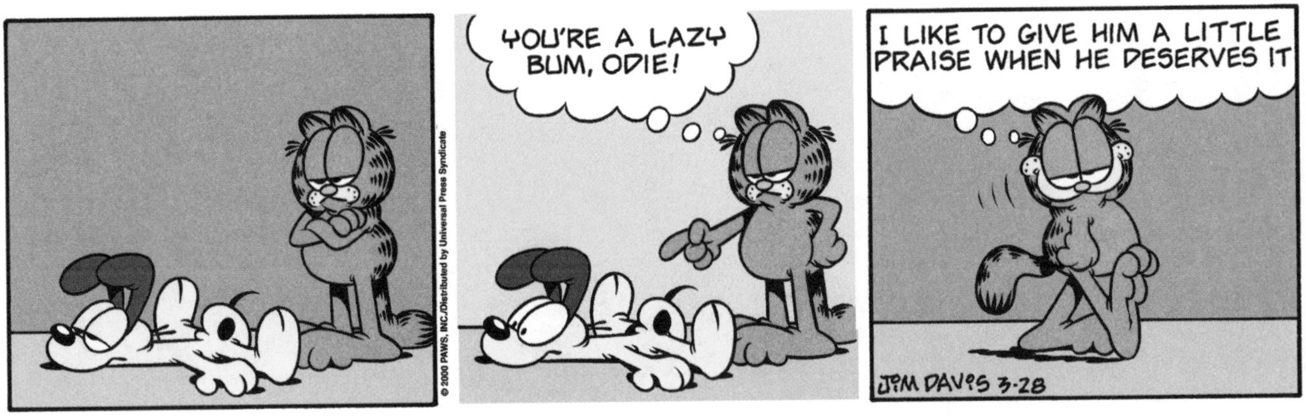
© 2000 PAWS, INC./Distributed by Universal Press Syndicate
YOU'RE A LAZY BUM, ODIE!
I LIKE TO GIVE HIM A LITTLE PRAISE WHEN HE DESERVES IT
JIM DAVIS 3-28

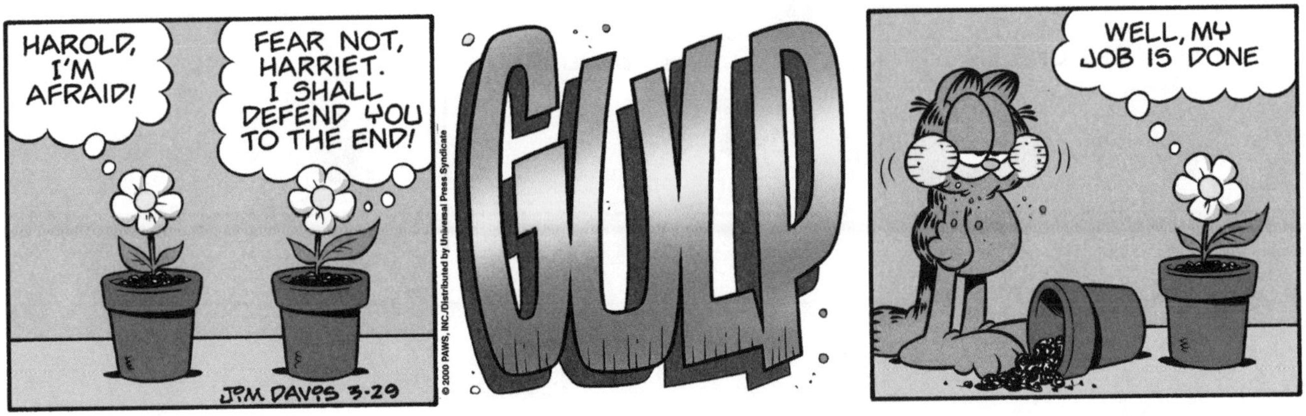
HAROLD, I'M AFRAID!
FEAR NOT, HARRIET. I SHALL DEFEND YOU TO THE END!
JIM DAVIS 3-29
© 2000 PAWS, INC./Distributed by Universal Press Syndicate
GULP
WELL, MY JOB IS DONE

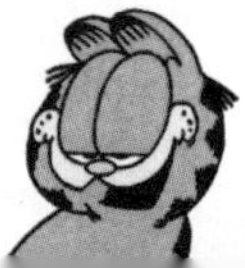

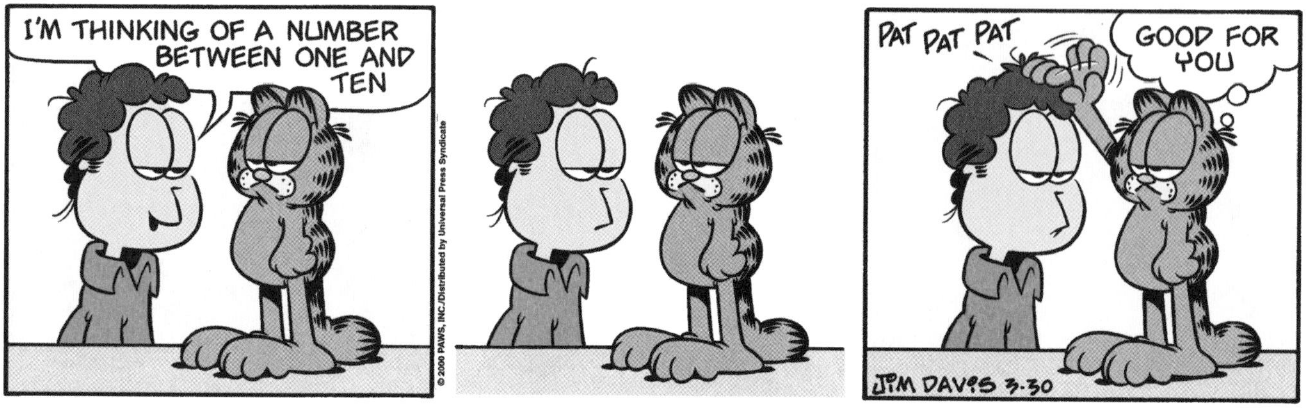
I'M THINKING OF A NUMBER BETWEEN ONE AND TEN
© 2000 PAWS, INC./Distributed by Universal Press Syndicate
PAT PAT PAT
GOOD FOR YOU
JIM DAVIS 3-30

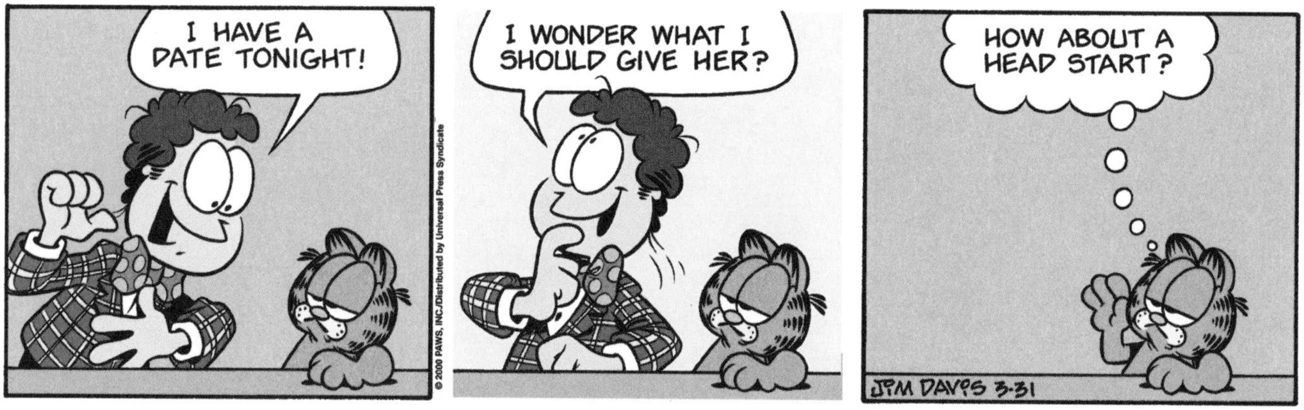
I HAVE A DATE TONIGHT!
© 2000 PAWS, INC./Distributed by Universal Press Syndicate
I WONDER WHAT I SHOULD GIVE HER?
HOW ABOUT A HEAD START?
JIM DAVIS 3-31

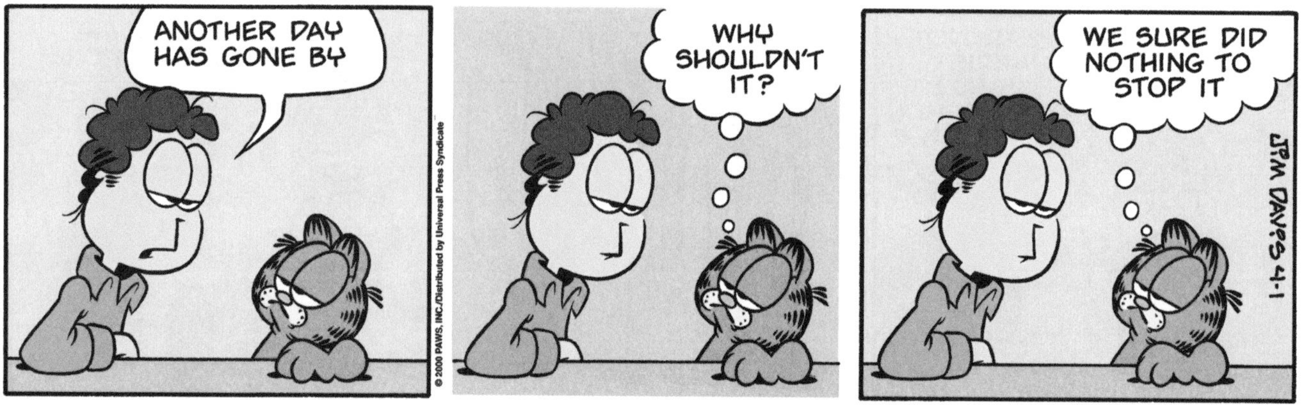
ANOTHER DAY HAS GONE BY
© 2000 PAWS, INC./Distributed by Universal Press Syndicate
WHY SHOULDN'T IT?
WE SURE DID NOTHING TO STOP IT
JIM DAVIS 4-1

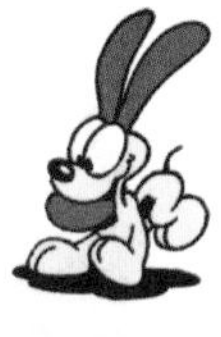

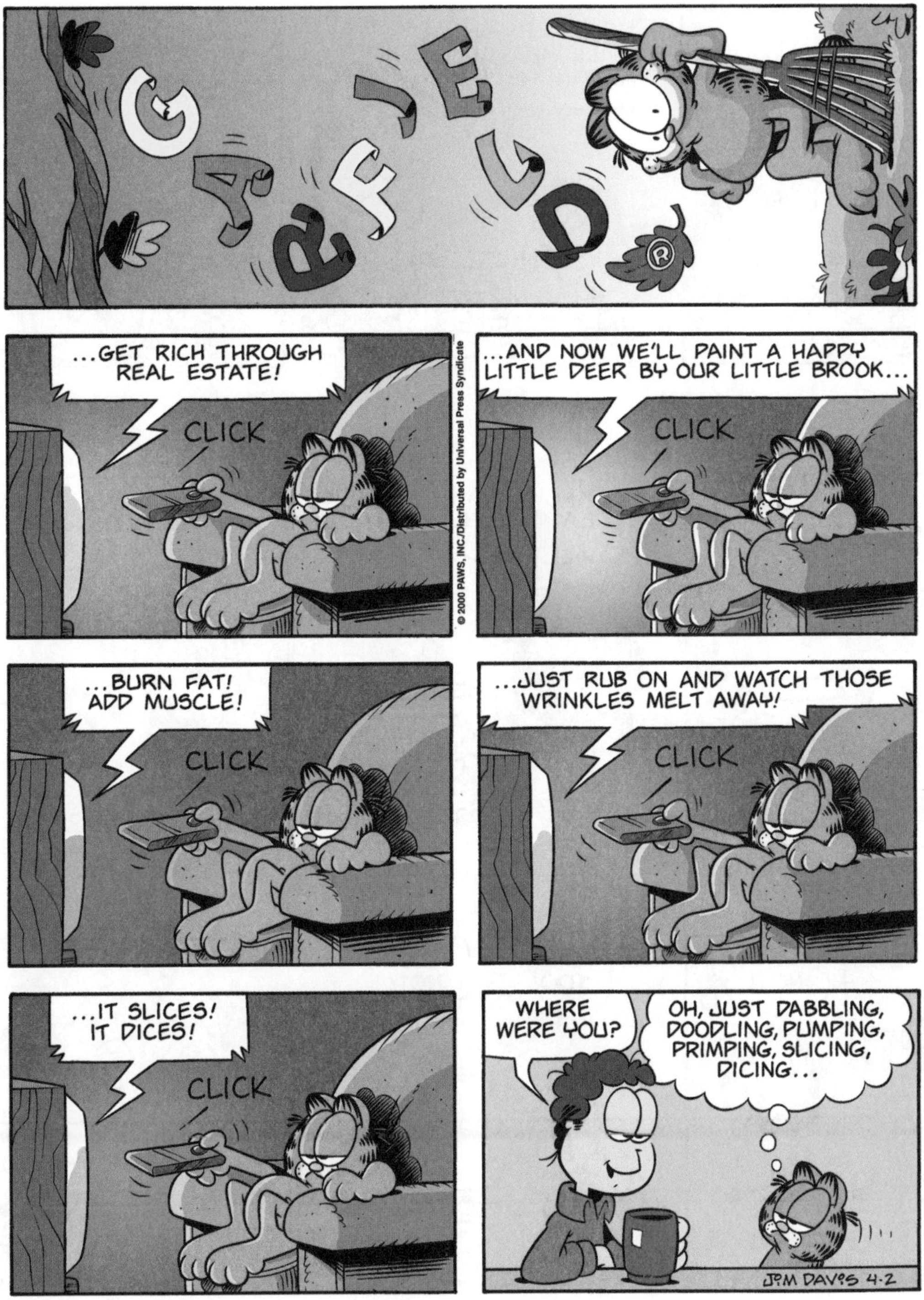
GARFIELD®
...GET RICH THROUGH REAL ESTATE!
CLICK
© 2000 PAWS, INC./Distributed by Universal Press Syndicate
...AND NOW WE'LL PAINT A HAPPY LITTLE DEER BY OUR LITTLE BROOK...
CLICK
...BURN FAT! ADD MUSCLE!
CLICK
...JUST RUB ON AND WATCH THOSE WRINKLES MELT AWAY!
CLICK
...IT SLICES! IT DICES!
CLICK
WHERE WERE YOU?
OH, JUST DABBLING, DOODLING, PUMPING, PRIMPING, SLICING, DICING...
JIM DAVIS 4-2

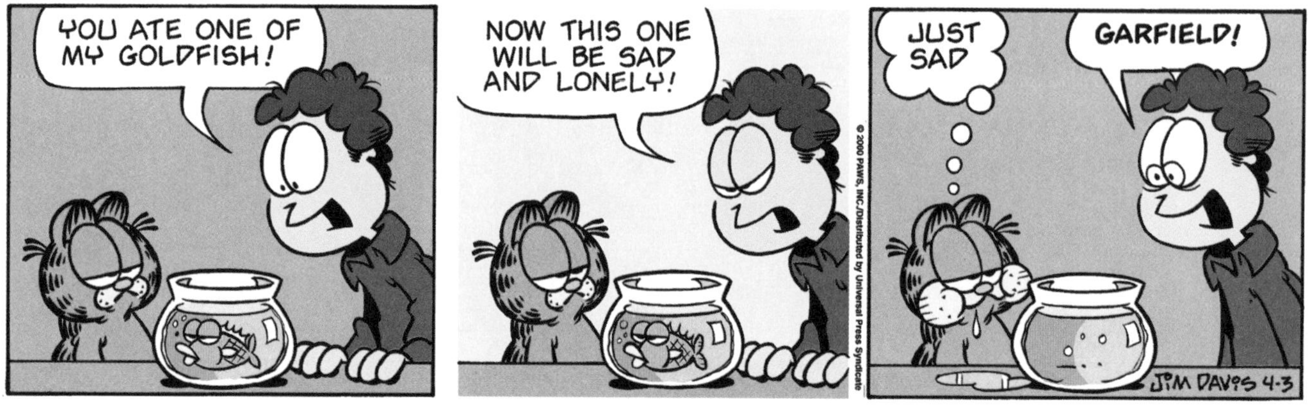
YOU ATE ONE OF MY GOLDFISH!
NOW THIS ONE WILL BE SAD AND LONELY!
© 2000 PAWS, INC./Distributed by Universal Press Syndicate
JUST SAD
GARFIELD!
JIM DAVIS 4-3

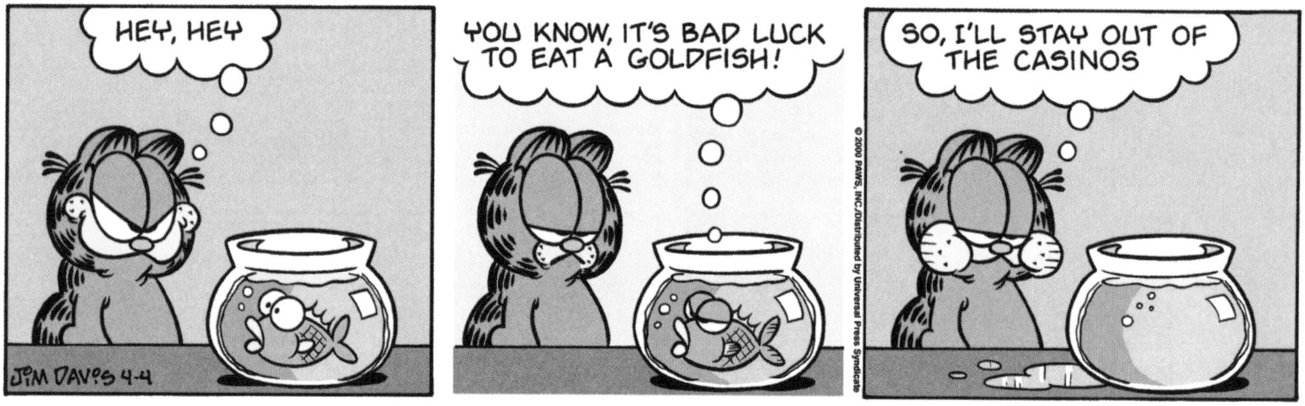
HEY, HEY
JIM DAVIS 4-4
YOU KNOW, IT'S BAD LUCK TO EAT A GOLDFISH!
© 2000 PAWS, INC./Distributed by Universal Press Syndicate
SO, I'LL STAY OUT OF THE CASINOS

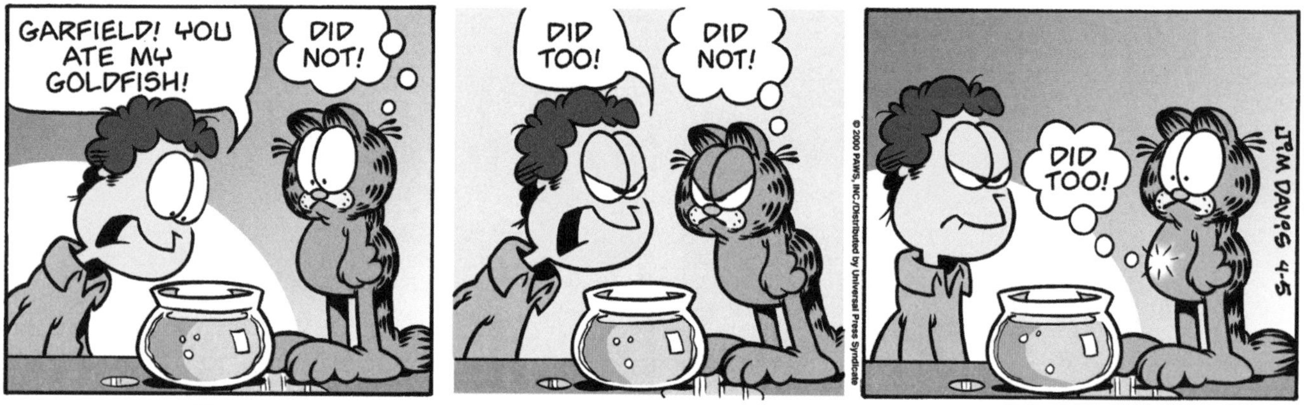
GARFIELD! YOU ATE MY GOLDFISH!
DID NOT!
DID TOO!
DID NOT!
© 2000 PAWS, INC./Distributed by Universal Press Syndicate
DID TOO!
JIM DAVIS 4-5

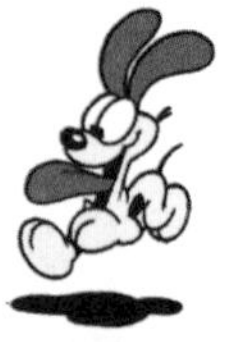

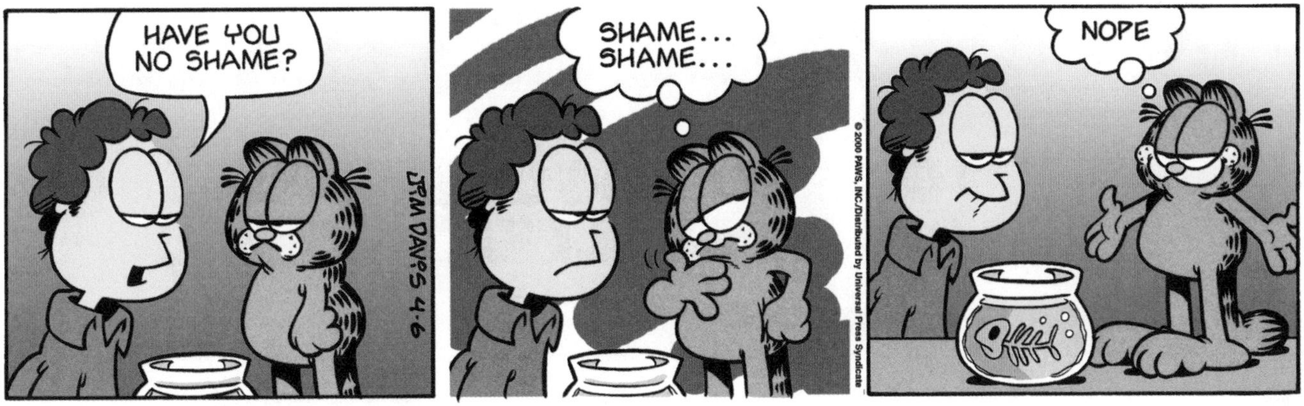
HAVE YOU NO SHAME?
JIM DAVIS 4-6
SHAME... SHAME...
© 2000 PAWS, INC./Distributed by Universal Press Syndicate
NOPE

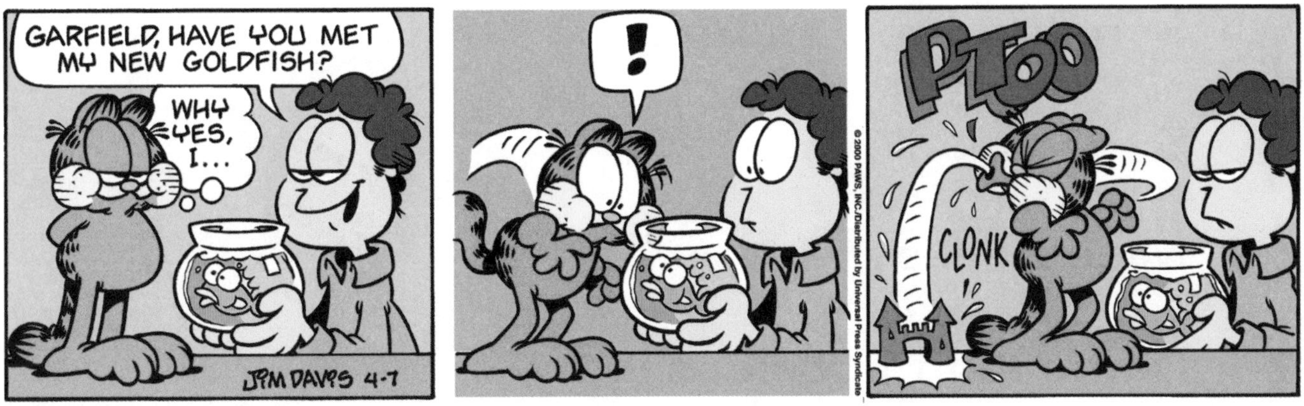
GARFIELD, HAVE YOU MET MY NEW GOLDFISH?
WHY YES, I...
JIM DAVIS 4-7
!
© 2000 PAWS, INC./Distributed by Universal Press Syndicate
PTOO
CLONK

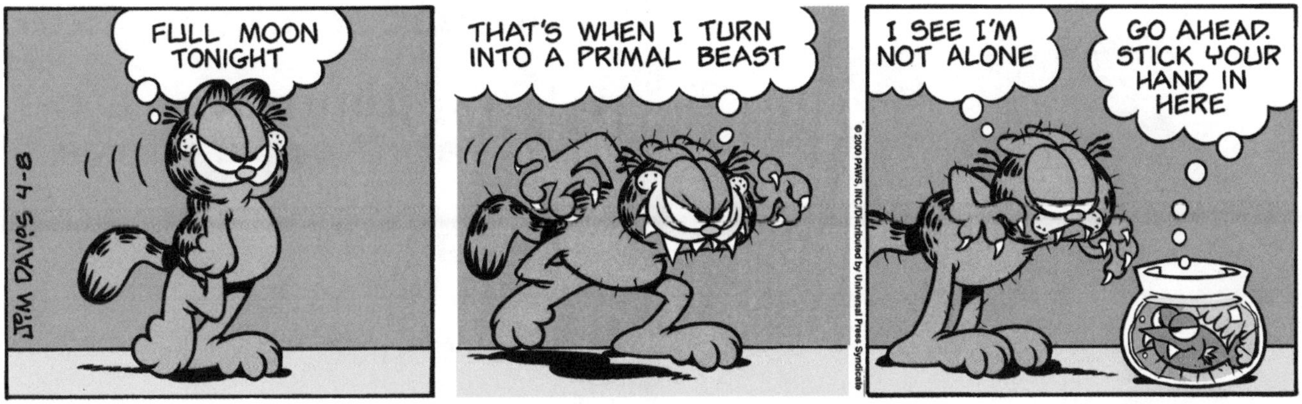
FULL MOON TONIGHT
JIM DAVIS 4-8
THAT'S WHEN I TURN INTO A PRIMAL BEAST
© 2000 PAWS, INC./Distributed by Universal Press Syndicate
I SEE I'M NOT ALONE
GO AHEAD. STICK YOUR HAND IN HERE

# GARFIELD'S
## TOP TEN SUGGESTIONS FOR NEW ATHLETIC EVENTS

 **10** The dogput

 **9** Synchronized snoring

 **8** Speedsnacking

 **7** Mice hockey

 **6** Demolition bobsleds

 **5** 90-meter ski jump onto unsuspecting grandma

 **4** Long jump over a pit of rabid wolverines

 **3** Fridge lift

 **2** Hairball hack

 **1** Eat till you explode!

©PAWS

# STRIPS, SPECIALS, OR BESTSELLING BOOKS...

# GARFIELD'S ON EVERYONE'S MENU

*Don't miss even one episode in the Tubby Tabby's hilarious series!*

__GARFIELD AT LARGE (#1)    32013/$6.95
__GARFIELD GAINS WEIGHT (#2)    32008/$6.95
__GARFIELD BIGGER THAN LIFE (#3)    32007/$6.95
__GARFIELD WEIGHS IN (#4)    32010/$6.95
__GARFIELD TAKES THE CAKE (#5)    32009/$6.95
__GARFIELD EATS HIS HEART OUT (#6)    32018/$6.95
__GARFIELD SITS AROUND THE HOUSE (#7)
32011/$6.95
__GARFIELD TIPS THE SCALES (#8)    33580/$6.95
__GARFIELD LOSES HIS FEET (#9)    31805/$6.95
__GARFIELD MAKES IT BIG (#10)    31928/$6.95
__GARFIELD ROLLS ON (#11)    32634/$6.95
__GARFIELD OUT TO LUNCH (#12)    33118/$6.95
__GARFIELD FOOD FOR THOUGHT (#13)    34129/$6.95
__GARFIELD SWALLOWS HIS PRIDE (#14)    34725/$6.95
__GARFIELD WORLDWIDE (#15)    35158/$6.95
__GARFIELD ROUNDS OUT (#16)    35388/$6.95
__GARFIELD CHEWS THE FAT (#17)    35956/$6.95
__GARFIELD GOES TO WAIST (#18)    36430/$6.95
__GARFIELD HANGS OUT (#19)    36835/$6.95
__GARFIELD TAKES UP SPACE (#20)    37029/$6.95
__GARFIELD SAYS A MOUTHFUL (#21)    37368/$6.95
__GARFIELD BY THE POUND (#22)    37579/$6.95

__GARFIELD KEEPS HIS CHINS UP (#23)    37959/$6.95
__GARFIELD TAKES HIS LICKS (#24)    38170/$7.95
__GARFIELD HITS THE BIG TIME (#25)    38332/$6.95
__GARFIELD PULLS HIS WEIGHT (#26)    38666/$6.95
__GARFIELD DISHES IT OUT (#27)    39287/$7.95
__GARFIELD LIFE IN THE FAT LANE (#28)    39776/$6.95
__GARFIELD TONS OF FUN (#29)    40386/$7.95
__GARFIELD BIGGER AND BETTER (#30)    40770/$6.95
__GARFIELD HAMS IT UP (#31)    41241/$6.95
__GARFIELD THINKS BIG (#32)    41671/$6.95
__GARFIELD THROWS HIS WEIGHT AROUND (#33)
    42749/$6.95
__GARFIELD LIFE TO THE FULLEST (#34)    43239/$7.95
__GARFIELD FEEDS THE KITTY (#35)    43673/$6.95
__GARFIELD HOGS THE SPOTLIGHT (#36)
    43922/$6.95

## GARFIELD AT HIS SUNDAY BEST!
__GARFIELD TREASURY    32106/$12.50
__THE SECOND GARFIELD TREASURY    33276/$12.50
__THE THIRD GARFIELD TREASURY    32635/$12.50
__THE FOURTH GARFIELD TREASURY    34726/$12.50
__THE FIFTH GARFIELD TREASURY    36268/$12.00
__THE SIXTH GARFIELD TREASURY    37367/$12.50
__THE SEVENTH GARFIELD TREASURY    38427/$12.00
__THE EIGHTH GARFIELD TREASURY    39778/$12.50
__THE NINTH GARFIELD TREASURY    41670/$12.50
__THE TENTH GARFIELD TREASURY    43674/$12.50

## AND DON'T MISS...
__GARFIELD'S TWENTIETH ANNIVERSARY COLLECTION!
    42126/$14.95

Please send me the BALLANTINE BOOKS I have checked above. I am enclosing $_____. (Please add $2.00 for the first book and $.50 for each additional book for postage and handling and include the appropriate state sales tax.) Send check or money order (no cash or C.O.D.'s) to Ballantine Mail Sales, Dept. TA, 400 Hahn Road, Westminster, MD 21157.

To order by phone, call 1-800-733-3000
and use your major credit card.

Prices and numbers are subject to change without notice.
Valid in the U.S. only. All orders are subject to availability.

Name_____

Address_____

City_____ State_____ Zip_____

30

Allow at least 4 weeks for delivery

11/00